Deanna Maclaren had the idea for *The Single File* while she was still married, but after her divorce found she needed to rewrite some chapters in the light of active experience – good, bad and hilarious – of living alone. She says the best aspect of living alone is the freedom to be herself. And the worst, having no one to blame on the days when she finds herself unbearable. She has been a professional writer for ten years and has published four novels: *Little Blue Room, The First of all Pleasures, Dagger in the Sleeve* and *Your Loving Mother*.

Also by Deanna Maclaren in Sphere Books:

YOUR LOVING MOTHER

The Single File

DEANNA MACLAREN

SPHERE BOOKS LIMITED
30–32 Gray's Inn Road, London WC1X 8JL

First published in Great Britain by
Sphere Books Ltd 1983
Copyright © 1983 by Deanna Maclaren

TRADE
MARK

Set in 10/11 Compugraphic Times

Printed and bound in Great Britain by
Hunt Barnard Printing Ltd, Aylesbury, Bucks

For Catherine Murray,
with thanks for all the shared laughter
on the other side of the wall

ACKNOWLEDGEMENTS

My grateful thanks to the following for giving me permission to quote their words:

Madelon Dimont from *Homes and Gardens*, December 1980 (p. 59)
Russell Harty from the *Observer*, March 1981 (p. 123)
Catherine Olsen interviewing Elizabeth Jane Howard in *The Standard*, November 1981 (p. 159)
Penelope Mortimer in *The Sunday Times*, January 1980 (p. 163)
Dorothy Parker's poem, *Resumé* by kind permission of Duckworths (p. 170)

CONTENTS

INTRODUCTION

Living alone. Most of us have to do it sooner or later in our lives.

It may be when we initially leave home as students, or when we take up our first jobs. Perhaps when our careers direct us to a strange town where we know not a soul. We might be divorced, separated or widowed. Or maybe we'll find ourselves living alone on a part-time basis, as a travelling salesman for example, or as a woman married to a man who works on an oil rig.

Rapidly increasing numbers of the population live on their own. Already, there are $4\frac{1}{2}$ million of us in this country, and this figure is leaping by 120,000 a year. By 1990, official estimates indicate that the number of people living solo will have risen to 6 million.

Yet whenever and however it happens, living alone is something we come to woefully unprepared. The majority of us grow up in a family unit. We live in association with other people at school, college and university. Despite the fact that nearly one in three marriages ends in divorce, most people at heart do expect to marry and enjoy the companionship of a partner for life. So when a girl sits in screaming isolation in a bedsit ... when a wife dies ... when a husband falls under a bus or for the blonde next door, the reaction is one of sick terror at the prospect of coping with life alone. For as we have received no education, training or advice in how to think and act as independent adults, most of us have no idea how to set about functioning as self-reliant single people. Without the presence of

1

another person, supporting, encouraging or providing our *raison d'être*, we often feel vulnerable, purposeless and afraid.

When we are suddenly obliged to live singly, we are often made to feel freakish and unnatural, because we are not conforming to a socially acceptable pattern. Ever since Adam and Eve it has been the commonly held belief that living with one or more persons is the right and proper thing to do. Independence, in fact, is frequently regarded not as desirable, but more in the nature of a penance. The widowed, in particular, frequently find themselves cruelly shunned by society, which reacts to a death in the family as if it were akin to a contagious disease. *A widow,* declares an old Japanese saying, *is a woman waiting for death.*

Waiting. It's a word much employed by the married when they're discussing the one in four British adults who are single. Time and again one encounters the attitude that single people are merely marking time in a gloomy transit lounge, waiting for a partner to come along and gain them admission to the social Ark. (Yet, intriguingly, legend has it that Mrs Noah fought tooth and nail against embarking on her husband's craft. I suspect that Mrs Noah was a free spirit with a vision of all the hassles that lay ahead. She saw that two-by-two does not necessarily equal balance and harmony.)

Society, however, will insist on telling us otherwise. From birth we are led to believe that living singly equals being lonely, depressed, frustrated and unfulfilled. With collective eyes blurred by double vision, society parrots that to be on one's own is to have failed. It was this sense of failure which led to one of the most disastrous advertising campaigns of all time: *You're Never Alone With a Strand.* Advertisers stay in business by keeping a finger on the public pulse, but the Strand cigarette campaign bombed because they unwittingly touched a nerve. The same nerve which commonly causes single people to be regarded as objects of pity. How often have you winced at the remark, 'Poor thing, all on his

2

own . . .', 'Oh dear. All by yourself, then?'

It's not surprising that some single people feel so damply sorry for themselves. When a widower starts every other sentence with the apologetic whisper, 'When you're on your own . . .' he is succumbing to centuries of community brainwashing. When a single woman launches into an unnecessarily long explanation about why she's never married, the defensive note in her voice is there to appease society.

After all, if she hasn't got a partner, there must be something wrong with her, mustn't there? I mean, it's not as if she could positively enjoy living alone, is it? Pigs don't fly, do they?

Sadly, this kind of propaganda all too often hits its mark. Do any of the following remarks sound familiar to you?

'I do like living alone. But sometimes, after a really rough ride at the office, I feel it would be nice to come home and have someone to talk to over a drink about my day.'

(Any married person will tell you that in reality what happens is that *you* are required to sit and sympathise for hours over *his* awful day. Or she'll welcome you at the door with a spanner and the news that Junior has attempted to spin dry the video. And forget that longed-for Scotch. Any suggestion that you need a drink will be greeted with the sour accusation that you are hitting the bottle too hard and too often these days.)

'It would be so useful to have a man/woman about the place to lift heavy things for me; put up shelves/cook me some decent grub; darn my sweater.'

(Do you honestly believe that all little boys spring from the womb wielding Black and Deckers, and all little girls are born Mrs Beatons? There's nothing wrong with wanting a relationship, but not if you're merely intending to use your partner as a handyman or nanny.)

'On Sundays and Bank Holidays I stand by my window watching everyone setting off on happy family outings, and I do feel a pang of envy . . .'

(Do you really want to be them, stuck in a traffic jam on a

3

broiling hot day, screaming abuse about her inability to read the map, why the air conditioning won't work, who forgot to bring the jar of pickled walnuts for Uncle Fred, what he said to her mother, women drivers, whether that lorry driver was right to shout what he did at the traffic lights, who's driving this car anyway – and when they get home, who left the puppy shut in and who is going to clear up the mess?)

It is they, in fact, who should be envying you. Just consider the advantages enjoyed by the person who lives alone.

You can sleep when it suits you. You are free to read till dawn and lie in bed all day on Sunday. You are at liberty to eat what you like, when you like. You have the luxury of being able to live to your own rhythm, not one imposed on you by someone else.

You have freedom of movement, with no one to interrogate you on why you're late home, and why you left your room in such a state. When you feel gregarious, you can invite your friends round without having to ask anyone's permission. And when you're tired of people, it's your privilege to shut the door on them and bask in the peace, secure in the knowledge that there will be no strident demands for a three-course dinner, or a hand with the washing up.

One of the most exciting aspects of being single is the number of choices life offers you, in comparison with your married counterparts. As a single person, your horizons are yours to set. They aren't imposed upon you by partners or families. The options are all yours – and so is the control. *You* decide what you want to do, where and with whom. *You* decide how to plan your life. You're assisted in these decisions by the welcome fact that your income is your own, to spend as you choose.

At work, being unmarried is a tremendous advantage. Unhampered by marital pressures you can devote as much time and energy as you wish to the single-minded pursuit of your career. This applies especially to single women, for despite the increased participation of some married men in domestic responsibilities, in most homes the working wife is still the one doing two jobs. Because you are free to travel on business or transfer to a new area, you have a distinct edge on your married colleagues in the promotion stakes. Already, the journal *International Management* has noted that an increasing number of married managers are turning down offers of promotion on transfer unless their companies make the effort to find their spouses jobs in the new area.

With more available leisure time than those in permanent relationships, the single person enjoys more opportunity to travel for pleasure and to pursue new interests and hobbies. You have the time, too, to look and listen, to stand and stare – especially at yourself. For anyone living in a family, this is a nigh unattainable indulgence. But you, unfettered by domestic distractions, are at liberty to meditate, to find out who you are and what you want. Amidst the rush and bustle of modern life, you have the luxury of quiet time to collect your thoughts and revel in the tranquillity of being at peace with yourself. Because you are free to *be* yourself. When you live alone you have no need of façades, pretences, defences. The public face can be left outside the front door, as with a sigh of relief you relax in your own space and make yourself at home with yourself.

When you first start living alone you may not have a clear idea who the real you is. But as time goes on, you'll discover strengths within yourself and facets of your personality that would probably have remained submerged had you been living with someone else. And if you do decide to live with someone again, you can come to the relationship saying with confidence, 'This is me. Not perfect, admittedly. Flawed here and there. But at least I know my assets and my limitations, my good points and my bad. I'm not seeking an emotional prop. Despite all my insecurities, I've proved I can survive on my own. I've proved I'm grown up.'

An increasing number of single people, however, are finding that independence is too addictive to give up. As Felicity Bosanquet, ex-wife of the former ITN newscaster put it, 'Divorce has made a new woman of me . . . If my life goes on as it is, it would take someone pretty exceptional to drag me to the register office. To be honest, I've never been happier in my life.'

Having learned to be self-reliant, many single people are reluctant to relinquish what they've won. And there is a distinct sense of victory, because none of us learns to live alone overnight. Of course it takes time, sometimes years, to adjust to a way of life that previously inevitably included the presence of another person. Whether it's sleeping or eating alone . . . seeing a film or taking a holiday by yourself . . . learning how to rethread a tap or a sewing machine . . . each achievement is a minor triumph, a small battle won. It's one less thing to be afraid of, one more thing to feel positive about. Eventually, you don't look automatically to others to fulfil your needs – either practical or emotional. You learn to believe in yourself, and in your capabilities. You gain a reassuring feeling of personal security which gives you confidence, and in turn makes you more attractive to others.

That's an important spin off, because no single person wants to live in haughty isolation from family, neighbours, lovers and friends. Of course people need people. Friends are especially important to anyone who lives alone, and here again the single person has the edge over those in permanent relationships. Married couples usually find it more convenient to draw their friends from one social stratum, but as a single person you are not so confined. You are free to have friends from all walks of life, and to enjoy to the full the variety of experiences that they offer.

Having this opportunity to taste, enjoy and experiment with so many different lifestyles gives you an enviable breadth of vision as well as a deeper understanding of other people's pressures and pleasures. Being privileged to dip into numerous social pools helps you to eliminate in your own mind what you don't want from life, and to concentrate your energies on that which does suit you.

Yours is the choice, and yours the control. And with an extra 120,000 of the population every year living alone, the signs are that, increasingly, people are choosing to retain their options and their independence. Faced with a society conditioned to harness everybody into couples, more and more people are now fighting back. Single people are demanding changes in the tax laws, rating assessments, housing allocations, any aspect of life which discriminates in favour of the family unit over those who live solo.

The Tory Bow Group, in a 1982 report, recognised that 'single people – who are a rapidly growing sector of the population – can suffer many injustices'. They recommended the abolition of the married man's tax allowance where the wife is working, and the replacement of local rates by a local income tax system – or the provision of allowances for people living alone. The reform group also urged that widows' pensions should not be taxed and that 'local authorities should as a matter of course allocate a proportion of their accommodation to single persons each year'. *Stop putting us down* is the message from singles to the rest of society – underlining an active demonstration from those who live alone that they regard it not as an unsatisfactory interlude, but as a highly attractive alternative lifestyle.

Because it is a relatively new concept, you may not yet be convinced. Which is why I've written this book. *The Single File* is for every man and woman, of whatever age, who lives alone. It's for everyone who's ever said, 'Oh, I'd love to do this, or that – but I don't fancy doing it on my own' . . . for everyone who has been made to feel that there is something to apologise for in living by themselves . . . for all those people who have been encouraged to think of themselves as inadequate, misfits or social failures because they are single.

The Single File once and for all demolishes the myth that living alone is something endured by people who, because they are single, have been stamped sub-standard by society. That is not to say that the purpose of this book is to assert that living alone is one great jamboree, and to gloss over all the difficulties and frustrations of the single state. The idea is to bring all the problems out into the open and suggest

7

sensible and practical ways of dealing with them. Deliberately, I have not carved up each chapter into bite-sized chunks labelled Divorcees/Widows/Men aged 18–30. Obviously, depending on your age, sex and situation in life you'll find that some aspects of each chapter have more impact than others. But it's worth reading even the bits that at first sight may not seem relevant to your way of life. Because people who live alone always have something in common, and it's often reassuring for three people aged, say, 17, 37 and 70 to hear one another talking about a certain experience and to realise, 'Oh, but that's just how *I* feel. What a relief to know that other people, of a different generation too, feel exactly the same way.'

When you reach the last page of this book I hope you'll agree that living alone is not something to be feared. That on the contrary, anyone who approaches it in a positive spirit, prepared to seize every opportunity and capitalise on all the benefits, will find living alone a thoroughly rewarding experience. One which, whether it lasts for a month, a year or decades, has the promise of being the most enjoyable time of your life.

CHAPTER 1

HOME HUNTING

Where to live – What to choose – How to find it

Time was when single people had a tough time finding somewhere to live. Home hunting is always a hassle – and that applies whether you're single, married or something in between – but for many years the situation was worse for those on their own, due to a dearth of compact but attractive accommodation suitable for a solo lifestyle. Landlords found it more lucrative to shove as many beds as the law allowed into a room, and if you asked for a room to yourself you'd be offered, if you were lucky, the cupboard under the stairs. Meanwhile those wanting to buy their own homes were nobbled by the myth that houses are occupied by (and built for) couples or families, never by people who want to live on their own. And absurd though it sounds now, until comparatively recently, single women who wanted a mortgage had to pretend to the building society that they were engaged.

Fortunately, there are signs that the situation is changing for the better. Signs that the more enlightened of councils and house builders have woken up, at last, to the fact that not everyone wants to live as a pair.

In London, for example, Westminster City Council is offering bedsits and one-bedroom self-contained flats at very reasonable rents to young singles. Both Wimpey and Barratt Homes, no doubt goaded on by a survey suggesting that there are 4.3 million single people who qualify as potential housebuyers, are building studio flats specially designed for solo living. You can even buy an Easybuild one up, one down cottage-style home by mail order. It comes in kit form, and a competent builder or skilled self-build group should be able to erect it within six weeks.

Having been neglected for so long, it seems that the singles market is now getting too big to be ignored. Certainly, the increasing number of people who either want or are obliged to live alone should give us more clout in our demands for housing suited to the needs of solo living. We are, after all, highly desirable tenants and homeowners. We don't demand large gardens or luxury family kitchens. We're quieter than people with children. And if we're female, the building societies, in a complete reversal of their previous disdainful attitude towards us, now positively purr their approval:

'Women tend to be more financially responsible and better mortgage payers than men,' a Building Societies Association spokesman declared. One in five single women in the 25–29 age group has taken on a home of her own, and despite earning less than single men, women invest in more expensive properties.

Environment

When you're looking for a new home, the most important question to be decided is the area you're going to move to. You're not just paying for bricks, mortar and a roof over your head, you're also investing in a lifestyle. The kind of community you live in, whether it's a village, town or suburb, the type of neighbours you have, the variety of shops, the availability of public transport, sports and cultural facilities, all these factors will have a large influence on your day-to-day routine. This is especially important if you're recently divorced or widowed. As it's likely that your style of living is going to change, this is a unique opportunity to sort out in your mind exactly what *you* want from the area you're moving to.

Obviously, there are certain fixed factors which are going to limit you in your choice of area. You have to be near your place of work and most people like to be within striking distance of their families. Most, but not all.

British-born actress Jenny Agutter has revealed, 'I chose to live in Los Angeles because I could never feel as though I was really on my own in England. Family and old friends were always just around the corner. I wanted the feeling of being entirely alone – to deal with everything without help.'

'That's all very well,' I hear you snarl, 'but I don't happen to be earning Jenny Agutter's sort of bread. What's the use of having a passion to live in Millionaire's Row when I can only afford £15 a week rent?'

Yes, of course your budget is a key consideration. It would be fruitless to lash out 75% of your income on your ideal flat in the heart of theatreland, only to find you couldn't afford a seat up in the gods. (As a rough guide, 30% is the maximum of your income you should allocate to accommodation.)

But look at it another way. Think of the most grisly place you've ever been to. Now, if your fairy godmother offered you unlimited funds to build the house of your dreams on condition that you sited it in Grimsville, would you accept? I'd guess not. And no, you wouldn't accept harbouring the secret intention to flog it at a profit a year later and move somewhere better. If Grimsville's that awful, you're not likely to have a flood of eager buyers.

If you start by choosing an area you like, drawing a circle round it and concentrating your search solely within that ring, providing you're determined enough, it's likely that you'll find your niche there. It'll take time and a lot of footslogging, but it's worth having a go. All right, in the end you might have to concede defeat and start all over again in a neighbourhood you don't favour quite as much. But what's the point of caving in and compromising right from the beginning? Even in the most expensive areas there is still reasonably priced single accommodation available. And often, there's a reason why the rent isn't sky high. It's all a question of what you're prepared to put up with in order to achieve the style of life you want. An attic room with a glorious view may be freezing in winter and stiflingly hot in summer. If you're a nautical type who yearns to live near a river, you may suffer damp. New acquaintances used to be terribly impressed when I told them my address, which at the time was a posh street right in the heart of Mayfair. When they came to visit, they were horrified. 'It's like living in a coal hole,' they cried, viewing the heap of nutty slack used to fuel the block's central heating piled up outside my basement flat. 'However do you keep the place *clean*? Do you ever get *any* natural daylight?'

None of these considerations mattered to me. Having spent three years cloistered in a small mining town in the heart of Africa, I was delighted to be within walking distance of my job, theatres, restaurants, clubs, leafy parks – all that the best capital city in the world has to offer. It wouldn't suit me now, fourteen years on. But at the time it was perfect.

How do you decide which area is right for you?

Young people leaving home for the first time naturally tend to gravitate towards the big cities. But however exciting it may seem in prospect, a large city can be a frightening and bewildering place as, with well-thumbed A–Z in hand, you pound endless grey streets trying to find somewhere to live. What helps is to get hold of someone who knows the city well and is in a position to tell you the difference in feel between each area. London, for example, is surprisingly village-like for its size. Anyone really familiar with the capital will recognise instantly the difference between, say, the relaxed atmosphere that prevails in the riverside area of Putney, and the faster, more cosmopolitan air north of the river around Swiss Cottage. Anyone coming absolutely cold to a city, and knowing no one to advise them in this way, could do worse than to approach one of the doormen, porters, or security guards in a large office complex or block of flats. Most of them not only know London intimately, but also have time to sit and talk to you. A person who knows the area will guide you away from snapping up a flat in a notorious red light district, and at the same time they'll point out certain pitfalls that might not have occurred to you. If you like to go to bed late and rise late, for instance, it's no good taking on a pad near a noisy morning market.

Winter or early spring is the best time to look for accommodation in London. In the summer, the capital is crowded with tourists who take flats on short lets. Then in September all the students are searching for digs, so rooms and flats are harder to find. While you're looking for a permanent place of your own, you might find it convenient to stay at a hostel – but you need to book at least two or three weeks in advance. The London Accommodation and Advisory Service has a booklet, *Hostels in London*, listing more than 130 hostels in the London area. Outside London, write to the nearest YMCA or YWCA.

When you're choosing your area, obviously you'll want to be reasonably near your work, so you don't spend a fortune on fares. But keep your social life in mind as well. If squash, or jazz dancing is your thing, you'd be foolish to take on a dirt cheap flat in an area that's so far from the sports or dance centre that you land yourself with prohibitive transport costs.

For those who find themselves on their own after years of living with a partner – the divorced, separated and widowed – the decision of where to live is often made for emotional rather than practical reasons. Because of bittersweet memories, or a straight loathing for a place that made you unhappy, the temptation is to turn your back on the way of life you had before, and opt for a complete contrast of environment.

When Robert's marriage came to an acrimonious end, he couldn't wait to see the back of the smart town house he had shared with his ex-wife. He bought himself a cottage in a sleepy Gloucestershire village and revelled in the peace, after so many years of aggro. But after a while he found he felt unsettled. 'It takes years to become accepted in a small community like this, and as my job takes me away a great

13

deal, it's difficult for me to establish myself as a regular in any of the village activities,' he says. 'And frankly, I do feel a lack of companionship. Not just with regard to women – though the problem there is that if you're seen with a woman strolling through the village, everyone tends to have you married off in minutes, which is obviously embarrassing for both of us. But apart from that, when I lived in town there were always people around who shared the same goals as me, who spoke the same language. Here, kind though everyone is, I find it limiting being restricted to endless conversations about runner beans and whether the postmistress's daughter is pregnant.'

After a relationship is ended, whether by divorce or death, it's wise to wait six months before deciding on a move. Estate agents and solicitors make a lot of money out of people who chuck up everything, move to a new area, hate it, and then decide to come back again. When you're under emotional stress, neighbourhood friends and a familiar way of life are invaluable supports which you'd be foolish to cast aside lightly.

One aspect most of the younger divorced and separated people I've spoken to are agreed on is the advisability of steering clear of the suburban sprawl of big cities. As one newly separated woman summed it up, 'The last thing you want is to be stuck in an area where couples are the norm. At the weekends it's dominated by the men cleaning their cars and mowing the lawns. During the day it's overrun by mums, kids and those juggernaut pushchairs designed for twins. And at night it's deader than the grave.'

Some people in this situation head straight back for a big city and get themselves back into circulation. But others, who've done the bright lights bit when they were younger and dread going back and starting all over again, find that the best place for them to live is in a medium sized, bustling town – small enough for them to recognise friendly faces in the street, but large enough to offer ample social, sporting and cultural activities.

'When I was eighteen I left my highland village and came south to Glasgow,' 28-year-old Fiona recalls. 'I was delighted to have got away from my family, and all the village gossip. I loved the anonymity of Glasgow. It was so exciting, so liberating! I married, and we moved to a suburb of the city. But when my marriage broke up, I dreaded the notion of returning to central Gasgow. I suppose my marriage had accustomed me again to being part of a small world, and had given me a sense of belonging. I'd feel adrift now in Glasgow. By moving to the smaller town of Inverness I still feel I'm part of a community. And I'm glad, too, that my family are within reach. Funny how you change, isn't it?'

When elderly people suddenly find themselves on their own, it's always assumed that they'll sell up and move to a nice quiet little bungalow down a country lane, or near the sea. In practice, this is often a disastrous course of action. However beautiful the views, it can be depressing being marooned down a country lane with no one to talk to but the milkman. In winter, you might not even see him if the lane is cut off by ice and snow. And if it's a seaside area you've got in mind, do you really want to be surrounded by people all your own age and older?

'I was on the point of buying my dream bungalow by the sea,' recalls Arthur, a 64-year-old widower. 'Then a friend said that the town I had in mind was known locally as God's Waiting Room and I realised I really didn't want to live in a geriatric ghetto. Another drawback was that although there were some grand walks, they were all over the cliffs, which I thought might prove troublesome with my arthritis.'

You may think you're after a bit of peace and quiet, but even so it's unwise to move anywhere where you feel isolated. When you're viewing properties, of course you'll check that you have easy access to transport, the community and health centres, shops and the library. You'll also find it an advantage to choose a house where at least one of the main rooms overlooks the road, and people, because

15

even the prettiest back garden will pall in time if you've nothing else to stimulate the eye.

The aspect is especially important for anyone who's at home all day – the retired, for example, or those who are self-employed who work from home. Check that you're not looking out onto a rubbish tip or a depressing blank wall. Even if you decide you can tolerate the wall, investigate who owns it. If it's a glue factory, you might decide to pass up that particular des. res. and keep on looking.

You'd do well, too, to decide whether you're an upstairs or downstairs person. A top floor flat will afford you not only wonderful views, but also an added feeling of security as burglars are disinclined to climb ninety-eight stairs on the offchance that you have an expensive camera worth stealing. But sky-high living means a hassle lugging shopping up and rubbish down. And you won't have a garden. Even if you have the use of one, by the time you've carted cushions, books, cool drinks and apples downstairs only to discover you've forgotten the suntan oil, you'll probably throw in the towel and decide to stay pale, interesting and upstairs. You won't suffer these problems with a basement flat. What you might have instead is a view of dustbins, a lack of natural light and burglar bars on the windows. Houses too, should be viewed in the same manner. Live on a hill, and you'll have to tolerate a great deal of wind, whereas a house in a sheltered valley will often be shrouded in mist.

Your age and general state of health are also important factors to take into consideration. A penthouse flat, a house with stairs or a hill to climb to the shops may suit you very well now – but think ahead a few years and give some thought to what your needs are likely to be then.

Renting

Deciding on the area is the relatively easy bit. The tough part is actually finding that room or flat. There's no point in running way from the fact that flat hunting is a hard, often dispiriting, slog. But stick with it, because if you know what you want and are prepared to search long and thoroughly enough, you'll find it.

Start at your newsagents, with the first edition of the local newspaper and the evening paper. Seasoned flat hunters read the Flats to Let column from the bottom up, hoping it will give them a flying start to be first to get through to the landlord on the phone. If you live in London, try also *The Times*, *Time Out*, the London Accommodation and Advisory Service, Capital Radio's flatshare list and the Piccadilly Advice Centre (01-930 0066). Notices in newsagents' windows, or on your office, club or college noticeboard may bring results. Only use a flat finding agency as a last resort. They often prove expensive at a time when you can least afford it. By law, they are not supposed to charge you a registration fee but many do and they often want up to a month's rent on top of that if they find you a place. Some of them also charge for alleged phone calls made on your behalf. The trouble is, of course, that the less reputable agencies see the desperate look in your eyes and take you for what they estimate they can get.

The best and often the fastest way of finding a place is by word of mouth. Tell everyone what you're looking for. Tell your friends, the people at work or college, the barman at the local. Hairdressers, so I'm informed, are particularly skilful at fixing their clients up with flats. Some landlords never advertise and will only let a room on the recommendation of friends. Often the most coveted rooms only get passed on in this way, so it pays to broadcast your needs.

If you're really desperate and literally have nowhere to lay your head for the night, contact your local Housing Aid Centre, who will direct you to a bed and breakfast hostel. It's worth remembering, though, that as single people we are not covered by the Homeless Persons Act and local authorities have no legal obligation to house us.

The same attitude prevails when it comes to council housing, with single people placed firmly at the bottom of the list. In Winchester, for example, single people are allowed onto the waiting list at age 30, but they have no chance of being allocated a house until they have waited five years. However, the charity organisation Shelter recommends that you do put yourself on the council house waiting list as a way of registering a protest in the hope that eventually the authorities will wake up to the fact that there are a lot of us single people out here and we all need somewhere to live. If you are already renting a home from the council and want to swop with someone in another area, contact Locatex who arrange exchanges between council tenants.

There is a glimmer of hope in the idea of local authority housing associations and co-operatives. You put your name on a waiting list, and eventually you may be able to become a tenant or co-owner of a property which has been cheaply leased by the local authority. Some of these schemes have, in fact, been specially designed for single people. The schemes, and the way they work, tend to vary from area to area, but more information can be obtained from your local Housing Aid Centre or from the Housing Corporation in London.

When the magic moment arrives and the landlord's phone isn't engaged . . . you don't arrive panting on the doorstep to be told the flat has just gone . . . OK, it isn't perfect, but it's the best you've seen and you want it . . . it's tempting to say yes on the spot and reel round to the pub for a rewarding double Scotch. Especially as the landlord will be pressing you for a quick decision, emphasising that there are a hundred more potential tenants hot on your heels.

A quick word here about landlords and landladies. With competition for flats so fierce, they are in the position of being able to pick and choose amongst possible tenants. So it's wise to do everything in your power to impress on them that you are a quiet, sober citizen who will cherish their property as if it were your own and, most important, that you will pay your rent on time. When you're viewing flats this is not the occasion to deck yourself out in your most funky gear. Pretend you're going to tea with Aunt Maud. Dig out that nice, demure cotton dress or the sports jacket with the reassuring leather patches. Emphasise that you are in steady employment, or studying hard for your exams, and be prepared to give references from your employer, previous landlord or bank. Once you've agreed to take the flat, expect to give a month's deposit plus one month's rent in advance immediately. But make sure that in return you receive the key of the door and/or a receipt.

However, before you snatch the key and rush off to celebrate, make sure you check out the following first:

* What sort of tenure are you being offered? If it's a 'shorthold tenure' it will last only for a fixed term of between one and five years. Make sure you know when you have to get out, or renew the tenure.

* What does the rent include? Lighting, heat, porterage? Do you have to pay extra for general rates and water? Is there a phone installed? It's expensive to have one put in yourself, and there may be a waiting list in your area.

* Are you allowed to redecorate?

* Are there laundry and/or drying facilities?

* Has the rent been registered with the local Rent Officer? Either you or the landlord can apply for a fair rent to be registered, and this amount will then be the most the landlord can charge you.

* If you're sharing a bathroom, landing, stairs and kitchen, who is responsible for cleaning them? Who supplies basics like cleaning materials and loo paper?

* Is there any storage space anywhere in the house (like the attic or garage) which you are allowed to use?

* Are you permitted to use the garden, if there is one?

* Many landlords are absentee types who operate through agents. Ensure that you have the name and telephone number of the person responsible for dealing with an emergency, or repairs.

Buying

When you're searching for a house or flat the logical place to start is at an estate agents. Read their blurb and you get the impression that you sit down with a sympathetic, know-ledgeable agent and explain that you're looking for, say, a two-bedroomed character cottage with a price ceiling of £18,000. The agent is then supposed to flood you with details of suitable properties. However, in some people's experience, you will indeed be swamped, but with four-bed estate semis at prices calculated to send your bank manager through the roof. I have also come to the conclusion that even if you walked into an estate agents and said you just wanted a two-room shack, in any condition, anywhere, and you had a million pounds to spend, they would still shake their heads sorrowfully and murmur that there's been such a run on that sort of property, they haven't much to offer you . . .

But despite the love-hate relationship we seem to develop with estate agents, most of us do find our houses this way. If you're moving out of your area, try to contact an agent who is a member of the Home Relocation or the National Net-work of Estate Agents. They operate countrywide and will ask their members to look for suitable properties for you in the area of your choice.

Something every house hunter soon learns to do is to interpret estate agents' blurb. Euphemisms which tend to crop up regularly are:

* compact – no room to swing a cat
* characterful – infested with cats
* distant views – if you stand on the chimney pot
* garden flat – basement with no light
* spacious – draughty and impossible to heat
* scope for improvement – falling down

Apart from going to estate agents, it often pays you to explore other avenues. Literally. Walk or drive around your chosen area in the hope of finding For Sale signs put up by vendors trying to save themselves hefty estate agents' fees. One enterprising divorced woman told me how she not only carefully selected the road in which she wanted to live, she then decided by the position of the sun on which side of the road she preferred her house to be. 'I get home from work at 4.30 and I wanted to be able to have my tea outside and relax in the sun for a bit. If I'd made the mistake of buying a house on the other side of the road, my garden would have been in shadow by half past four.' Pat then popped a note through every door, asking the occupiers if they were thinking of selling. It happened that one person had idly been contemplating a move and Pat's letter proved to be the catalyst. And because she knew he was saving on estate agents' fees, she was able to negotiate a price with him which was considerably lower than that being asked by agents handling similar properties in the area.

Cheaper than estate agents, though not always providing the same range of services, are the property shops and computer-matching agencies. Property shops such as Seekers operate rather like Job Centres. Details and photographs of the properties are displayed in the shop for you to browse through. It is then up to you to contact the vendor to arrange an appointment to view.

The computer-matching system, such as that operated by Homeline, is to feed details of properties and buyers' requirements into a computer. The buyers are then sent a comprehensive print-out of suitable properties, and again it is up to them to contact the vendor and take matters further.

As I mentioned earlier, both Barratt and Wimpey are pioneering custom-built singles' homes. In the past, very little has been built for this market. Yet, as a Barratt spokesman pointed out, 'The number of single households has grown very rapidly in the last few years, while the number of flats available for rent has shrunk.' In a Barratt Studio Solo, you are offered a living/sleeping area, kitchen, bathroom and dressing/storage room. The advantage of the Studio Solo and the similar Wimpey Super Single is that they have been designed to allow you to move in with little more than your suitcase. They are decorated, carpeted and have all the basic furnishings included in the price. Crest Homes, too, are building one-bedroom houses specially suited to the first-time single buyer.

Those with more money to spend, who yearn for elegant surroundings and the suggestion of gracious living, might be tempted to take a flat in a converted beautiful old country house. Both Period and Country Houses and Hunt Thompson Associates specialise in these conversions, but the lordly lifestyle doesn't come cheap. In 1981 a 99-year lease on a one-bedroom flat would have set you back £58,000.

Developers are beginning to realise that the elderly will be an important growth market in the next decade. AMSA Retirement Homes are concentrating on building specialised housing which is quiet, manageable but also central to the local community and amenities. One-bedroom flats, mostly with balconies and spectacular views, cost from £40,000.

If you already own your home, but find it too large for you to manage, you could consider giving it to Help the Aged. They will convert it and in return give you an expense-free flat within the property.

When you go to view a house or flat, don't be beguiled by the weather or the time of day. Visit it in the rain, in the evening and at a weekend. You may discover that a road which is a haven of peaceful tranquillity during the week is deluged on Saturday afternoons by soccer fans en route to the nearby football ground. If, on your second visit, you find the vendor's aunt still standing casually in the fireplace recess, move her out of the way. She has probably been planted there to conceal a damp patch, or a hole. Watch out, too, for strategically placed house plants, positioned to draw your eye away from the peeling plaster. Above all, take someone with you for a second opinion. This is especially important if you're the type, like me, who tends to concentrate on the lovely view and ignores that smell of old socks which could be dry rot. Buying a house is probably the biggest investment you'll ever make in your life, and it's a nervewracking decision to have to make on your own. An excellent aid is the Consumers' Association *Which? Way to Buy, Sell and Move House.* It takes you step by step through the processes involved in buying or selling a house, and in particular contains pages of sound advice on what to look for when you view. Despite this, I find it rather endearing to learn that most of us still choose our homes not for purely practical reasons, but on gut instinct. Time and again you hear people say, 'Oh I just walked in and knew at once I wanted to live here. It was my house.'

But however much in love you are with the place, before you commit yourself you should check on the running costs of the property:

* Rates
* Water rates
* Ground rent, if leasehold
* Upkeep charges, and whether you have any control over them.

The next step, of course, is the finance. A building society is most people's first option when seeking a mortgage, and if you're a first time buyer it helps if you've registered with the society for the government 'Homeloan' scheme. If you can save £600 in two years, you qualify for a £600 loan which is added on to your mortgage advance and is interest free for the first five years. When you're viewing properties, it's worth remembering that building societies prefer to lend on houses rather than flats, especially if the latter are conversion jobs with leases that have less than 50 years to run.

If you are refused a mortgage, always ask why. Then walk a hundred yards up the road, and try the next building society, and the next. (Some years ago there was discrimination against single women, but this is now illegal.) Alternatively, banks and local authorities are also in the business of offering mortgages. Although government spending cuts mean that local authority loans are not as easy to get as they used to be, they have the advantage that local authorities will often lend on properties which building societies are wary of. Converted flats, for example, or older properties which the purchaser wants to renovate.

'Should it happen that you've tramped the length of the high street and had all the bank and building society doors slammed in your face, don't despair. It's only a house you're trying to buy, remember, not *The Times* or the Empire State Building. The mortgage you need may seem a frightening amount to you, but in terms of what's borrowed daily by city whizz kids and international industrialists, what you're asking for is peanuts. Somewhere, there is someone willing to lend you the money. Approach your trades union or professional association for help. Try your employer – but if your firm is willing to make you a loan, check whether it would have to be repaid if you left their employ. Your solicitor or accountant may be able to arrange finance for you (for a fee) or if you're buying a brand new property, ask the developer if he has mortgage facilities available. Finally, there are the mortgage, or insurance, brokers. As one broker told me, 'I arrange mortgages for out-of-work actors, struggling writers, students . . . all the people who are supposed to be bad risks. There are very few people I can't fix something up for.' It's essential, however, to go to a reputable broker. The Corporation of Mortgage, Finance and Life Assurance Brokers will give you a list of their members in your area.

Before they offer you a mortgage, the organisation who is lending you the money will send in their surveyor to value the property. Some building societies will now let you see a copy of the surveyor's report. But bear in mind that this is a *valuation*, not a full *structural* survey. For this, it's essential to employ your own surveyor (although some building societies will, for an extra fee, arrange for their surveyor to carry out a structural survey for you at the same time as the valuation). The Royal Institution of Chartered Surveyors,

The Incorporated Society of Valuers and Auctioneers or the Incorporated Association of Architects and Surveyors will provide you with a list of their members in your area.

A structural survey isn't cheap – but it's vital for your peace of mind if you live alone. At first sight, the lengthy report will probably scare you witless. Page after page of faults in the place you want to call home. But when you analyse the report, you'll see that many of the defects are in fact quite minor and easy to repair – a broken window catch, perhaps, or a rotted piece of weatherboarding on the back door. Remember, no house or flat is perfect. You may think when you viewed it that you inspected it pretty thoroughly, but every house has its secrets and you only learn about them once you've paid the money and it's too late to get it back. At least if you move in armed with your surveyor's report, you know the worst. You aren't going to find yourself sucked into a nightmare saga starting with your amused discovery of a mushroom growing behind the cooker and ending with all the floorboards and staircase being ripped out because the place is riddled not just with mushrooms, but with dry rot. (A true horror story.) And if you do have the misfortune to have something like this happen to you, then providing the rot wasn't mentioned in his report, you might be able to sue the surveyor.

Jobs with Accommodation

At first sight, it looks as if you're solving two problems at a stroke if you take a job with accommodation attached. *The Lady* magazine, for example, has pages of advertisements for people wanting live-in domestic help, or companions. The obvious drawback is that if you leave the job, you've lost a roof over your head as well, and you're back to square one. The other pitfall, especially for women, is sorting out the genuine advertisers from the dodgy ones.

Divorcee Alison recalls, 'Years ago I answered an advertisement in a quality national newspaper inserted by an artist who wanted a personal assistant. I'd just left my husband and was camping out with friends, so lured by the offer of a free flat I went along to meet the artist. He was a white-haired man in his fifties who seemed suspiciously vague about just what my duties would be. Every time I pressed him for precise details about the job, he offered me a sherry and commented admiringly on my tan. Obviously, I bolted for the door at the first opportunity. But I was interested to see that over the next six months that same advert cropped up again and again in the newspaper – at intervals just long enough for some innocent to have taken the job and then left rather hurriedly.'

The moral here is first, to follow your instincts. If the vibes are wrong, don't take the job. Secondly, adopt a businesslike attitude from the start and make it plain that you expect your prospective employer to do the same. Don't let on that you're totally alone in the world, even if you are. Invent a posse of supportive male relatives and bring them casually into the conversation.

When you're discussing the accommodation, don't leave any vague areas. Ensure that it's made clear whether you're free to come and go at whatever time of day or night, if you can entertain your friends and whether you have a separate, private entrance. Do you have to share a bathroom or kitchen? If you do have to share, say, a kitchen with your employer, establish right from the start what principle is being used for your food and his/hers, and who is responsible for the cleaning. Sharing facilities can cause enough aggro when you're a private tenant, but when you're sharing with your boss it can put you in an impossibly difficult position. Make sure your time off is clearly defined and that you have a written contract which covers both aspects of your job (salary, hours, holidays, etc) and your tenure of the accommodation.

Moving In

This is not something you should attempt to do by yourself. Even if you reason that you own so few possessions, you could just hire a van and manage the entire operation alone, it's advisable to have someone with you to revive your spirits if the van breaks down or simply to make you a cup of tea when you surface from the last packing case. Don't go to the other extreme, however, and enlist too many helpers. A surfeit of carnival atmosphere has been known to result in an arm being cut off a sofa when it got stuck in a doorway.

The easiest way to move is to ask a removal firm to do all the packing for you. Because of the expense, however, most people do some or all of the packing themselves. The important thing here, for people living alone, is not just to label each packing case with its contents, but to ensure that when filled they aren't too heavy for you to move by yourself. You won't unpack all your boxes on the day you move. Some, containing less essential items, may sit unopened for months, but if you want to redecorate the room they're in, or put a carpet down, it's galling to find they're too weighty to shift.

If you're loading a van yourself, remember to put in last things like carpets, which you'll want to come off first. Anyone using professional removers should avoid:

* getting in the way
* wincing as your packing cases are thrown into the van
* giving the men advice on how to load your precious set of drums.

This is their job. They do it every day and they know more about it than you do. Just make the men gallons of tea and smile your apologies nicely when they produce from the back of cupboards the smelly fishing socks and sweaty T shirts you forgot to pack. Even so, make sure you keep your wits about you and ensure that everything that left your old home turns up at your new one. A check list will help.

Label each piece of furniture with the room for which it is intended. Hopefully, you'll have done your stuff with the graph paper and thought this out well in advance, to enable you to take full advantage of strong removal men or helpers on moving day. Tomorrow, when there's only you in the place, is no time to decide that the grand piano needs shifting down two floors.

Whatever you do, don't let your kettle go with the rest of your gear on the van. A tea-making survival kit is vital and should travel with you as hand luggage to your new home. It's best to stick to tea and coffee. If you succumb to the temptation to see the day through in an alcohol induced haze, you'll probably end up sawing both arms off the sofa. Save the booze until everything's unloaded and, most important, you have made up your bed. One thing's for sure. When everyone's gone and you're left to spend your first night in your new home, you won't feel lonely. You'll be feeling so elated and exhausted you'll crash out, thankful that you haven't had time to unpack the alarm clock.

Some Useful Addresses

AMSA Retirement Homes, P.O. Box 9, Henley-on-Thames, Oxfordshire.

Barratt Developments, Barratt House, 2 Grosvenor Road, Wallington, Surrey.

Capital Radio, Euston Centre, Euston Road, London NW1. (01-484 5255)

Corporation of Mortgage, Finance and Life Assurance Brokers, 24 Broad St., Wokingham, Berkshire RG11 1AB. (0734 785672)

Crest Homes, 39-41 Thames St., Weybridge, Surrey.

Easybuild, 24 Sandy Lane, Camberley, Surrey.

Help the Aged, 146 Queen Victoria St., London EC4V 4BX.

Homeline, 3 Kensington Mall, London W8. (01-221 3838)

Home Relocation, Suite 303, Radnor House, 93 Regent St.,

London WIR 7TE. (01-439 3611)

Housing Corporation, Waverley House, Noel St., London W1V 3PB.

Hunt Thompson Associates, 69 Parkway, London NWI. (01-267 3895)

Incorporated Association of Architects and Surveyors, Jubilee House, Billing Brook Road, Weston Favell, Northampton NN3 4NW.

Incorporated Society of Valuers and Auctioneers, 3 Cadogan Gate, London, SW1X OAS.

Locatex, P.O. Box 1, March, Cambridge PE15 8HJ. (03542 4050)

London Accommodation and Advisory Service, 16 Great Russell St., London WC1B 3LR.

National Network of Estate Agents, Refuge House, Watergate Row, Chester. (0244 316695)

Period and Country Houses Ltd., 61 Harcourt Terrace, London S W 10. (01-373 5180)

Royal Institution of Chartered Surveyors, 12 Great George St., London SW1P 3AD. Scotland – 7 Manor Place, Edinburgh EH3 7DN.

Seekers Property Shop, 48 Market Place, London N W 11. (01-458 8035)

Wimpey Homes, Hammersmith Grove, London W6.

Further Reading

Bradshaw's Guide to DIY House Buying, Selling & Conveyancing – Castle Books, 5 Blackdown, Leamington Spa, CV32 6RA.

Buying a Home – SHAC, 189a Old Brompton Road, London SW5.

Which? Way to Buy, Sell and Move House – Consumers' Association.

CHAPTER 2

HOMEMAKING

A place of your own

'Quite simply, this is my place,' said divorcee Joan as she ushered me into her cosy flat. 'It's not just somewhere to rest my head, it's my home. The one small area in the world where I can really be me, where I don't have to pretend. It's comfortable, it suits me and my way of life, above all it helps me to feel at peace with myself.'

Your home, we agreed, should be a welcoming refuge, a place where you're at ease, content – where you want to be. Yet sadly, many people who live alone don't view their homes in this light. To them, the place they live in is somewhere to be seen as infrequently as possible. It may be because they feel driven out by unhappy memories; by a lack of warmth or comfort; or just because their pad is so filthy it makes them feel sick. But the major reason why so many single people don't bother to create a relaxing environment for themselves is that society has led them to believe that being at home is a non event. How, asks society, can you possibly be enjoying life if you spend some of your evenings and weekends stuck at home, alone?

Just consider, as a single person, the advice most often thrown at you: *Don't stay in! Get out and meet people!*

'Why sit at home staring at your own four walls?' the Agony Auntie scolds Separated Steve. 'Join a club. Enrol at evening classes. Learn to windsurf. There's a fascinating world outside your front door. Go out and meet it half way!'

Well yes, Agony Auntie is right – up to a point. It's important for all of us to keep in the social swim. But not if we're diving into a whirlpool of merrymaking purely to escape from drowning with boredom in a room, a flat, a house we can't stand. The trouble is that, albeit with the best of intentions, people like Agony Auntie tend to endorse the widespread belief that if you spend a few evenings at home by yourself you're a failure. Lost out. Life passing you by. Boat not just missed but steaming over horizon issuing derisory hoots at forlorn figure alone on quayside.

What you *are* in danger of catching, though, is the plague of believing that a frenzied social time is the passport to a fulfilling life. So if all a man wants to do is flake out at home with a book he still feels obliged to pretend to the world the next day that it was Bunny girls instead of Charlotte Brontë he had spread out on the fireside rug last night. It's hard enough for Joe Soap next door having to keep up this charade, but when a screen romeo like Omar Sharif admits that he has far fewer girl friends than anyone he knows, and he'd rather go to bed with a book, his statement is considered amazing enough to make headline news.

Then again, we've all encountered 'One for the Road Roger'. He's a stalwart down at the local with a regular order for a pie and a pint as soon as the doors open, organising the darts, chatting up the birds, jovially insisting that you can't leave yet, the night is still young, and usually staying to help the bar staff clear up. Good old Rog.

Sad old Rog. He's so terrified of going home, he'd rather spend every night in a noisy, smoky pub, with comparative strangers who he knows at heart don't give a damn about him. He regards the place he lives in as alien territory. Somewhere he has to force himself to return to – especially if his ex-wife has made off with most of the furniture. Soaked in self-pity, he doesn't realise that he doesn't *have* to camp out on dusty bare boards, staring at the space where the telly used to be as he spoons baked beans from a tin.

(No, I haven't forgotten how wretched it is to feel lonely, insecure and frightened. We'll be looking at those aspects of single living in a later chapter. What this one is about is the need to create a restful home environment tailored to suit

31

your way of life. Because if you feel comfortable with your surroundings, you're more likely to feel at home with yourself – and that, in turn, is half the battle in learning to live successfully with other people.)

But back to Rog. If he doesn't watch it, he'll find himself gratefully proposing to the first woman who comes along willing to wield a feather duster and unearth the Rennies he's crying out for after all those indigestible pub pies. So desperate will he be to rush her to the Registry Office that he'll ignore the voice of experience warning him that an enthusiasm for cleaning up after him and baking wholesome homemade pies is hardly the recipe for a happy marriage.

What Roger has, in common with every other single person, is the ideal opportunity to create a totally individual living style. It may not seem so at first, but eventually it must dawn on you what bliss it is not being obliged to consider the whims, tastes and demands of parents, partners and children. Because we grow up in families and accept as second nature the necessity to be mindful of the needs of others, it often takes some time when we live on our own to appreciate the full liberation of being able to do our own thing with our homes.

Vera was sixty when she was widowed. 'My husband was a very conservative man who decorated our house in subtle, muted earth shades. It looked very tasteful, very nice. But two years after his death I stood in my sombre bedroom with its parchment walls and oak wardrobes and rebelled. What I'd always longed for and never had, even as a child, was a really feminine bedroom. I gave the oak bedroom suite to my daughter and bought a new set in white, with gold relief. The rest of the room is now pink, lavender and white, with lace-edged pillows and frilled flowery pelmets. My son is appalled. He says it's more suitable for a sixteen-year-old girl than a woman in her sixties. But I don't care. It's what I want and it makes me happy to wake up to every morning.'

What makes you happy only you can know. It might be rainbow-coloured ceilings, murals, sunken baths or suspended beds. Whatever your fancy, if you can afford it, why not indulge it? If it doesn't work you can change the whole thing back again, without having to suffer the piercing screams of *I told you so*.

For all sorts of groans-from-back-of-hall reasons to do with conditioning and mothering, men seem to be singularly inept at turning their houses into homes. Yet when men like One for the Road Roger do nerve themselves to make a pit stop they often prove to possess far more verve and imagination than women at homemaking.

Take 30-year old Stuart. After his divorce, he took a cool look at his life style and in particular at his elegantly furnished dining room.

'My marriage was punctuated by squeals of, "Don't put that hot dish down on the polished table . . . mind you don't scratch the table . . . watch that wet glass on the table". I hated the bloody table. What's more, now I'm single again I never use the thing; if I want to entertain I prefer to take people out to a restaurant. And if I have a few friends round for supper, it's more relaxing to make it a fork and fingers affair in the comfort of the sitting room.'

The table went, along with the ladder-back chairs, the sideboard and the Wilton. Stuart's dining room is now a motor cycle workshop. 'It's great having the space to experiment,' he enthuses. 'I can cover myself and the walls with grease without anyone nagging. It's warmer than the garage in winter and I have the added satisfaction of the room being used to full capacity, instead of twice a year when it was a dining room.'

A change to single status often necessitates a move to smaller accommodation – when a marital split forces the sale of the family house, or the widowed find their homes too large for one. The way you view this depends on whether you look at half a glass of wine as being half full or half empty. Naturally, it's distressing leaving a house which has been your cherished home for many years. But there are unexpected compensations.

'When my husband and I split, I sobbed for days at the thought of selling our lovely country house,' recalls Wendy, a dancer in her mid twenties. 'But it had to go and by the time all our debts were paid off, I was left with just enough for a one-bedroomed flat. I wallowed in self-pity for months, until in the end I'd bored not just my friends with my agonising, but myself too. Then something snapped, and I started to see the positive side of my situation. I could, I realised, indulge myself – as far as my finances allowed – in new colour schemes and furnishings for my flat. I held a huge garage sale, delighted now to have a legitimate opportunity to get rid of those op art curtains, the pleated lampshade, the rattan chair that gave me backache – all those things which you hated as soon as you got them home from the shop, but couldn't admit to loathing because they'd made such a hole in the housekeeping money.

'Once installed in my new home, I discovered other advantages. My flat was on the first floor, in the middle of a terrace. After running a large house, I found my heating bills for the flat laughable. "How you'll miss your pretty garden," said my friends. I thought I would too. But my flat had a balcony big enough for me, my deckchair and some tubs of fuchsias. Best of all, the balcony faced south, whereas my old garden was north facing and never got the sun in the afternoons.'

Whenever you're moving from larger to smaller accommodation, the golden rule, and the hardest one to follow, is to be ruthless about chucking out furniture that won't fit or that you don't need for your new way of life. Easier said than done, I admit, when that six-foot oak settle was one of your late wife's most treasured possessions. But would she really want you to break your back every time you heave it out of the way to get to the kitchen? Far better to give or sell it to a home with the space to set it off in style. If you offer it to relatives first, at least you'll have the comfort of knowing it's still in the family.

By the same token, it isn't disrespectful to your late partner's memory to change things around in your home. It's healthier to keep a special place in your heart for them rather than allow a shrine of their memorabilia to crowd you out of your own living room.

If you're living in a small space, then however much it hurts, you are going to have to learn to be reasonably tidy. Naturally, it's your place and if you want to keep it like a tip that's up to you, but there is a danger that you'll be so reluctant to come back to it that you'll be joining One for the Road Rog propping up the bar till closing time. Even more infuriating is deciding you will pop out for a livener and then spending hours of precious drinking time on an enforced treasure hunt for your wallet. Obsessive tidiness is a bore, but a reasonable degree of it saves you time in the long run. (The worst example of excessive zeal in this direction is the woman who apologised to her guests for the drifts of cherry-blossom 'cluttering up' her lawn.)

It helps if you've got enough storage space – even if it's only a box under the bed into which you heave all your dross as the doorbell rings. Beds with fitted drawers underneath are practical, but expensive. A cheaper solution is to fit casters to some junk shop drawers and slide them under the bed.

If you live in an older house you're lucky, as there will probably be numerous alcoves and landing space which can convert to good storage use. Modern houses, as we all know, don't have these accommodating features, so you're obliged to employ more cunning in those uncompromisingly straight-edged rooms. Apart from cupboards and drawers, utilise the wall. A foot-wide shelf fitted round the wall at picture rail height makes use of space that would otherwise be wasted, and will take an amazing amount of books, bottles and boxes.

Take a look at the bathroom. Box in the sink and give yourself cupboard space beneath the basin. You may also find there's room for a surprising amount of clutter behind the panels that mask the bath. I know about this because when I was living in a rented flat and writing my first novel, I was so terrified of prying eyes that I used to hide the manuscript at the back of the bath. Much later it transpired that all the other tenants knew of this hiding place and were reading each instalment of the novel as it was finished, lying in the bath and enjoying a steamy scene in more senses than one.

During all this heady talk about painting your walls puce if it pleases you I've assumed that the place is yours to do as you like with. But what if you're in rented accommodation and forbidden even to wave a tin of Dulux in front of the walls?

To hell with all that, I said, when I lived in a rented basement flat decorated throughout in an interesting shade of untreated sewage. Aware of the beady-eyed landlady upstairs watching for tell-tale paint smudges in my hair, I smuggled down the gear and redid the place white by stealth, at night. I had reckoned without my landlady's sense of smell, however, and there was a very acrimonious row, with me being accused of deceit and ordered to return the flat to its original tone of diarrhorea (taupe, my landlady called it). In the end, after I'd put in a suitable amount of grovelling, she calmed down and admitted it did look fresher in white. 'But,' she admonished, 'you should have asked me first. I know it says in the rent agreement that you can't redecorate, but I don't mind if you ask and let me know what you want to do.'

Rule one, then, is to chat up your landlady. Knock on her door occasionally armed with a bottle of her favourite tipple and suggest she joins you for a glass. Try to ensure that these jolly drinking sessions are conducted in her flat rather than yours – the last thing you want is her getting into the habit of popping into your flat whenever she feels like a bit of company . . . or has exhausted her own cache of booze. Establish a rapport with your landlady and you'll benefit: not just from being able to paint the place as you wish, but also because she might be amenable to your removing the more ghastly pieces of her furniture as well.

She might ... but we all know in reality we're going to remain stuck with that overstuffed armchair and all we can do is disguise it with an enormous, pretty shawl. Anyone who's lived in rented rooms soon becomes very adept at the art of camouflage. Cheap cotton bedspreads transform ugly sofas or chipped tables. An alcove piled with junk disappears if you hang up a curtain the same colour as the wall. The antediluvian standard lamp provides an admirable support for a climbing grape ivy. (Remember to water the plant away from the lamp flex.)

Mark is a management trainee whose firm moves him round the country to a new office and a new bedsit every six months. 'In my last place, I developed back trouble so I invested in an orthopaedic bed,' he says. 'Then I realised my small flat looked like a dormitory. There was my bed, my landlady's two single divans, and a convertible sofa. I pushed one of the divans against the wall, piled it with cushions and found it a useful adjunct to the sofa. That left me with the second divan to dispose of. I took off the mattress and hid it under the box cushions on the sofa. Then I dragged the divan base into the kitchen, upended it against the wall and hung a piece of corked hardboard down the length, which I used to display postcards and messages. It still looked something of an eyesore, but at least it gave me six feet more room in my living area.'

Obviously, the place isn't going to seem like home until you've bought a few of your own things that reflect your taste, your personality. Mark always starts in a new flat by bringing in his own lamps.

'The landlady's lighting is bound to be hideous – stuff she wouldn't give houseroom to herself. I bung it all under the bed and position my own favourite lamps – an Anglepoise for reading, and others with cotton shades for a soft background light.'

Clever lighting can do a great deal to improve the appearance of your room. Brighten up a gloomy corner, for example, by hanging a mirror there and placing a pretty lamp in front to reflect in it. Artfully positioned spotlights will draw the eye to objects you find pleasant to look at – a favourite picture, perhaps – leaving that moth-eaten stuffed owl in the shadow of obscurity. Don't buy ordinary light bulbs – a delicate pale pink like Phillips Argenta Rose is much kinder on the eyes. Though for a really flattering light you can't beat candles. The scented variety have the advantage of not only bathing you in a soft glow, but also masking the smell of the pork you burned in the kitchenette.

'I would never buy anything for a rented flat that's heavy or needs fixing permanently to a wall,' says Mark. 'I've invested in some fold-flat beech bookshelves, a Persian carpet, some good lithographs and a compact music centre.'

Other good buys, which you can pick up and take with you when you move, are bright scatter rugs and cane or wicker furniture.

If you're canny, you'll make a point of getting on friendly terms with the other tenants in the house, in case it's possible to effect a few stealthy furniture swops. It'll probably have to be a moonlight flit because most landladies tend to screech with rage if their beloved stuffed owl migrates up or down a floor. But if Grizelda and Gerald from downstairs get a migraine from their red and yellow striped curtains, and you know they'd brighten up your drab decor, it's only sensible to arrange a quiet exchange.

Grizelda and Gerald should also prove useful for gen on how the house works – or doesn't. Tap them for information on the eccentricities of the hot water system, and the best time to take a bath. What day the dustman comes, and when therefore to make sure you're around to grab a black plastic bag before Guy in the garden flat snaffles them all. Whether you're entitled to use the garden – it may be that you are, but have been put off by Guy staking claim to the only sunny spot and making out it's his territory. Then there's storage. Officially, you may be forbidden to use the garage. But if Grizelda and the rest have been getting away with sticking their bikes in there, you may as well quietly follow suit.

Buying the Basics

'I love coming to your little flat, Sylvia,' gushed her mother. 'It's such a home from home. Everything looks so *familiar*.'

Naturally. Student nurse Sylvia had approached all her friends and relatives and found that most of them had something they wanted to turf out. Admittedly, not everything was to her own taste, but she recognised that setting yourself up with all the essentials all at once can be a frighteningly expensive business. Even if you're moving from a larger house crammed full of furniture, you often find it either won't fit or won't suit your new place, obliging you to give or sell it to people like Sylvia and go out and buy more. An afternoon spent wandering round the high street stores is likely to leave you shell-shocked at the price of the most basic household equipment. But setting up a home doesn't have to cost a bomb. It's worth keeping an eye on those high street stores, because they are all in cut-throat competition with one another and often have excellent special offers, with up to a year's interest-free credit thrown in. And if you time your spending spree to coincide with the June or January sales you could do very well – providing you don't get lured into buying a whole load of stuff you don't need just because it's plastered with a beguiling red reduced ticket.

The small ads in local newspapers are an excellent source of second-hand bargains, both for individual items and notices of garage sales. Experienced bargain hunters tell me there are two tricks attached to local rags.

First, find out in which part of town the paper comes out earliest (you can often gain half a day's advantage here) and start ringing the moment you spot a likely item. Remember, you're competing not only against other householders, but dealers too, and the best bargains tend to get snapped up very quickly. Dealers can be a suspicious lot. They usually manage to get to the vendor's house first and block the door as I pant up the steps, greeting me with the keen enquiry, 'What are you after then, love? A new chest?' I used to take this personally, until I realised they were only trying to suss out if I was a rival dealer in stripped pine.

The second strategy worth bearing in mind is to choose a newspaper which circulates in a prosperous middle-class area. People here will often be giving their cooker the heave, not because it's clapped out but because they've been tempted to replace it with the latest split level model advertised in the Sunday colour supplements. Another advantage of these vendors is that being proud of their homes, they tend to take care of their possessions, so the appliance you're buying from them has a good chance of being well maintained and serviced.

The same principle applies to newsagents' noticeboards. Choose your area wisely and you'll have a choice of bargains. But the reverse seems to be true of junk shops. Prices are often higher in the better class areas, so it will pay you to travel a few stops further down the line to a seedier neighbourhood. Never offer the full price in the junk shop. The owner will expect you to haggle.

If you have the courage, and the time, then auctions can provide the best bargains of all. It depends who you've got bidding against you on the day. The time factor is important, though, as you need a day to view before the auction itself.

Most big towns have a shop specialising in reconditioned cookers and electrical goods. They may have the odd chip or scratch, but most reputable shops guarantee their equipment. It's also worth calling in at the Reject Shop if there is one near you. They don't just sell seconds, but good value manufacturer's end of ranges as well.

When you're buying on the cheap, it's essential to keep your wits about you and examine every prospective purchase very carefully, both for defects and to ensure that the item really is what you want, and will fit where you want it to go. A serious defect to one person, however, may be only a minor irritation to another. If you discover woodworm in that knockdown price set of spoonback chairs, for example, you'll either recoil in horror and cancel the sale, or calmly decide to devote a day treating the holes with Rentokil. (If you're me, you'll then gnaw your way through a packet of aspirins to get rid of the headache brought on by worrying if you've done a thorough job with the woodworm fluid.)

Whatever you're purchasing, one of your main considerations should be how you're going to get the thing home – and up the stairs. Obviously, it's false economy to buy a table for £25 at the local market if you've got to lash out another £10 for the hire of a van and a strong man. It would have been cheaper to pay £30 for the table at the high street store which delivers free. You must also spare a thought for the size of your door frames and whether there are any tight corners to be inched round. It may look hilarious in movies when the piano gets stuck on the stairs, but the other tenants in your block won't be hysterical with mirth, especially if the wedged piano is blocking the way to the loo.

One way to dodge the carting home hassle is to buy by mail order. Many people are finding it far more convenient to sit by the fire with their feet up, choosing what they want from a catalogue instead of battling their way through high street crowds. Most mail order firms claim to give you cheaper goods by cutting out the middleman (ie. the retailer) but it's often a swings-and-roundabouts operation, as what you would have paid to the middleman you are now sometimes shelling out on mail order postage. The reputable firms offer goods on seven days' or a month's approval and will return your cheque without delays or inquests if you decide to send your purchase back. The two main drawbacks with mail order buys are first that if you are out at work all day you have to arrange for someone to be there to take your parcels in. Secondly, if you've ordered something that needs to be assembled at home you often find that a vital screw or nut is missing from the parcel. You then have the aggro of either writing to the mail order company and waiting for their reply – or you're obliged to make a foray down to the high street for the nuts and screws, which is what you ordered by mail specifically to avoid.

As several of my single friends have jobs which require them to move on and set up a new home in a new area every year or so, I asked them to take a look at their basic household equipment and pass on any tips that the rest of us might find useful:

Carpets

Living alone, your sitting room carpet isn't going to get the same wear and tear that a family would inflict on it. So you can save money by having a bedroom quality wool carpet in your living area. Watch out for useful room-size remnants. Avoid rush matting. It traps the dirt and soon looks tatty.

Beds

They take up a lot of precious room. Wesley-Barrel, the London Bedding Centre, The Space Saving Bedding Centre and Adeptus all have an ingenious selection of folding, stacking and triple purpose beds. If you intend using your bed as seating it's worth investing in a firm-edge mattress or a foam rubber one such as 'Charisma' by Dunlopillo which can stand the strain of being sat on. Ordinary sprung mattresses are not designed for this purpose, which is why your mother bawled at you so often not to sit on the edge of the bed.

Sheets

Mail order are excellent value. Beware street market sheets. They are often composed of more starch than cotton. Check how tight the weave is, and also the size, if the stall holder will let you!

Pillows

Buy the best you can afford – otherwise they soon go limp or lumpy.

Curtains

Do you need them? If you're not overlooked, why bother? Hanging baskets with trailing ivys or a row of Mother of Thousands on a sash window make an attractive alternative. If you do need curtains, sheeting is cheap and easy to sew as it comes in a wide width which reduces the number of seams. John Lewis has a marvellous range of prints and plains in lovely colours. Make top loops to eliminate the need for expensive tape and hooks. Keep an eye on the reject box in any store which makes up curtains. They sell off at reduced prices curtains which have been ordered but not collected. (Who are all these people who submit themselves to the headshrinking hassle of measuring up windows, choosing material, lining, headings etc. and then don't bother to pick up the finished product?)

Blinds take up less room than curtains and are safer in kitchens. Make sure your measurements are exact.

Tables

Aim for flexibility. Drop leaf tables are best as they don't take up room when not in use. Watch out with gatelegs, to ensure you and your guests can sit comfortably without bruising your legs. Alternatively, simply join up two shelving or low cupboard units with a piece of chipboard.

Seating

Folding dining chairs are sensible, but always try before you buy. It's worth paying extra for those with padded backs as hard-edged wood or plastic will hammer your spine. Folding garden chairs are more comfortable but listen for tell-tale creaks heralding collapse if entertaining a heavyweight guest. Crumble-filled huge floor cushions are cheap and cheerful. High-backed seating that provides neck support is more comfortable than low-backed. Two 2-seater sofas take up less room than a 3-piece suite.

Cookers

Vary in width. When buying, especially second hand, make sure it will fit your space. It's essential to have your cooker checked and installed by a qualified fitter from the gas or electricity board.

Crockery, Cutlery, Glasses

Markets give good value, also reject shops. Check that the handles are put on properly. Do you really need a matching set of plates? Toning colours in different patterns look attractive and won't bore you as quickly.

Cooking Pots

Oven-to-table ware saves space and washing up.

Freezers

A boon for many single people. Not because you're going to spend your Sundays blanching basketfuls of beans, but to save you endless treks to the shops. However, if you live near the shops, you might as well save your money and use the shopkeeper's freezer (and electricity, insurance, maintenance).

Anyone unaccustomed to being responsible for choosing household furnishings and appliances can find themselves quite at sea at first. What are the features you're supposed to look for in a fridge or carpet? How do you decide whether you need an upright or cylinder vacuum cleaner? An excellent handbook to help you shop successfully is the illustrated *Which? Shopping Guide*, which gives you practical advice on all aspects of household purchasing, from deciding what you need through to maintenance and servicing. On a lighter note, William Rushton's book *Superpig* contains a wealth of basic information and wry humour (it's especially good on how to wash clothes).

Luxuries . . . and False Economies

One of the many advantages of being single is that we have

the liberty to spend far more time in bed than people who have children. Since we all spend a third of our lives in bed anyway, it makes sense not to economise on such an important basic item. Get the best you can afford and don't be shy about ordering the size of bed you want. If you hanker after a king size four poster, then have one, and to hell with what the neighbours think as they watch it being delivered to your bachelor apartment.

Bed manufacturers emphasise that it's vital to try out the mattress by lying on it before you buy. Advertisements croon lullabies about the infinite variety of our sleeping positions . . . they show us pictures of clever glasses of wine balancing on the springs . . . they worry endlessly about your bad back, offering you mattresses that are firmapaedic, orthopaedic, posturepaedic, supportapaedic . . . But what no bed manufacturer or salesman ever seems to mention is what you and I know a bed is used most for, after sleeping. I just wish I knew a couple with the nerve to march into Heals and ask the salesman's advice on sexapaedic mattresses – before thoroughly testing each bed for its spring under stress, the strength and squeakiness of the legs, and whether the casters are liable to make it whizz alarmingly round the room.

Bedcoverings, too, are items you can really go to town on. A luxurious goose-filled quilt with a gorgeously pretty cover – a patchwork spread – Hollywood white fur – whatever your taste you can indulge it, secure in the knowledge that no child is going to come romping in at 6 a.m. and throw Ribena and egg all over it. And if you should happen to spill red wine on it, well the mess is all your own and there's no one to nag about the cleaning bills.

The bedside table is the ideal place for your telephone. Telephone engineers seem to me to be sadists in their insistence on connecting the instrument up in halls, so you suffer the draught either from the stairs or the front door blasting down your neck as you take a call. Admittedly, it is expensive to have a telephone installed if there isn't one there already, but if you live on your own it's an essential, rather than a luxury. Not just for late night calls to friends when you're feeling a bit low and not just to keep your social life on the boil, but also for those inevitable times in life when either you or the heating system suffers a temporary breakdown and you need help.

It is absolute madness to over-economise on heating. Whether we're fuelled by oil, coal, gas or electricity, we all feel like electrocuting ourselves when the bills arrive. But if your home is cold, you're only going to be miserable. Then you'll feel driven out, and before long you'll be joining One for the Road Rog at the bar – probably spending more in the pub than you would have done turning up your gas fire to a comfortable level. Heating *is* expensive. It's a horrid fact of life, like our unpredictable summer climate. We all moan about it, but it's an occupational hazard of living in one of the most civilised countries in the world. If you can't tolerate either the weather or the price you have to pay for fuel, go and live in Australia or Greece – then you can sit in the sun and winge about the scarcity of water and the prohibitive price of Scotch.

Obviously, it's only sensible to conserve as much heat as you can. Newspapers and magazines are full of intelligent advice on how to insulate your loft, lag your pipes, draught-proof your doors and either double glaze or cling film your windows. Clearly, it's absurd to heat half the garden and the sky over the roof, but this apparently is what we are doing if we allow expensive warmth to escape.

Watch, though, that you don't get so carried away buying goodies for your home that you neglect to attend to an investigation of the support systems you'll need to make you truly independent. Which of your neighbours can you rely on to keep a spare set of keys for you? Ask them to recommend a good local doctor and dentist. Keep their phone numbers handy along with those of a reliable plumber, electrician and general handyman. Check out which of your corner shops will deliver or stay open after you return from

work. Locate the nearest branch of your bank, the launderette, the council rubbish tip.

Don't wait until the moment when you need these people
or services. Seek them out well in advance and you'll save
yourself a great deal of time and worry in the long term.
Make sure, too, that your property and its contents are fully
insured, preferably with a new-for-old index linked policy.

Maintenance – Avoiding That Sinking Feeling

If the loo overflows every time you flush it, it's tempting to
think, oh I'll just ignore it and use the one at work . . . I'm
not at home much in the evenings anyway . . .

This is an attitude generally more prevalent amongst
women than men. As a sex, women seem stubbornly
unwilling to learn how to maintain and mend things. Deep
down we know it's unreasonable, but when the door handle
falls off or the sash cord breaks, the assumption is that it's a
man's job to put it right. If there doesn't happen to be a man
around, far too many of us will suffer in a stinking room with
a window we can't open rather than tackle the repair job
ourselves – or pay a professional to do it. But if you as a
woman can bring yourself to appreciate the difference between your spanner and your screwdriver, it's wonderful the
sense of liberation that sweeps over you when you do cope
with a small job yourself instead of having to charm a man to
do it for you.

No one is suggesting that anyone, man or woman, should
attempt to mend the gas cooker or re-wire the house by
themselves. But things like changing plugs, fixing fuses,
putting on new tap washers, unblocking sinks, adjusting loo
cistern ballcocks and changing car tyres are within anyone's
capabilities. They are fiddly jobs, admittedly, but not impossibly difficult, and you'll save yourself pounds on what it
would cost to hire a professional to come in.

A good set of basic tools is the first essential: screwdrivers, spanners, brad awl, saw, hammer, pliers and electric drill are adequate to start with. You don't need to buy them all new – second-hand stuff is often better value if it was made in the days when tools were fashioned to last. Make friends with the staff in your local do-it-yourself shop. Explain that you're a novice at the game and ask them to help you with everything you need to see each particular job through. That way, you won't get home with wood, brackets and screws for your new bookshelves and find that no one told you about the all-important rawl plugs.

Take the trouble to learn where the water mains stopcock is located and the mains switches for gas and electricity. Make sure you have a good, stable torch (complete with batteries), candles and assorted fuses to hand.

The wise course is to think ahead, expect equipment to break down periodically and budget for it. It's shaming how many of us will subscribe to a private health scheme, antici-pating that our bodies will give up under the strain occa-sionally, yet when the roof springs a leak or a joist gives way, we are outraged at the inconvenience and expense we're burdened with. It saves a lot of time and hassle to put in a bit of spade work before things break down, building up a list of reliable plumbers, electricians, carpenters and general handypersons on whom we can call in an emergency. Wait-ing until the emergency occurs only throws you into the clutches of the cowboys, who regard you as the easiest way to make a fast buck. (There's more gen on what to do in an emergency later on, in Chapter Eight.)

Bear in mind that even in the best of circumstances, mov-ing to a new home can make you feel depressed and dis-orientated at first. You don't know anyone, and you don't know your way around. At home you're surrounded by practical tasks that need your attention, and you don't know where to locate a plumber, or the best places to shop for all your household necessaries. Adrift and overwhelmed by it all, it's easy to feel like giving up and letting everything go hang.

Don't. Living in a place where nothing works properly is bad for your morale. Try to tackle one job at a time, so you at least have the satisfaction of seeing something, however small, completed every day. Drifting from job to job is unproductive, and mentally disruptive.

You'll also do wonders for your state of mind if you make an effort to keep the place clean. Of course it's tempting to think, oh well, there's only me to see it, so why bother? It would be different if I had someone to clean it up for.

You have got someone to clean it up for. You. Obviously, it's boring to get so fanatical that every time someone drops biscuit crumbs on the floor you rush the Hoover under their feet. But taking a balanced pride in the way your home looks is a reflection of the value you put on yourself. You'd be horrified at the notion of going out in dirty clothes, so why live in a room that reeks of stale cigarette smoke, cooking smells and the overturned bottle of beer behind the sofa? There's no need to spend a fortune on lavender-scented spray-on polishes. A damp cloth and a dry duster work just as well (even on wood) and cost a fraction of the price of all those aerosols. Vacuum the floor, open the windows, stick some fresh flowers in a vase and you're through.

Oh – I forgot the washing up. It may be tempting to leave the dirty dishes piled under the sink for a week, but I can vouch from experience that it's extremely unpleasant having to clean up mice droppings, especially when apart from the left-over food they've also chewed their way through your favourite beaded evening bag.

Dig for Victory

'I shall miss my garden dreadfully,' a widowed lady told me recently, 'but since my husband died, I've found it impossible to manage by myself. I've really got no choice but to sell up and move to a flat.'

Since she had already sold her house and the reason we

met was that I was buying her wheelbarrow, it didn't seem a diplomatic moment to discuss ways and means of coping with a domestic jungle on your own. Even those of us who love gardening find it daunting being placed in a situation where we alone are responsible for what seems like acres of wilderness. But the degree of difficulty in coping with a garden isn't always dependent on size. A small patch with a sloping lawn, terraces of heavy clay and high hedges can be more time consuming than an acre of land designed to look mainly after itself.

The first thing to do when you take over a garden is to decide what you want from it. Not what the previous owners wanted, or your ex, or your late wife. What *you* want. A sunny spot for your deckchair, with a blaze of summer flowers in the borders? A fragrant herb garden? A vegetable plot to keep you fed all year round? A sheltered Mediterranean courtyard, filled with flowering tubs? A water garden, complete with pool and jacuzzi? A putting green?

Purists insist that it's essential for your garden to match the style of your house. 'You cannot,' they shudder, 'have a cottage garden outside a neo Georgian terrace.'

Why not? Whose garden is it, anyway? Who's going to tend it, weed it, water it? Mr Purist? Obviously, you have to temper your imaginative bent with the amount of time and money you have available to spend on your dream. It's no good hankering after a romantic rose garden if you don't have hours in the day to spare for all the unromantic pruning, spraying, mulching and dead heading such a vision entails. You'd do better to settle for bulbs, which take care of themselves and multiply in a satisfying manner from year to year.

One thing you won't be short of is advice. Gardeners are a sociable lot and weeding the front garden is one of the quickest ways I know to make friends. And bookshop shelves are crammed with gardening books. Whether you want to fill your patch with wild strawberries or York stone paving, you'll find something written specially with that in mind.

We all have our own favourite gardening writers – those who seem to be on our wavelength; for me, the best gardening books are those with lots of colour pictures, and written by people who considerately refer to Foxgloves as well as Digitalis. I always enjoy anything by Anne Scott James. She doesn't talk down to amateurs like me and, unlike certain more celebrated gardeners, she isn't afraid of admitting when she's failed with a certain plant or shrub.

There's no need to spend a fortune at expensive garden centres stocking up your garden. Neighbours, local fêtes, markets and bring-and-buy sales are excellent sources of cuttings. A trip to someone else's beautiful garden makes a pleasant Sunday outing, as you'll come home loaded with cuttings and ideas. *Visit an English Garden* (available from the English Tourist Board and some bookshops) is a book featuring over 250 gardens well worth looking at.

Many people are put off gardening because they assume it's hard, back-breaking work. It needn't be. Tools and equipment have become lighter and far more efficient in recent years. Spring loaded spades, hover mowers, plastic wheelbarrows, versatile hand cultivators and small electric rotovators all help to take the grind out of gardening, leaving you more time to sit back and enjoy what you've created. And just about everything you may need, from secateurs to cypress trees, is available on mail order – so if you don't have transport you're saved the chore of lugging your new holly bushes home on the bus.

If you love the look of a pretty garden, or a well stocked vegetable plot, but have neither the capacity nor the energy to manage it yourself, why not investigate to see if there is a share-a-garden scheme operating in your area? Young people in flats, for example, are often delighted to have the opportunity to share in a garden. The usual arrangement is that you divide up the produce 50/50, or if it's a lawn and flower garden, your helpers can pick what they like, within reason. It's a useful arrangement when you're away on holiday, too.

There's something both soothing and stimulating about gardening. Even friends of mine who've been convinced they've not got green fingers have found, once they recovered from their initial horror at inheriting a garden, that they gained surprising fulfilment from it. And gardening has a way of satisfying your every mood. Quite apart from the thrill of watching things that you've planted grow and blossom – it's marvellously therapeutic if you're in a tearing rage to have a furious session pulling up weeds or slashing at the blackberry bush. (I can always tell when the girl next door has had a blazing row with her boyfriend. The smoke from her enormous bonfires blacks out the entire neighbourhood.)

But you don't need half an acre to enjoy the pleasures of gardening. A window box, a few tubs on a balcony or the outside stairs can be a source of endless delight, especially if you fill them with fragrant flowers and shrubs. Imagine the lift to your spirits as you stagger in at 3 a.m., feeling distinctly jaded, to be greeted by the heady scent of night flowering Nicotania (Tobacco Plant). All for the price of a packet of seeds.

And yet, over the intoxicating scent of Nicotania, do I sense a chill in the air?

Look, you are saying grimly, I have found somewhere to live. I have turned my house into a home and cultivated my garden. My place smells of fresh paint and roses. There is nothing I'd like more than to go out to a party and come home feeling tired and emotional. But how do I get invited to parties when I live alone and don't damn well know anyone?

Some Useful Addresses

Adeptus, 110 Tottenham Court Road, London W1. (And countrywide.)
English Tourist Board, 4 Grosvenor Gardens, London SW1W ODU.

London Bedding Centre, 26 Sloane St, London SW1.
Space Saving Bed Centre, 14 Golden Square, London W1.
Wesley-Barrell, 86 Tottenham Court Road, London W1.
(And countrywide.)

Further Reading

Superwoman – Shirley Conran (Penguin)
Reader's Digest Repair Manual (The Reader's Digest Association)
The Sunday Times Book of Home Maintenance (Times Books)
How to Buy (Almost Anything) Second Hand – Richard Ball (Astragal Books)
The Decorating Book – Mary Gilliatt (Michael Joseph)
How to Cheat at Gardening – Hazel Evans (Ebury Press)
The Which? Shopping Guide – Consumers' Association
How to Cope at Home – Barbara Chandler (Ward Lock)
Superpig – William Rushton (Futura)
The Smaller Garden – Penelope Hobhouse (Collins)

CHAPTER 3

THE SOCIAL SCENE

Meeting people – Where to go and what to say

Once you've discovered the pleasures of staying at home and enjoying your own place and your own company, it's only natural that you'll feel the need to start extending your horizons. But you're in a new neighbourhood and you don't know a soul. The folk next door are no help – they're out all day and appear to barricade themselves in at night. You're longing to get out and meet people. So where do you start?

Ideally, you start weeks or months *before* you move. Ask your newsagent to order the local paper of your new area. Read it from cover to cover – the sport, the small ads, the jumble sale notices, W.I. meetings – everything. It will all appear coldly alien at first, but as the weeks go on you'll find yourself growing more comfortable with the paper. The reason local newspapers are so successful is that they reflect very accurately the character of the area in which they circulate. By immersing yourself in the local rag, you'll get a feel for your new town and the people who live there.

Gradually, you'll notice that certain names keep cropping up again and again. By the time you move, you'll know that Major X is the man leading the anti-motorway campaign. Miss Y, secretary of the Theatre Club, runs jazz dancing classes on Tuesdays, while Mr Z, the plumber, is also captain of the local cricket team which came top of the league last season. Even if you don't give a damn about the motorway, hate the theatre, jazz dancing and cricket, and are capable of handling your own plumbing, just being familiar with the odd name or two is useful conversationally, if only to stop you dropping monumental bricks.

Another tactic to try before you move, is to contact the secretary of a sports, social club or activity group that interests you in your new area. After my divorce, I decided for various practical reasons to move to Winchester, although I knew no one there. From *Spare Rib* magazine I learned the name of the contact at the Winchester Women's Group and rang her up, explaining my situation and asking if I could come down and have a chat. Jill was marvellous. She very kindly laid on a buffet lunch party and invited three other women to meet me. When I moved, it made the world of difference knowing four friendly faces in a sea of strangers.

Moving to a new place is an exhausting business, both physically and emotionally, so while you're first getting your bearings it's wise not to try and jump into too many social pools at once. Concentrate your energies, initially, on just one or two activities that attract you. When I'm in a strange town, my first port of call is always the library. I know I'll feel at home there, and it's a good starting point for making contacts, either with the staff themselves or through the clubs and societies listed on the notice board. Depending on your interests, your jumping-off point could be the sports centre, the social club at work, the film society, the W.I., the local history society, the church ... Tune in, too, to your local radio station for up-to-the-minute info on what's going on in your area.

Men, of course, have always found it easy to get to know people through the camaraderie of the pub scene. But it's not so simple for a woman. Even in these liberated times, a woman drinking alone is all too often regarded as a scarlet harlot, and, therefore, fair game. When you've dropped into a pub hoping to find friendly companionship, it's infuriating to be leered at and treated as the good time who's been had by all.

One way round this is to choose a pub whose ambiance you like and gradually get yourself known there, especially to the landlord. Jane, a trainee manager for one of our top chain stores, is transferred to a new town every nine months. At first she dreaded each move and the readjustments and loneliness it involved. Because her job necessitates short-notice travelling and late hours, she found it wasn't practical for her to join local clubs or societies – especially as she knew that by the time she'd established herself as a member, her firm would have wafted her to a town 100 miles away.

Jane realised that for someone in her position, the ideal solution would be to centre her social life on her local. A pub scene is more easy going than a club, in that people are dropping in and out all the time and there's no hassle about why you didn't turn up for the AGM last Thursday. What Jane did was to start by calling in at her local for a quick drink on her way home. At first, she never stayed longer than half an hour. Just long enough to have a brief chat with the landlord and get her face known.

'But don't grab a glass of wine and retreat to the darkest corner of the saloon,' advises Jane. 'Sit at or near the bar for that half hour. It shows you're feeling sociable, and you're on hand to join in the general conversation.'

Jane also popped in to the pub after she'd been to the launderette on Saturdays and sometimes for a drink Sunday lunchtimes. It didn't take long for the landlord and bar staff to get to know and like her, and once she expressed a willingness to learn how to play darts, her place in the local social scene was assured. The darts, she says, have proved an unexpected asset. Not just for easing her way in to a new group when she moves to a new area and a new local. But with her darts in her coat pocket, she feels more secure walking home on dark nights.

It goes without saying, of course, that women in pubs do not sit and wait for men to buy the drinks. Neither do you take your purse out and peer half-heartedly inside as you pray for a man to flash a fiver at the barman ahead of you. Nor do you give a man the money to go and fetch the refills. You get up off your backside, pay for your round and bring the drinks back to the table. Cheerfully.

Friends and ...

Neighbours, logically, should be the perfect people to take you under their wing and introduce you to a new area. Unfortunately, we British seem to take a perverse pride in cultivating a chilly attitude towards those on the other side of the wall. You do hear stories about kindly, smiling women who turn up after the removal van is gone, bearing tea, home made cake and a stream of useful advice about the neighbourhood. All too often, however, the folk next door remain firmly on their side of the fence, warily eyeing you and your washing line through the slats and reporting back to their other halves about your bizarre taste in underwear.

Once again, it's up to you to make the first moves. Take a stroll round the area one Saturday afternoon, stopping to talk to everyone you can. Chat over garden walls, admiring your neighbour's roses or enquiring about the acidity of the soil. Ask that man who's washing his car where would be the cheapest place to get yours serviced.

Most people who take the trouble to make the first overtures of friendship towards their neighbours discover that they weren't being standoffish at all. What they were displaying was a typically British respect for your privacy. They didn't want to intrude. As you get to know your neighbours, hopefully you'll achieve a balance between frosty reserve and the sense that you and they are living in one another's pockets. Being a good neighbour generally boils down to being supportive in a crisis, lending them things, not complaining about the noise, and keeping an eye on the place for them while they're away. In return, they are supposed to do the same for you.

But because you live alone, you may find that your neighbours tend to take advantage of you, assuming that of course you'll be free to babysit, or dish out tea and sympathy. This is the point at which, gently but firmly, you must establish your boundary lines. Make it clear that it isn't convenient for them to pop in for a chat as soon as you get home from work, as it's a time when you feel extremely irritable and need to be by yourself. But if they'd like to drop by for a drink after supper, they'd be more than welcome.

Once you've got to know your immediate neighbours, there's nothing to stop you looking further afield. Pause at the bus queue and find out from the people in line how reliable the service is. Linger during a lax time at the nearest general store – shopkeepers are a mine of local information. It doesn't matter that you aren't interested in where the best fish and chip shop is, or know already. Your aim is to make contact, and get across that you're new to the area. You may find that the man at the bus stop lives just across the road from you, or the girl at the sweet shop whom you've asked for gen on the local cinema is at a loose end tonight and fancies taking in a film.

Shortly after my mother was widowed she stopped in the park to admire a young baby in her pram. It transpired that Jenny, the mother, was a freelance woodcarver desperate for a few hours peace to get on with her work. My mother, with time on her hands, offered to take care of baby Hannah for a few afternoons a week and as a result has been drawn very happily into Jenny's lively social circle. Not only that, but when she takes Hannah out lots of women pause to smile at her … invitations to tea are exchanged and as a result I get peevish calls from the rest of my family complaining that my mother is never in when they ring up.

The Untouchables

It isn't just moving to a new town which can place you in the position of having to establish a social life from scratch. If you're widowed, or newly divorced or separated, you may have lived in a neighbourhood for decades, yet suddenly find yourself adrift, as if your new single status has branded you as an outcast from the safe haven comprised solely of couples.

You don't fit in any more. As recently divorced Wendy put it, 'My married friends ask me round for coffee mornings, or for drinks when their husbands are out. But what they won't do is invite me to dinner, because they're terrified I'm going to seduce their husbands. For their part, the husbands are wary of having me around in case their wives think I'm having such a wacky time as the gay divorcee that they're tempted to have a bash at it themselves. Either way I can't win. I feel as wanted as a contaminated can of corned beef.'

The widowed often find themselves left out in the cold for quite the opposite reason from divorcee Wendy. Journalist Madelon Dimont wrote in *Homes and Gardens*, after her husband died:

'There's all the difference in the world between being a bachelor girl, independent and single by choice and being the leftover half of a couple. Parties can be hell. You feel a freak, on your own when the others have either come in pairs or are in the process of pairing off, untouchable the moment you admit you're a relatively recent widow. *Widowhood attracts respect and, frequently, unease*' (my italics).

It's at this juncture that the divorced and widowed often find it helpful to associate for a while with people who have a shared experience of their situation and don't make them feel like pariahs.

The National Council for the Divorced and Separated organises countrywide groups, with outings, theatre parties, etc. where people can make friends and discuss mutual problems at weekly meetings.

Cruse is an organisation with over sixty branches in England, Scotland and Wales, and offers advice and support to the widowed.

But not everyone wants to dwell on the private agony of their newly acquired solo status. 'There is nothing worse,' my friend Stuart declared vehemently, 'than arriving at a dinner party seeking diversion and lively company, to have your hostess hiss at you in the hall, "Darling, we're very cosy tonight. Only one other guest and I know you're going to get on so well. Blodwyn's newly divorced like you so you'll have lots in common. Poor lamb, she's still frightfully weepy about it all – her ex was a superpig by all accounts – but I know as you've been through it all yourself you'll be terribly sympathetic. Strictly *entre nous*, I think Blodwyn would like nothing more than to settle down again . . . with the right man this time . . ." '

Everyone finds it disappointing at first when old married friends either want to pair you off, or only invite you round when their spouses are out. But gradually you may find that it is you who are severing the bonds with them – for the time being. Their values, interests, topics of conversation won't be the same as yours. With your new independent lifestyle, you may come to regard their twosome set up as stiflingly smug, and prefer instead the company of the single people with whom you have more in common.

Just about every single person I've interviewed for this book has given me the same piece of advice to pass on to those who are seeking a more varied social life: *never refuse an invitation*. Accept everything you're offered, however uninspiring the people or occasion might seem at first sight. You may not be remotely interested in the Sewage System of Southern England (who is?) but if you're invited to a talk on the subject, at worst it could be so awful that it'll make an amusing story to relate to your colleagues at work over coffee . . . and you never know, you might find at the lecture that the girl working the slide projector is having a party next week which she'd love you to attend . . .

That's all very well, you may say, but I haven't got time for this kind of hit or miss socialising. After a hectic day at work, what I want is to get out in the evening and go somewhere where I can be sure of meeting a friendly crowd of people – preferably some of whom will be of the opposite sex. But just where do I go? Where do all these people hang out?

Here are some suggestions to start you off. Most of them are London orientated – it's not that I don't believe the rest of Great Britain exists, it's just that London is the place I'm most familiar with – but these ideas can fairly easily be adapted for your own area.

Where to Meet Men

First the bad news. Men abound in any *milieu* which is muddy, wet, windy or cold. Kit yourself out with some snazzy, weatherproof gear and track the beasts down at:

* Rugby grounds, sailing, golf and archery clubs, race tracks and sports centres, ski-ing, windsurfing, pot-holing, mountaineering
* On hills, flying model aeroplanes
* Private aerodromes, learning to fly real ones
* Jogging
* Playing cricket or bowls in the park
* Backpacking anywhere in Greece (especially if you fancy Scandinavian men)
* Allotments or the local gardening club
* Under second hand and vintage cars
* On walking/cycling holidays (don't under-rate youth hostels)
* Archaelogical digs
* If you're not the outdoor type, get a job in a sports shop

After braving the elements, you deserve a reward. Treat yourself to:

* A drink at the Connaught bar. It teems, discreetly, with Gucci-shod men. I dropped in there once simply to rest my aching feet, and within two minutes I'd been bought a glass of champagne.
* Suss out the City. Have lunch at one of those places which used to be working men's caffs, but that are now chock full of pin-striped types gleefully spooning up the roly poly pudding they're not allowed to have at home.
* Take tea at the Ritz. Film producers favour it for concluding deals.
* Call in for an early evening drink at a big hotel

catering for sales conferences and exhibitions.

* Pretend you want some insurance. Within a week of filling in the coupon you'll have eager underwriters beating a path to your door.

The following venues also come highly recommended:

* Beer festivals
* Speakers Corner, Hyde Park
* First class train and airline compartments
* Political rallies
* Casinos
* Teachers' residential courses
* Swans Tours (expensive but worth it)
* Pubs with dartboards and billiard tables. Learn to play! Or at least keep score.

Where not to waste your time trying to meet men

* Singles holidays
* Theatre clubs and drama groups
* Art galleries
* Most evening classes

Where to Meet Women

* Wine bars, especially at lunch time
* Dance classes
* Department stores – working, shopping or eating
* Singles holidays
* Art and craft exhibitions
* Art galleries on Sundays
* Cruises (especially to Cape Town)
* Any patch of city green, on a summer's day
* Companies employing a large secretarial staff
* YWCA and nurses' hostels – go to one of their dances
* The South Bank – Festival Hall, National Theatre, Film Theatre, etc.
* Local theatre clubs

* Fringe theatres
* Walking her dog in the park
* Health farms
* Salad bars/vegetarian restaurants
* Flea markets
* Weddings
* Tea dances – try the Café de Paris, Coventry St, London W.1., or the Winter Gardens, Weston-Super-Mare. And no, you don't have to be a wizard at the waltz.
* Discos
* Late night shopping in supermarkets
* Churches
* Flower shows
* Women's Institutes and Women's Clubs – offer to give a talk, show your holiday slides, teach them car maintenance.
* Libraries
* Charity shops
* Any event involving royalty, animals, or both
* Kew Gardens
* Writers' and painters' residential courses
* Clean betting shops between 1–4 p.m.
* Selling Avon cosmetics (don't you need some new aftershave?)

Where not to waste your time trying to meet women

Anywhere cold, wet, muddy, smelly or potentially fattening.

One cautionary note. Finding someone via the activity or sport that they are interested in is all very well, as long as you're prepared to take second place to it for as long as your friendship lasts. It's no good revving up with a vintage car enthusiast and then complaining that the most you ever see of him is his feet sticking out from under it as he spends the entire summer lovingly examining the big end.

The difficulty, of course, with even the most exhaustive and inventive list of suggested meeting places is that a good percentage of the people you encounter are going to be already spoken for. The most obvious way to overcome this is to join a singles club. They usually rendezvous at a hotel or pub near you and arrange a varied programme of parties, theatre visits and outings. Scan your local paper for details, or write to the National Federation of Solo Clubs for the address of a group in your area.

Alternatively, if you find the idea of a singles club too much like open warfare, you might feel easier employing guerrilla tactics through organisations like Dateline and Nexus.

Dateline is one of the oldest established computer dating agencies. They fix you up with dates through a comprehensive questionnaire: you indicate the type of person you're looking for and in return for a sizeable fee you are sent the telephone numbers of allegedly suitable people. After that it's up to you. Everyone who's ever tried a computer dating service has hilarious stories to tell of arranging to meet their blind date 'under the clock' and then both of them dodging behind pillars to try and suss out what the other is like. The fun of it is (and you must treat it as fun – wade in desperately searching for a committed relationship and you're doomed to disappointment) that you never know who your blind date will turn out to be. As I type this, it's rumoured that if you write 'Broadcasting' on the Dateline questionnaire under Occupational Preferences, you might find yourself under the clock with a celebrated TV presenter who is on their books under a false name.

The people who run an organisation called Nexus say that it provides all the information and facilities for people to enhance their social life and widen their circle of friends and contacts. It's essentially a communication service. If you join you'll be sent a collection of open letters – Icebreakers – from those who welcome phone calls from other members. There is also a facility for choosing friends by listening to their voices on tape. In addition, Nexus offers a Skill Bank, whereby members who are carpenters, seamstresses, linguists, accountants, etc. will offer their services to fellow members, free.

The problem with solo clubs and dating agencies is that they are regarded (unfairly) as an unnatural way of making friends. As a result, people who have used them tend to be defensive and disparaging.

'All the women I met through computer dating were randy bitches just after my body,' one man complained to me. (Yes, really.) 'If you were feeling too tired to screw them through to their seven o'clock alarm, or if you just wanted to talk, for heaven's sake, they gave you the big heave.'

Widowed Elizabeth Dix, writing in the *Guardian*, summed up many women's experiences of singles clubs:

'Through the clubs I have indeed met many interesting, intelligent, widely-read, well-informed women, but Dear God! the men! . . . there are those who walk around with a permanently bewildered look, as if they cannot possibly believe that anyone could be so unkind as to leave them; those whose wives got lost behind in the push for success – "She doesn't give me what I want anymore" – what did they want – Superwoman? And those who have had an extramarital fling, come a cropper, and ended up with neither wife nor mistress.'

The most positive approach came from another *Guardian* correspondent who was adamant that the most painless way to meet men was through the lonely hearts columns. Not by answering the ads, but by placing them herself.

'Having waded through the 90 replies I got at the first attempt – always bearing in mind that I didn't have to answer any if I got cold feet – I was able to pick six "likelies" and arrange to meet them when, where and, having spied them from a distance, if I wanted, knowing that there were 84 back in the brown paper bag at home.'

Breaking the Ice

It's bad enough walking up to a perfect stranger under the clock and stammering your way through those first embarrassed introductions which leave you floundering in a swamp of hesitant, half-finished sentences, but parties are even more of a nightmare. Is there anything more chilling than strolling into a room full of people, all of whom appear to know one another, to be greeted with the numbing realisation that there isn't a familiar, let alone a welcoming, face in sight?

Before you hit the panic button, remember that it helps to have in mind, right from the start, a plan of campaign and a few opening gambits. Begin while you're dumping your coat. If anyone else has arrived at the same time, this is the moment to smile and say. 'I don't know a soul here, do you? My name's Chris . . .' Or why not strike up a conversation by admiring your fellow guest's perfume, aftershave, T-shirt or dress? That way, you'll be able to move into the main arena in the reassuring company of your fellow guest, which at least gets you over the first hurdle.

But suppose you're really thrown in at the deep end, into the midst of fifty strangers all of whom, you are convinced, are laughing like hyenas at the sight of you standing there, conspicuously on your tod. What to do?

Resist the urge to bolt, flee to the loo, or subside in a corner behind the Swiss cheese plant. Sitting down, in fact, is fatal. You'll only find yourself marooned, smiling glassily at people's knees while they shout at one another over your head.

First, take a few deep calming breaths, and then go and help yourself to a drink. Circulate slowly once round the room. If by this time your hostess hasn't surfaced and no one has stopped to talk to you, don't allow yourself to be browbeaten into settling for a quiet evening in front of the TV instead. Remind yourself that even the most magnetic personalities have suffered just the same sort of agonies. Take heart from superstar Donald Sutherland's ex-wife who says of their first meeting, 'He was afraid to enter the room and tripped over a dog as soon as he did.'

What you have to do now is take the initiative by employing one of your rehearsed conversational icebreakers. The opening gambit you choose will depend very much on the type of gathering, your own personality and whether that first drink was a single or a stiff double.

Openers I've had great success with are:

* *The direct approach.* 'Hello, I'm Chris. I don't know anyone here. Do you mind if I talk to you for a while?' (They can hardly reply, 'Yes I do mind. Piss off.' And if they do, they're obviously not the sort you'd want to be friendly with anyway.)

* *The blatant lie.* 'Hi! Aren't you Joe Soap? Weren't you at Felicity's do last week, when she set fire to her husband's mistress?'

You are, of course, at liberty to escalate fictional Felicity's behaviour to whatever outrageous heights you choose – say anything, just so long as it intrigues your new acquaintance enough to want to prolong the conversation.

Actress Pamela Stephenson has been quoted as favouring the *full frontal attack*, recommending that you walk boldly up to an innocuous looking man and shriek, 'Jonathan, I'm *so* sorry I behaved like an animal last night.'

I have to report that I tried this on a man at a party in deepest Surrey. Looking hunted, he stared desperately round and muttered, 'My wife will be here in a minute. I call her Mummy. You'd like talking to her.'

I'm always surprised (and encouraged) to learn how many celebrities are, in truth, extremely shy but hide it under aubergine hair, sequinned trilbies and shrunken gym slips. It's a successful *passive policy* which ducks them out of having to make the first move, as their appearance provides an instant talking point. If pink and green striped hair is likely to get you the sack, try a witty badge, brooch or T shirt instead. You might find yourself being chatted up by Oliver Reed, who has been known to inform pretty girls, 'For years I've never known how to undo a lady's bra. Could you show me?' Personally, I think I'd be inclined to show him the door . . .

Those of us not blessed with Oliver Reed's brio are best sticking to a *non-contentious campaign*. Ask how long your fellow guest has known the host or hostess, find out where they live, what they do, where they went on holiday last year, whether they like the music on the stereo.

Best of all is an *active approach*. It always helps, at any gathering, if you can find something to do. No, not fetching someone another drink. Save that ploy for when you need to escape from a bore.

Fortune telling and character reading are sure-fire ways to kindle interest. Forget the yawn-making 'Ah, now don't tell me, let me guess! You're a Leo, aren't you?' tactic. Instead, learn to read Tarot cards, handwriting or – if you're endowed with cool hands – head bumps. After all, don't we all love to hear fascinating and flattering revelations about ourselves? (No, of course all you say doesn't have to be true. You're at a party, not a Girl Guide rally. No one ever extended their social circle by telling the tedious truth all the time.)

The key word here is flattery. Don't do as I did recently, attempting to be Ms Super Cool when in the company of a devastating man. 'Really,' I informed him, 'you ought to do something about your appalling handwriting. It reveals the most terrible things about your character.'

Laying down his pen, he replied coldly, 'I may be no great calligrapher – but your sense of timing could certainly do with some attention.'

Too late, a chastened Ms Super Cool realised that what he was writing was a very large cheque for the expensive lunch she'd just enjoyed.

One of the most imaginative icebreakers I know is 81-year-old Phyllis, who arrived at my last party knowing no one, clutching a loaf of home made bread in one hand and a small cloth-bound book in the other. The bread, she informed me, was for all the people staying on who'd want toast in the morning. She was sure I'd have forgotten to order extra. (She was right.) Phyllis then hurled herself into the fray and charmed all my friends into signing their names in her birthday book whilst she read aloud the (often scandalous) verse appropriate to their day. By the end of the evening she was on first name terms with everyone and all my guests were fighting for her phone number.

If your name's not Dave Allen it's wiser to refrain from telling jokes, as, in the unlikely event that you remember the punch line, you'll only fluff it. And don't be tempted into bounding into the middle of a group and slaying them with a smart question like, 'What I've always wanted to know is, in those pictures of Atlas holding up the world, what's *he* standing on?' People only feel intimidated by this sort of attack and are likely to give you the cold shoulder as they take refuge in a heated discussion about their rip-off baby-sitters. Above all, don't let nerves stampede you into murmuring, 'God I'm so bored. Isn't this a ghastly party? And who is that fat woman in beetroot red who looks like a stand-in for Miss Piggy?' Inevitably, you'll find yourself with egg on your face, talking to your host about his wife.

I say, I say, I say . . .

Once you've made contact, your next objective is to keep the conversation going. Many single people find this the hardest part, pointing out that if you have a partner you can have a rest whilst your opposite number puts in some conversational spade work. When there's just you, you're obliged to expend more effort and make every word count if you're to prevent your new acquaintance murmuring vaguely about just popping off to find you a nice hot vol au vent.

69

The traditional advice here is to cultivate the art of Being a Good Listener and Asking the Right Questions. This is fine just so long as you don't turn the questioning into an exhausting and exhaustive interrogation. Show your interest in other people, of course, but avoid wearying them by posing as a Robin Day clone.

Much as we all relish talking about ourselves, it is sometimes stimulating to have someone else (you) chatting in an interesting and arresting way about themselves.

Interesting and arresting is not 'Me? Oh, I'm just a teacher, salesman, nurse.'

Pep it up a bit.

'I spent two hours today trying to discuss the irony of Jane Austen with my O Level class, whilst one of them insisted on turning somersaults across my desk. What would you have done?'

'I've just come back from an international sales conference. Most of the delegates were half asleep, complaining that the trouble with Concorde is that you arrive at your destination hours before you leave home.'

'I bandage bishops' bottoms.'

Remember, people aren't clairvoyant. You can't expect them to be interested in you unless you give them some clues, hints, handles to latch on to about who you are and what you've done. Be positive about yourself and your achievements, and eliminate 'I'm only' and 'I'm just' from your conversation. Self-deprecation is a turn off, *unless* you've achieved something fantastic that will make everyone else sick with envy – having your firm give you an all expenses paid winter holiday in Kenya – finding a riverside penthouse at a peppercorn rent – receiving red roses from Robert Redford. With anything in this league emphasise that you were *lucky*, *fortunate*, etc. Even if you did give yourself varicose veins pounding the city streets on your flat hunt or migraines doing overtime to earn that Kenya trip. If you got red roses from Redford, please write immediately and tell me how you did it.

The easiest way to keep a conversation going is to find an area of common ground. Either in the form of mutual interests – gardening, golf, vintage cars, bad midnight movies on TV, music, travel, etc. Or mutual aggro – British Rail, estate agents, communal changing rooms, landladies, late night vending machines that spew out dust instead of milk . . .

Naturally, you read the newspapers and tune into news-based television and radio programmes to keep yourself informed. But don't bleat pathetically, 'Yes, I watch a lot of telly. I've nothing else to do, you see, being on my own. The voices are company for me.' It may be true, but utter it too often and you'll find yourself dumped by the Swiss cheese plant waiting for those non-existent vol au vents whilst your new acquaintance chats up a more positive personality on the far side of the room. Keep up with current affairs, but there's no need to feel obliged to have a firm view on everything. Admit you can't quite make up your mind on a topic and people will rush in, eager to convert you to their way of thinking.

The Wheat, the Chaff – and the Wait

Right. You've made contact with a lively group of people who seem your sort. You said all the right things. You were friendly, approachable, interested. You neither hid behind the Swiss cheese plant nor got drunk and puked all over it.

Great. So why, you wonder, fixing me with a beadily accusing glare, is your phone not ringing? Why is the mantelpiece not groaning with invitations?

Give it time! Think back. Were your most satisfying friendships and attachments formed within hours or days of a first meeting? Chances are, any time you've walked into a new set up and been greeted with overwhelming bonhomie, that group has turned out to be not your style at all. If they're falling over themselves to make you one of them, there's often a sinister reason why. Establishing a worth-

71

while rapport is a gradual business. It pays to take it slowly. Otherwise you'll lumber yourself with the neurotics, the deadbeats, the clinging vines, the people with more chips on their shoulders than a carpenter's block.

Have the courage to wait and discriminate. But you don't need to wait passively.

Just because no one from the new social circle you want to crash has rung up and asked you round for coffee, it doesn't mean they can't stand the sight of you. They are not, at this very moment, gathered in a merry little group shrieking with laughter over your clothes, your accent and the spot on your chin.

What they are doing is getting on with leading the active, absorbing lives that attracted you to them in the first place. It's not that they don't like you. It's just that they're too preoccupied to remember to include you in things.

What you have to do now is insinuate yourself into their lives. It helps enormously if you are passably good at some activity like tennis, squash or bridge, where people will be keen for you to partner them. Or if you possess a useful social skill – anything from being able to thump out a tune on the joanna at the local, to knowing how to fix the strobes at the disco, or being a dab hand at knocking up a hundred profiteroles for a party.

If, like me, you possess no social skills whatsoever and your main hobby is sleeping, then I recommend to you the books and records ploy. Ignore the old saw about Never a Borrower Nor a Lender Be. Borrowing and lending books and records is a splendid way of furthering an acquaintance in that it gives you an excellent excuse to drop by at their place to deliver or return. It also gives you a conversational jumping off point.

And the more you listen to people, the more you'll discover of how you can make yourself useful to them. This may sound cold blooded, but remind yourself that part of friendship is lending not just the new Frederick Forsyth but a helping hand when necessary.

72

Fran may have flu and be desperate for someone to pick up a prescription. Joe might have bought an antique desk and need someone to help him heave it into the house. Lucy could have got landed with the catering for the dance and need a hand with the washing up . . .

If they're people you like, and whom you want to like you, get involved. Do anything. Stuff envelopes, paint walls, climb ladders, chauffeur children, cheer on touchlines. You'll probably end up enjoying it. And it'll certainly help to ease you in to your new social circle.

It makes good sense when you become involved in any new group to keep a low profile at first. This gives you time to sort out who you like and who you don't, and familiarise yourself with any long standing cliques or warring camps. If you breeze into the local drama group and declare that you've a Masters Degree in electronics and they can safely leave the lighting to you, you run the risk of alienating old George who's been happily blowing the fuses for years.

All this is not to suggest that as you expand your social circle you should attempt to submerge your own identity. To join the poetry circle not because you have a feeling for verse, but because you've heard that it attracts the prettiest girls in town, is a waste of time. The pretty girls will soon find you out and speedily transfer their attention to people who aren't frauds, but who display a genuine interest in poetry.

Here again, it's a question of balance. Living on your own, it's important that you take the initiative and go out and meet lots of people. But from the wide variety of new acquaintances you make, try to recognise and cultivate the few who will become soul-mates, likely to join those whom you number as your real friends. For as a single person, it's your friends who provide you with a vital support system. When you're feeling blue, lonely or ill . . . when you're in an agony of indecision or delirious with joy, it's your friends who you call on to help, listen, sympathise or share the champagne.

But there's more to it than that. Apart from providing you with emotional support, your friends can also give you a valuable sense of continuity. Offered so many choices and so much freedom, many single people find themselves feeling rootless, unhappy that they don't belong anywhere or to anyone. But by acting as your extended family, your friends can help to fill this void. They are usually the people who know you best. They've seen you in all your moods, through good times and bad, probably over many years. When everything else is in a state of flux, it's immeasurably comforting to know that your friends are there – representing an enduring feature of your life. They're part of your past. They'll support you today. And they'll still be around tomorrow.

But they won't be there if you don't take the trouble to keep in touch with them. Make the effort to ring them up. Drop them a line. Invite them round. Remember their birthdays. Good friends are hard to find, so don't neglect them or let them drift away. Living alone, you *need* them.

The Right Lines

Letters and postcards are another invaluable way of forging social links. We all love getting letters, but living on our own, the postman's knock can be a special highlight, not to say lifeline, in our day. To receive, of course, we have to do some pen pushing ourselves first. As single people we have the advantage of being more mobile, socially and in our careers, and it's important that we make the effort to keep in touch with our friends even when we're living countries or continents apart.

I wonder why men are so hopeless at continuing a correspondence? Nearly all the men I know are infuriatingly lazy about letter writing – but that doesn't stop them complaining that all the postman ever brings them is bills.

Where men do score, however, is in the knack many of them have of being able to further a friendship by sending a nicely timed brief note, pertinent newspaper cutting or witty cartoon. When reticent Jonathan wanted to get through to popular Sylvia he showered her not with flowers, dinner invitations or reams of purple prose. Instead, every other day he sent her a postcard of the home town he knew she hated. Views of skyscrapers by day ... the underpass by night ... the hideous statue in the main square ... the hideous statue – floodlit ... Sylvia appreciated the joke, and the man who initiated it.

Let Us Praise ...

Apart from being a courteous gesture, a thank you letter often provides a useful lever for continuing a new friendship. It gives you the ideal opportunity to enclose that back issue of a colour supplement your host wanted ... the address of the people who mend cane chairs ... or to ask for the telephone number of that dishy redhead ...

All hostesses remember (and tend to ask back) guests who take the trouble to write a brief, appreciative note. Even if the evening was an unmitigated disaster and you had a lousy time, there must be something you can pick on to praise.

I once spent hours stuffing cabbage leaves with mincemeat and sewing them up with cotton. It sounds revolting and it was. If it happened now, I'd cheerfully chuck the whole mess in the bin and send out for some fish and chips. But I was younger then and still conditioned to believe that if I admitted failure no one would love me. My guests waded their way wordlessly through the soggy cabbage, but more embarrassing was to receive, the following day, a fulsome thank you letter in which the man enthused for pages about how he appreciated all my efforts, how valiant it had been of me to try so hard, what strength of character I had shown in not giving up, etc., etc. I felt *awful*. It would have been much better if he'd complimented me on the wine, my perfume, the conversation, even the cat.

Not So Alien Corn

Love letters are the most difficult of all to write and as a consequence frequently never get sent at all. Which is a pity, as even the most hard bitten of us are secretly thrilled to receive a love letter. A phone call, however loving, is swiftly forgotten, for try as we might, we can never remember the content of every verbal caress just whispered to us down the line. The pleasure of a love letter lies in its permanence. We carry them around in our handbags, our wallets and keep them tucked at the back of our lingerie chest, or in the third drawer down of our executive desks. And we read them – again and again.

Learn to write a memorable love letter and you will ever be assured of a special place in the recipient's affections, for we always think tenderly of anyone who took such pains on our behalf. Being single, we have an unrivalled opportunity to pursue the art of the *billet-doux*. Of course married couples can and do write romantically to one another, but often the loving tone tends to get warped by domestic intrusions. So when a woman writes to her husband, 'I long to lie in your arms and kiss the breath out of you,' she's liable to follow it up with the douche of a wifely reminder to 'remember to wear the thermal vest I packed for you as you know how those Cornwall mists affect your chest' (i.e. I don't want you coming back wheezing bronchially and demanding that I take a week off work to nurse you).

Men and women vary considerably in their opinion of what constitutes a good love letter. When you're writing to women you should above all be *romantic*. Say what you feel, and what you'd like to do with her and to her, but phrase it lyrically. Keats, in his last exquisite sonnet, did not inform his lady that he couldn't wait to chew her tits off. Instead he said he longed to be 'pillowed on my fair love's ripening breast'.

Men are turned on by word pictures, so you can be as

forthright as you like and they'll be delighted. (So will the blokes they work with.) Flowery prose and sugary sentiments will only embarrass the guy. The message he really wants to hear, over and over, is that he's the biggest and the best. The only drawback is that although in the first frantic fever of lust it may seem hilarious to write a brilliant limerick in praise of his private parts, are you going to cringe when you realise that the boys in his office have enjoyed chortling over it too? Worse, how are you going to feel about it when all passion is spent?

Men may squirm at the overly sentimental, but they are deeply affected by any message with a bitter-sweet quality. Dorothy Parker got it right in a poem to an absent soldier lover, when she wrote,

'When in sleep you turn to her,
Call her by my name.'

We'll never know how many stabs Dorothy Parker had at those two poignant lines, but few of us ever get a love letter right first time. We all need a trial run or two to get the ink and inspiration flowing. The fatal thing, however, is to neglect to burn those early attempts. It's passion killing, as I can vouch, to come across drafts of a love letter written to you, and find yourself musing critically that actually, you prefer version two instead of opus eight which you finally received.

Two Into Three CAN Go

Falling in love is wonderful – until it happens to your best friend. For years you've gone around together. He or she is like an extension of yourself. You've shared secrets, joys, disappointments. You know whatever the hour of day or night, you can ring up or drop round and be made welcome.

Then comes the day your friend announces that he or she is getting married. You're delighted for them of course, but beneath your sincerely expressed good wishes, it's hard to

77

repress a sense of betrayal. Inevitably, everything will change. The support on which you relied, the unquestioning twenty-four hour loyalty and interest just can't be there with the same degree of reassuring intensity as before. Your friend is now half of a couple, and with the best will in the world just isn't going to have as much time as before to devote to you.

Sadly, this is the point at which many long-standing friendships break up. When people are in the honeymoon stage it's natural that they should become totally immersed in one another and old friends are relegated to the sidelines for a while. Then there's the time-consuming business of setting up home, first for two and then for three, or more. As a single person, it's often impossible to take a keen interest in endless discussions about pinch pleats and prams. It's easy to decide that really, you don't have much in common with your friend any more – and so you drift apart.

Women have a harder time of it here than men. When women marry, it isn't just their husband's name they usually take, but his entire lifestyle as well. Women tend, without thinking about it, to adopt their partner's family and friends as their own. Whereas Jim will take it for granted that he is free to have a night out any time with his mate at the pub, Mary might find that there's a hostile atmosphere at home if she suggests splitting a bottle with a friend at the wine bar. For some reason, men are suspicious of one's unmarried women friends. I imagine men resent the implication that you don't want to be at home with them, and fear that you and Mary intend chewing the nostalgic cud about the old days, and ex-boyfriends in between tearing hubbie's character to shreds.

But despite the conflict of interests, it's foolish to jettison all those years of friendship – both for your sake and for that of Jim or Mary. The emphasis may have changed, but it's important that true friendship should survive changes in lifestyle. Jim and Mary may now have their respective

78

partners, but they still need you in their lives, just as much as you need them.

Because you, as a single person, are the one without anyone else at your back, hassling you over the relationship with your friend, it is your job to make the situation easier for Jim or Mary. The first thing you have to accept is that they are not going to be as available as in the old days. So it is up to you to fit conveniently into their timetable.

If Mary's husband is in the habit of nipping off every Saturday afternoon to watch football, this could be the ideal time for you two to get together and have a chat as you touch up one another's roots. If Mary is wise, however, she won't fall into the trap of only asking you round when HE is out. Naturally, it's important for you to establish a good relationship with both of them.

You'll go a long way to achieving this if you –

* Avoid arriving just as he's getting home from work
* Don't sit in his favourite chair and read his newspaper before him
* Try not to monopolise Mary
* Resist the urge to treat him as your tame, unpaid handyman. Ask advice by all means, but don't lumber him too often with requests for practical help
* Keep quiet about the racy social life you're leading – he might fret that you're trying to lead wifey astray
* Offer to babysit occasionally (for free, naturally!). They'll appreciate it, and you might reap the benefit of a rewarding relationship with the child as it grows older.

And when visiting Jim watch out that you don't –

* Keep calling in just before his wife is serving supper
* Turn up looking pathetic in a shirt with the buttons off. It'll work once, but the novelty will soon wear off
* Try and get off with his wife
* Keep taking him out and getting him drunk
* Embark on stories about the hairy things you and old Jim got up to in his bachelor days. Talk about your girlfriends by all means, but keep your wilder sexploits to yourself.

79

Above all, as a friend of either Jim or Mary, it's essential to develop nimble footwork to avoid getting caught in the crossfire of their marital flak. If a row blows up between them and you sense that they're using you to score points off one another, never, ever take sides. Make an excuse and leave. At once.

You'll probably find that when the heat's on at home, both Mary and Jim will use your pad as a bolt hole. It took me some time to realise that the role of the single friend in this situation is not as a marriage guidance counsellor, but more in the nature of an echo chamber. What your mate needs to do is spew out all the aggro whilst you uncork another bottle and murmur, 'So you turned the hose on him? What happened then? . . . You really flushed all her warpaint down the john? Hell, what did she say?'

Naturally, you'll want to indicate your support for Jim or Mary, but it's wiser not to go over the top and weigh in with abuse against their respective spouses. By the time your friend has cooled down and is rushing home for a grand reconciliation, he or she will view your acid remarks with resentment. It's OK for Jim to call his wife a prize slagging bitch but fatal for you to clap him on the back and agree wholeheartedly.

The real difficulty comes, of course, if the rows become more prolonged and your friend's marriage breaks down. From your point of view, it's easier if you like one of them but not the other and have no problem deciding to which mast you're going to nail your supportive flag. But what do you do if they're both valued friends of yours, and you'd dearly like to stay on good terms with each of them?

Ideally, you remain neutral and keep friendly with both. In practice, this rarely works out. If Mary spends hours crying on your shoulder one night, she's going to feel betrayed if she sees you the next day in the pub, lending a sympathetic ear to the husband she now loathes. Agonising though it may be, you'll probably be forced to take one side or the other in this situation, at least in the beginning. But give it twelve months, and by then hopefully Mary will be so involved in her new life that she won't give a damn if she spots you tangoing with her ex. By then she'll probably like him a lot more herself, anyway.

Weekending

You've kept your old friends. You've made new ones. Now you're at the point when you can reap one of the huge benefits of being single. You are at liberty to accept weekend invitations without being obliged to consult anyone else . . . 'No I don't want to go and stay with the Browns. Her cooking gives me indigestion and his home-made beer tastes of the dustbin he made it in' . . . and without having to turn yourself into a walking timetable: 'I don't see *why* you can't just stick your head round the door and ask your secretary to give me a ring if your meeting's going to drag on after 4. Otherwise I'll have to get right across London in the rush hour to pick you up and if we miss the 5.00 from Euston, it'll mean changing at Peterborough and Peter will have to meet us which is terribly inconvenient as he has to drop the boys at a basketball tournament and if they're late they'll only whine for the entire weekend . . .'

There's no one you have to leave a casserole for and instructions about paying the milkman. You don't need to leave your place tidy if you don't want to. You're free to pack a bag, flick up all the switches, lock the door and *go*.

What you won't forget to do, of course, is pack a thoughtfully chosen present for the people who've invited you. If you're in a tearing rush and couldn't get to the shops, you can always rely on flowers – but not, please, a large cellophane wrapped mixed assortment. Take a mass of freesias, a huge bunch of sweet peas or roses out of season.

Flowers are always welcome, but what's appreciated even more is the weekend guest who has clearly taken the trouble to suit the present to the person. Some suggestions:

* *Hostess*: Dior tights; champagne; champagne flavoured toothpaste (from Heals)
* *Host*: Booze
* *Teenage sons and daughters*: A Swiss army knife; a beautifully shaped antique scent bottle; blank cassettes
* *Aunt Maud*: an exquisitely pretty flowering plant; a beribboned box of sugared almonds
* *Uncle Fred*: his favourite pickled walnuts, gift-wrapped from Harrods or Fortnums
* *Mothers*: Mary Chess or Floris toilet water; a hand-stitched silk scarf
* *Fathers*: The latest risqué novel that he daren't be seen buying himself
* *Grannies*: a record of the music she danced to in her youth
* *Grandpas*: A T shirt with a saucy message printed across the chest

One of the most relaxed hostesses I know is Maggy. I'm always delighted to be invited to her rambling country cottage because although common sense tells me that she's obviously gone to a lot of trouble to ensure the comfort and entertainment of her guests, she doesn't let it show. She has an absent-minded husband, three children, a soppy dog and (the local fox permitting) several geese, but nothing seems to throw Maggy. She seemed the ideal person to give me a few pointers to pass on to those of us aiming to be asked back for another weekend.

What she appreciates most, she said, are guests who make it quite clear from the outset what time they are arriving and (more importantly) when they intend to leave. As Sunday afternoon draws on and the hostess is wondering frantically if the remains of the joint will stretch to a scratch cold supper, it's infuriating when Maggy asks politely, 'How long can you stay?' to receive the vague reply, 'Oh, I'll just play it by ear, if that's OK by you.'

Just as bad are the people who announce warily, within

five minutes of crossing the threshold, that they *might* have to leave early on Sunday morning. Maggy is quite well aware that this means they'll see how good a time they're having, and if the weather's lousy or the children are too stroppy, they'll cut their losses and run. This charming behaviour leaves Maggy with a fridge full of unwanted food, a wasted Sunday and a row on her hands as she and her husband argue about which one of them invited those people in the first place.

In my view, the only circumstance in which you can get away with slithering off because you've got something more exciting on offer is if you're a firm friend of the hostess, and you're honest. If I said to Maggy, 'Look, it's possible that this devastating man will ring on Sunday and ask me to fly over to Paris for lunch,' (yes, well I did say *if*) Maggy would laugh, tell me to have a great time, and lend me her best dress into the bargain. But if I lied, and muttered that I might have to get home, Aunt Maud might be calling in for elevenses, I'd immediately lose a good friend in Maggy.

All hostesses, says Maggy, adore guests who lend a hand with laying the table, washing up, walking the dog and amusing the children *without being asked and without making a great song and dance about it*. Let's face it, the very words hostess and guest are something of misnomers these days. They conjure an image of a hostess with nothing much else to do but arrange the flowers artistically and give Cook instructions for the *petits fours*, whilst upstairs the maid is laying out the guest's plus fours. It's much easier all round (and more fun) if you as the visitor show you're ready to pitch in and be treated as one of the family. After days of preparation, cooking, cleaning, fetching, carrying and smiling (often in between holding down a full-time job) many a hostess has been saved from a quiet nervous breakdown by a guest offering to make *her* a cup of tea.

It sounds simple enough, but it's surprising how many

people find it more convenient to assume that their hostess is so well organised, she'd resent any help. Especially in the kitchen. The only time this holds good, asserts Maggy with feeling, is in that final crucial half hour before she serves dinner. 'Just bring me a stiff Scotch, then get the hell out of the kitchen and prepare to lavish praise on whatever I'm capable of dishing up,' she pleads.

When you're accepting other people's hospitality it's only good manners to leave your diet sheet and calorie counter at home. If you're on a diet on medical instructions, or if you're allergic to particular foods, let your hostess know well in advance, and then shut up about it whilst you are in her home. Above all, don't range your bottles of pills among the dining table crystal and proceed to bore everyone with grisly, detailed explanations of what they're all for.

Kitchens and bathrooms, Maggy points out, are the two areas where even in the best run households, tension tends to run high. (Isn't it nervewracking when your hostess declares within minutes of your arrival: 'There's lashings of hot water. Do take a bath any time you like.' Does she mean *now*, you wonder anxiously, recalling how sweaty you got on that stuffy train.)

It's all so rosy in the colour supplements. Mr 1980s splashes cheerily in his en suite pampas shower. The children frolic in the bathroom. And in the spotless farmhouse kitchen (revealing no trace of debris from last night's drunken dinner) a smiling Mrs 1980s serves an enormous brunch as her guests relax in their monogrammed his 'n' hers towelling robes.

In truth, of course, you the guest have forgotten to pack your bathrobe so you are hovering near your bedroom door with your old mac clutched round your pyjamas. You are hopping from foot to foot because you are desperate to get to the bathroom, but every time you scuttle onto the landing, a child or Mr 1980s races in ahead of you and bolts the door. When at last you make it to the kitchen breakfast bar a bleary-eyed Mrs 1980s asks what you'd like to eat and without thinking you say, oh just bacon and egg would be fine. As she rescues the frying pan from the heap of greasy dishes under the sink you realise that everyone else is making do with black coffee and Alka Seltzer.

Obviously, it helps if you establish early on what the morning routine of the house is. Then you can find your own way of fitting in. It goes without saying that having discovered the best time to gain admittance to the bathroom, you won't leave soggy towels and talc on the floor, shaving cream or hair spray on the mirror or beard droppings in the handbasin.

Because of the children, Maggy finds it easier to organise a sit down breakfast, at a set time. That way, she says, you get it all over and done with in one go and everyone can then shoot off and do their own thing. But when she visits me, she appreciates that I don't 'do' breakfasts, so she'll happily make herself some tea and toast to take back to bed with the newspapers. What really drives me mad are the men (and it always is the men) who declare heartily that of course they understand that breakfast is a do-it-yourself affair, and then proceed to stand limply in my kitchen waiting for someone to show them how to fill the kettle.

They're the same type who expect their host to have a carefully arranged schedule of events to fill every moment of their stay. It never occurs to them to bring a map of the area, a book to read, or embroidery to do. Neither are they tuned into the warning signals that they have stayed too long.

Departure is often tricky to execute gracefully. You don't want to appear as if you're rushing off with a sigh of relief. But on the other hand you don't want your hosts to start exchanging those 'God, is she staying a fortnight?' looks. Maggy says you'll know if you have lingered too long if:

  * You're given instant coffee instead of the aromatic Blue Mountain you've been served with all weekend

* The roaring log fire is left to go out
* The heating is turned down
* You're asked if you'd like a cup of tea 'before you go'
* All the ashtrays are emptied, washed up, put away, and the windows are flung wide
* Your host starts taking a keen interest in your train timetable or your car mileage
* Your hostess reveals a motherly concern about the contents of your fridge. Have you any bread, or milk at home? Can she give you some to take with you, to see you through till morning?
* The pre-dinner gin and tonic doesn't materialise
* Dinner doesn't materialise.

Homecoming

Most times, you'll be glad to get back to your own place. To an undisturbed bathroom. To your own bed. To your choice of TV and radio programmes. Above all, to an atmosphere and an environment in which you can let go, and just be *you*.

But there are occasions, perhaps when you're feeling a bit down, or vulnerable, when it's hard coming home. When you're warm and cosy by your hosts' fire, well fed and watered, surrounded by amiable companions, it's tempting to overstay your welcome simply because you're reluctant to return to your solitary pad. One's torpor is often exacerbated by well meaning friends who make sympathetic remarks about poor old you, having to go out into the cold night, back to an empty flat with no one to make your bedtime hot chocolate . . .

The only way round this is to heave yourself out of that easy chair and *go*. Tell your hosts you'd love to stay longer but you've got an exciting lunch date tomorrow and you must press a silk shirt and catch up on your sleep.

When you leave the train at the other end, quell any whispers that it would be nice to have someone there at the barrier waving a welcome by reminding yourself that they'd probably be furious because the train was late. Remember the freedom that being on your own affords you. You're at liberty to splurge on a taxi home if you want, without anyone nagging about the expense. If you feel peckish you can stop off for a fast snack without suffering resentful remarks from a partner about spoiling your appetite for the nourishing meat loaf waiting for you in the fridge.

Yes, it can sometimes be depressing returning to a cold, empty, silent home. But not if you remember to be sufficiently well organised and plan ahead. With the aid of a couple of time switches there's nothing to stop you arranging matters so that at the hour of your arrival, lights, heat and radio are all on. Light, warmth and the sound of cheerful music will give an immediate boost to your morale.

So too will the anticipation of a treat you've promised yourself. A half bottle of champagne, a new record or best-selling paperback will all help to make your world a more cheerful place. Or if it's not too late, why not ring a friend and compare notes on your respective weekends? Most people who live alone appreciate calls on Saturdays and Sundays.

The Telephone

We're all familiar with the types who have an infuriating knack of ringing up just when you've got into the bath, or the timer is shrieking that if you leave the bleach on one minute longer your hair will fall out. When you make a call, it's considerate always to try and ascertain immediately if the person you're ringing is busy. Especially if you're telephoning with the intention of enjoying a long gossipy chat. It helps if you bear in mind the lifestyle, and therefore the daily routine, of the person at the other end of the line. Sounds obvious, maybe, but it's amazing the number of people who drift along in the blissful belief that because it's convenient for them to get to the office early and make all their calls before 8 a.m., then everyone else is happy with this arrangement too.

Some folk, of course, are too polite to scream that the house is on fire just when you ring to have a moan about the poisonous letter you received from your Aunt Maud. Or if their phone's in the living room it can be tricky for them to explain that they can't talk now because their Aunt Maud is sitting glued to every word. Listen carefully to the tenor of people's voices. If they're terse, tense, strangely hoarse or speak in a hissing whisper, assume they're tied up and tell them you'll call back later.

If you're the type who tends to ramble on, you'll save taxing your friends' patience (and keep your phone bills down) if you make a note of what you want to say. We've all had the maddening experience of chatting for an hour, then realising when we've rung off that we completely forgot to mention that tonight's dinner party has been postponed a week.

Answer phones have come down dramatically in price over recent years and are rapidly proving a great social asset for the single. It's heartwarming coming home in a raw, lonely state to find the little red light signalling that someone wants to talk to you. Everyone I spoke to about this emphasised earnestly the advantage of not missing important calls when they're out, but I have a sneaking feeling that many of my interviewees installed their machines to reprieve them from those strangled conversations when lover A rings up whilst they're in bed with lover B.

Some Useful Addresses

Cruse, 126 Sheen Road, Richmond, Surrey. (01-940 9047)
Dateline International, 23 Abingdon Road, London W.8.
National Council for the Divorced and Separated, 13 High
Street, Little Shelford, Cambridge.
National Federation of Solo Clubs, Room 8, Ruskin
Chambers, 191 Corporation St., Birmingham B4 6RY.
Nexus, Nexus House, Blackstock Road, London N4.

Further Reading

Select Magazine – monthly. Published by Dateline, it's for
and about single people
Ageing for Beginners – Mary Stott. (Basil Blackwell.)

CHAPTER 4

SEX

Let's do it – when, where and how

'Your place or mine?'

Ah, the bliss of living on your own, being free to take someone back morning, afternoon or night without having parents cramping your style or flatmates who've decided that today they must get on with pickling those onions. In this respect, single people are the envy of their married friends. Nevertheless, the question of your place or mine has its problems, especially for the solo woman who may only have met her prospective lover two hours ago at a party.

'If you asked me what I relish most about living alone I'd say it's the sense of control I have over my own life,' Sue told me after her divorce. 'But when I was first separated from my husband I must confess that when it came to sex all that hard won control went quite out of the window. After years of having my confidence undermined, it was wonderful finding myself admired by men again. It went to my head. Time and again I'd find myself at a party, flirting, fancying a man like mad and then asking him back to my new flat. Next morning, I'd wake up in a cold sweat when I realised what I'd done. I mean, I have a thicket of locks on my doors and windows, I never let the gas man in without asking for an identity card – I'm manic about security. Yet out of sheer lust, I invited a perfect stranger to share for the night my home, my bed and, most frightening of all, my unconscious hours. I could have been mugged, or murdered. How did I know, on such a short acquaintance, that he wasn't a sex freak who'd insist on stringing me up from the rafters?'

Is the answer to give your place a miss and use his? 'Even if you're sure he's straight, you still have the hassle of getting home if you don't have transport of your own,' Sue points out. 'There's nothing worse than trying to rouse a sex-sated man at 3 a.m. to persuade him to drive you home . . . failing, having to hunt through the phone book for a taxi service, paying a fortune for the trip and knowing you're going to be one of the walking dead at work tomorrow. However good the sex was, by the time that 7 a.m. alarm shrills, you really begin to wonder if it was all worth it.'

Niall, a 30-year-old bachelor, rarely invites a new lover back to his place because, as he says, 'I always like to take a woman home as I feel rotten about her going back alone late at night. And I never stay the night through with a woman I don't know very well. Getting involved in their breakfast routine is hell, especially when you both have to get off to work. Besides, I'm always too well aware that however desirable she may appear at midnight, she's going to look very different in the morning – and so am I!' Niall recommends that anyone who's not sure at the start of an evening in which part of the city they're going to end up, should keep a diary note of a mini cab service which covers a large area. 'Make sure you know your lover's full address – the name of the street and the number of the house. If he or she lives in a large block of flats, try and remember as you come in the route you'll have to take to get out again as dawn is breaking.'

Not every interesting encounter takes place after dark, of course. It often happens, particularly after a long, lingering lunch that you find the effort of raising the claret glass to your lips has made you both unaccountably tired. You yearn to lie down and rest for a while. But where, if you're not within striking distance of either your or your companion's pad?

Fortunately, there are some British hotels which recognise that not everyone requires accommodation for an entire night. Hotels and motels situated near airports, railway terminals and ports are accustomed to weary travellers who need a room just for a few hours in order to rest after a long journey or effect a wash and brush up and a change of clothes. Called a day let, it's recommended by many as a civilised way of reviving yourself for the rigours of the evening – providing, of course, you can stand the financial strain after all that expensive claret at lunch.

Make It Easy on Yourself (and your lover)

Whether it's a first night frenzy or a slow burner you've been tantalisingly leading up to for months, the occasion will be more mutually enjoyable if you make an effort to create a relaxingly romantic atmosphere.

* Tone down the sizzling decor. A surfeit of red light bulbs, cocktail shakers in the shape of naked ladies and umpteen editions of *The Joy of Sex* strewn on the coffee table can be most inhibiting.

* Don't rush things. That scene where the woman strips off as he's unlocking the front door only works in films – and then only if you've got a body like Bo Derek's.

* Do try and have clean sheets on the bed, and swill down the bathroom. Filth is a passion killer. (Admittedly, this only prevails in an ideal situation when you've had time to prepare. In practice what seems to happen is that you realise the clean sheets are stuffed under the sofa that she/he is on. Having wrecked the romantic build-up by wrenching them out, you notice that these are the sheets with the gory red stain on. *You* know the stain is only red wine from the time you used the sheet as a tablecloth. But will your new lover believe you? Do you really want to spend a boring five minutes eulogising on the versatility of the sheets in your household?)

* Remove all debris left by previous lovers. It's extremely off-putting to stretch out a languorous foot and find it entwined round another woman's knickers rolled up

in the sheets, or a crusty hanky that's clearly been used for previous mopping up operations.

* Stop fretting about what the neighbours will say if they see your bedroom curtains drawn at 3.30 in the afternoon. You can't win either way, as if you leave the curtains undrawn the neighbours will only be riveted by the sight of your naked lover peering out of the window to make sure the car isn't parked on a double yellow line.

* Don't make it obvious you're the neighbourhood stud, even if you are. All women like to feel they are something special, not just another notch on the gunstock of your ego.

* Turn your heating on, and up. Remember women feel the cold more than men.

* Take your socks or tights off *first*.

* Most people feel nervous about taking their clothes off in front of someone else for the first time. This is the stage at which you can't flatter your lover too much or too often.

Bewitched, Bothered and Bewildered

Hopefully, you'll have the time of your life with your new lover. But it's wise to bear in mind that because you are unfamiliar with one another, the occasion might turn out to be one of those first night flops.

Most men find this crucifyingly embarrassing and die a thousand deaths as they wait for the woman to ring down the curtain with an epilogue of scathing abuse. In fact, none of the women I know would dream of displaying anything but genuine kindness, understanding and gentleness in such a situation. She won't scream with derisive laughter, because she'll appreciate that there are many times in her sexual life when nerves or emotional pressures cause her to freeze up, too. But because she's a woman, it isn't manifested in such an obviously physical way as it is with a man.

It will help her to help you if instead of verbally scourging yourself for your temporary incapacity, you talk to the woman about it – let her get close to you by telling her what's on your mind. Alternatively, some men find it easier if they have a cup of tea, lie back and chat and laugh for a while about topics unrelated to sex. Others prefer the woman gently to take the initiative, and with mouth and hands gently caress back the desire into them. The important thing is for you, the man, to give the woman some indication of what you'd like her to do – chat, make tea, stroke your back or whatever. You'll find her a willing and understanding partner, but if you don't know her very well you can't expect her to be clairvoyant about your needs. Tell her. Show her. Encourage her. And she'll respond.

It may be that you realise this is one of those occasions when the flame has died and nothing she does is going to rekindle it. In which case you good-humouredly cast off your Casanova cloak, and tell yourself that there'll be other times. But before you leave the bed, have the consideration to pleasure that woman by your side. In the words of one man to whom such a scene was at one time a fairly frequent occurrence, 'It's unfair to leave her with ball ache as well.'

Touch Me In the Morning . . . .

* Do try and remember your lover's name.
* Be kind. Even if it was the worst amorous encounter of your life and you're convinced you never want to set eyes on your new lover again, try and find something encouraging to say. Very rarely does the earth move the first time. If you make a sour comment now about your lover being more paunchy than raunchy you may regret it later and realise that on another occasion you might be more in tune with one another.
* Women should avoid getting maudlin, or hysterical with remorse, sobbing that you've never done anything like

94

this before, he must think you're cheap, he must have lost all respect for you, etc., etc., *etc*. You made the decision to go to bed with him, so there's no point in taking it out on him because now you feel you made a mistake. As for feeling cheap, this is something women have been brainwashed over. Does *he* feel cheap? Have you lost any respect for him? Quite. You're just as free as he is to indulge in a night of reckless passion without being obliged to do the sackcloth and ashes routine in the morning.

* Men look absurd wearing women's flowered bath-robes. It's sexier to drape yourself in a towel.

* Have respect for your lover's home. Last night you were glad of the low lights, the soft bed and the poodle that broke the ice by licking your bare shoulder when you were paralysed with embarrassment over the grubby vest you forgot you'd put on. In the cold light of morn, it's not on to wander around kicking the poodle, and haranguing your lover that the lighting is straining your eyes and the downy bed is murder for anyone with a bad back.

* Men: Don't keep asking if you're the best.

* Women: Don't keep asking if you're the most beautiful.

* Resist the urge to bolt. If you have to depart quickly, to get to work or keep an appointment, leave an affectionate or witty word or note. (It is not at all amusing for a new man to leave a £10 note under a lady's alarm clock.) If you're making your exit at 3 a.m. have the decency to do it quietly, without pausing on the communal stairs to shriek a droll remark about your partner's prowess between the sheets.

* Don't assume that one night of love makes you an established twosome, and start agitating about 'when am I going to see you again?' If you both desire the affair to continue then it will, simply because you'll not be able to keep your hands off one another for very long. But if your lover is unsure, or doesn't want to be committed, then respect this and lay off. By giving someone enough space, you often bring them back to you.

It's bad enough someone assuming that because you've spent the night with them, you are now a bonded pair. What's worse is when that person actually tries to move in with you. The obvious sign to watch for is your new lover sighing and saying how awful his or her own flat is, so inconvenient being such a distance from yours, and the lease is up soon and it'll be such a drag looking round for somewhere else ... Unless you are very sure of your feelings, don't succumb in a moment of tenderness or passion and agree to let your lover stay indefinitely at your place. If he or she is genuinely looking for somewhere else it would be churlish to make him or her sleep on the pavement – but if you do take your lover in, make it clear that it's only for a week or two and Aunt Maud is coming to stay after that.

You'd have to be a dimwit not to recognise the 'I'm looking for a new place' ploy, but there are others which are subtler. Watch out for lovers who start reorganising your kitchen or wardrobe. Who, if the pipes burst on a frosty morning, assume it is they who will call the plumber. Be alert to them referring to your place as 'our place' or 'home'. And be especially wary of lovers who 'just want to hang a change of clothes in your wardrobe'. I once came back from holiday with a man and absentmindedly agreed that he could leave his suitcase at my flat until the next day. It took me six months to get rid of him and that damned case.

Can't Buy Me Love?

Isn't it wonderful to be so much in love that you rush out and happily spend a month's rent money on an extravagant present for your lover? And isn't it galling when your lover tears off the gift wrapping and you just know from the look on his or her face that you've made an expensive blunder and chosen the wrong thing. The difficulty is that men and women often have confused ideas about what the opposite sex regards as a desirable gift. Many women imagine, for instance, that men like to be given ties. They don't. Men who still wear ties usually prefer to choose them themselves. And contrary to popular male belief, women do not fall into an ecstatic swoon on being presented with crotchless panties and suspender belt in black and pink nylon.

Presents don't have to be expensive, or come garlanded in ribbons. One of the most thoughtful things you can give anyone is time. Drive your car to the office of the one you love on a rainy evening and offer to chauffeur your lover home to save him or her waiting for the bus. Or if, after a fraught week, your lover is run ragged at the prospect of hosting a big family reunion, offer to park yourself in the kitchen to make the endless cups of tea – and wash them up.

The most treasured gifts are either those of pure sentimental value, or those which carry with them an element of flattery – when you receive something which implies that the giver imagines that the gift reflects your lifestyle. Few of us, for example, can afford to drink champagne in any great quantity. Yet we'd all be delighted to receive a pair of crystal champagne glasses. That's one idea. Here are some more:

From Men to Women

* Champagne and strawberries – for breakfast
* Champagne-coloured silk lingerie. (Steal some undies from her drawer to check on the size. Should you still be confused, at least err on the right side. If you're a 34, it's not very flattering to be presented with a sexy Janet Reger silk bra in a size 32. Believe me, I *know*.)
* One hundred roses, in containers, to greet her at her flat as she walks in
* One perfect rose. (That means no greenfly, blackfly, mould, bitten off petals or stifling cellophane.)
* A taped, loving message left by her bedside
* A large bottle of her favourite perfume
* A flowering shrub which blooms in the month you first met (Watch out if you have a row, though, in case she

takes the shears to it.)

* An American edition of a book she's longing to read, but which hasn't been published in Britain yet

* A well-organised weekend in Paris (I stress well-organised, because if you're the muddling through, memory like a sieve type, forget this one, unless the lady concerned has a sensational sense of humour.)

* Laughter. Make a lady laugh and you'll have hit on one of the most effective aphrodisiacs known to man

* You – just when she thought there was no hope of seeing you. Women adore men who demonstrate that they are prepared to travel hundreds of miles just to snatch a few hours with them.

From Women to Men

* A portrait of himself, sketched from a flattering photograph

* A barrel of real ale, or a bottle of vintage wine from his favourite vineyard

* A thoughtfully chosen item that shows you are taking an interest in *his* interests or hobbies

* A ticket to an all-women mud-wrestling show

* Supper at the Savoy, on you (if he's rich, it's a gesture he'll never forget)

* An enormous wind-up bath toy – Hamleys in London do fetching hippos, tortoises and whales

* A hip flask

* A Noël Coward-type silk dressing gown

* A picnic hamper crammed with delicious gourmet treats

* A snakeskin wallet

* A crystal whisky decanter and glasses, or silver spittoon for his pad

* An early morning call to his office when you know he's got a stressful day ahead. Just say 'I love you' and put the phone down

The One I Love Belongs to Somebody Else

'I can't understand why it's supposed to be such a shock horror scene for us single people to have affairs with those who are married,' laughs Lucy, a freelance photographer. 'As long as you're careful not to let it get too heavy emotionally, married men and women can make ideal companions and lovers.'

The advantages, according to Lucy, are that married lovers are appreciative of what you have to offer, both physically and with regard to personality, too. You'll have a good time when you're together because they'll be light-hearted at being released from domestic responsibilities, and as your hours together are limited, you'll make the most of them. Usually, Lucy says, married men are more financially generous than their single counterparts, so you should get wined and dined very pleasantly. Although unless they're on super expense accounts, they won't be able to be too lavish in view of the wife at home scrutinising the bank account.

'An affair with a married man or woman can work like a dream,' says Lucy, 'as long as you bear in mind three important rules. First, don't allow your lover to indulge in long "my spouse doesn't understand me" sessions. The truth is that the husband or wife probably does understand your lover, only too well. If your lover's going to use you as a shoulder to cry on about his or her marital problems, then point to the exit sign. Find a lover who gets on famously with his or her partner, but just needs a few hours off occasionally to enjoy some amusing company and lively sex. Second, don't permit your lover to dictate what you do or who you see in the time when he or she is not available. You'd be surprised the number of women, in particular, who get involved with married men and spend their spare hours moping at home because HE gets jealous if they see other men. Third, accept the limitations of the affair. Your lover is not going to leave home for you. He or she is not going to be available at weekends, bank holidays or on your birthday. And you won't be able to go on holiday together, unless it's a snatched overnight stay in Birmingham or Dusseldorf.'

Not everyone would agree with Lucy about the charms of such a relationship. She's mentioned some of the disadvantages, but there are others too:

* Married lovers won't be there when you need them or want them. At least if your lovers are single, you're free to ring them up and make love verbally down the phone. You can't do that if they're married.

* There are heavy limitations on who you can introduce them to in your social and family circle.

* Married lovers always have one eye on the clock. Especially women who don't have jobs outside the home, and have to be back at 4 to pick up the kids from school.

* You're restricted over the places you can be seen in together. Be prepared for them to dive under the restaurant table if neighbours of theirs walk in or a photographer aims a lens in your direction.

* Your life will be disrupted by disjointed phone calls at odd hours. At 8 a.m. while he's out fetching the papers, or a snatched 3 minutes while she's busy putting the car away.

* Quite often, you'll find married lovers are using you as ammunition in retaliation at the infidelity of their partners.

* Inevitably, one or other of you will from time to time be wracked with guilt over the deceived husband or wife. This is bound to have a dampening effect on your sex life, leading to rows on the theme of 'We have so little time together, why do you have to foul it up by agonising over *him/her*?'

* You are obliged to accept that you will always have to take a back seat in your married lover's life. You always have to fit in with all his or her other domestic, social and work arrangements. You can never come first.

* If you fall heavily for them, you'll end up getting badly hurt. It can't be emphasised often enough or loudly

enough that married lovers rarely leave their partners, whatever they may say to the contrary.

'The most irritating men,' Lucy admits, 'are those who are coy about admitting they are married. Single men don't have this problem, of course, because most married women wear wedding rings. But many men don't, and it's so stupid of them to pretend they're bachelors when it sticks out a mile that they're married. At first, they'll only invite you to lunch rather than dinner, and naturally they are never free at weekends, unless it's a stolen hour on Saturday when they're allegedly at a rugby match. They go berserk if you smear lipstick on their shirts (which will be well pressed, along with their handkerchiefs) and if you mislay an earring in their car it's the signal for a full scale hue and cry. Then they're so vague about exactly where they live – you don't of course get given the home telephone number, and calling the office is dodgy if the wife is in cahoots with the secretary. They tend to be non-committal about what they do at weekends, and their conversation keeps harking back to how enviable your freedom is, how foolish you'd be to give it up . . .'

You might imagine that having a lover who is unmarried, but living with a man or woman, would be a considerably more open relationship, free of many of the conflicts mentioned above. You would imagine wrong. In practical terms there is little difference between an affair with someone who has a marriage certificate, and someone who enjoys a live-in relationship without it. In fact, in an affair with such a person, the blurring of the lines makes for increased pressure between you. At least with a married man or woman, you know exactly where you are. By getting married, your lover has made a public declaration that he or she has *chosen* to live with his or her partner. But people in live-in relationships are apt to come up with a series of inventively apologetic reasons for their domestic situation:

'Oh well, she didn't have anywhere to live so it seemed a good idea at the time for her to move in with me.'

'Poor Peter was dreadfully upset when Ellen left him. I

took him under my wing, you know, and he just sort of stayed.'

'Frankly, I couldn't afford the rent, so Chris moved in as a lodger and, well, things just drifted on from there.'

In a marriage, it is accepted that the couple will be spending most of their time together, but with people who live together there is the underlying (and often false) assumption that they are each free to pursue other relationships. Confused over the extent of your lover's commitment to a partner, understandably you agitate to see him or her more often than you would if she or he were married. But the more pressures of this sort you apply, the more it is likely to trigger moods of guilt or angst in your lover. So before you get involved in such an affair, it pays to establish exactly what your lover's relationship is with his or her partner, and to decide if it's worth putting up with all the attendant stress.

Until The Real Thing Comes Along

The gay divorcée, playing the field and leaving a trail of exhausted men lying on the touch line ... the born-again bachelor entertaining a bevy of Bunny girls on his king size bed ... the merry widow, gaining a new lease of life from a succession of younger lovers ... oh, the winks and nods directed by society at single people, the assumption that because we are free to do so, we are madly making whoopee with exotic lovers at every available moment. But as every single person knows, the reality is that finding a compatible sexual partner isn't as easy as it sounds – a fact that often comes as a nasty shock to many of the newly divorced.

Most of us have times when we feel anything from the longing for some gentle lovemaking to the urge to indulge our wildest fantasies – but there happens to be no one around with whom we can share the experience. Traditional advice on this aspect of living alone verges on the farcical. Men, it is tacitly assumed, may wander into a massage parlour or buy up a supply of *Playboy* or *Men Only*. Women, however, are briskly recommended to have a cold shower ... take the dog for a five-mile walk ... visit a friend with at least three children aged under five. Certainly, it never seems to occur to anyone that women over a certain age, especially the widowed, should yearn for sex just as much as girls thirty years their junior.

'The answer is simple,' says divorcee Laura. 'If there's no man in my life to make love to me, then I make love to myself. It took me some time to come to terms with this, because I was brought up believing that masturbation was self-abuse. But I got over all that when I realised how many of my friends, of both sexes, married and single, practice masturbation. When I'm smitten with a bout of erotomania, I soak in a warm bath, loaded with my most expensive smelling goo. Then I fall into bed with a glass of wine, a sexy novel and my vibrator. I know exactly what turns me on, and I lie there and indulge in an orgy of incredible fantasies – things I'd be too shy ever to reveal to a man. I'd never pretend that this sort of sex is as good as the real thing. You have to approach it from the point of view that making love to yourself is not an attempt to emulate the sensations you feel with a lover. It's a different, complementary experience, rather than an inferior substitute. And as far as I'm concerned, it's better than getting crabby because I'm sexually frustrated.'

Laura bought her vibrator at a sex shop. 'I didn't have the nerve to go in there by myself so I asked a woman friend to accompany me. The male assistant didn't leer, sneer or give us pitying looks, and my friend and I had a giggly half hour sorting through the wares. I'd no idea there was such a variety of sex toys – for both men and women.'

If you can't muster the courage to enter a sex shop, most sex aids are available by mail order, delivered very speedily to your door in an anonymous plain paper parcel. Magazines like *She* carry advertisements of reputable firms who will send you a free brochure. Another alternative is to obtain your sex aids from a travelling saleswoman, much in the same way that you might buy Tupperware. As far as I know, there is only one woman engaged in this work, and she operates mainly in the West Country; so if you live in this area and you're invited to a selling party where your hostess is mysteriously vague about what's going to be on offer, you could be in for an intriguing surprise.

Taking a Chance on Love

I can't imagine that any single woman in her right mind would go to bed with a man without first making an appointment at her local clinic for contraceptive advice. No woman who wants to stay single, that is. I hate writing this about my own sex, but regrettably there are still a few women around who regard a husband as a meal ticket and aren't averse deliberately to getting pregnant as a means to this end. The canny man will bear this in mind and take his own precautions. 'If I intend making love to a woman I don't know very well, I never accept her word if she says she's on the Pill. I always use a sheath,' I was told by a man who treasures his single status and intends to keep it that way. Fortunately, women intent on snaring men through 'accidental' pregnancies are now a dying breed. Most of the single women I know are so terrified of getting pregnant that they check and double check to ensure that they've taken their Pill, or squeeze twice the recommended amount of spermicide onto their caps.

If disaster does strike and you suspect you are pregnant, go at once to your GP or contact the British Pregnancy Advisory Service for their branch nearest to you. Don't rely on home pregnancy testing kits; if they've been stored incorrectly in the chemist the chemicals may have deteriorated, and you'll get a false reading. If you need an abortion, your GP should be able to arrange this for you. Should he be unable or unwilling to do so, organisations such as the

British Pregnancy Advisory Service or Release will advise you on how to obtain an abortion privately.

After pregnancy, the thing most people fear with respect to their sexual lives is catching VD. Though in a way, it is reassuring if you have had such a scare, as once you've been through the system of getting it checked out and treated you don't feel so alarmed if it happens again.

The important fact to remember is that most people who go to a special clinic or their GP worried that they're riddled with an infection that will turn them blind, have probably not got VD at all. Legally, there are only three diseases which are termed venereal: syphilis, gonorrhoea and chancroid (and this last is only common in the tropics). What you probably do have is one of any number of sexually transmitted diseases, all of which (apart from herpes) are easily and effectively cured.

What you *must* do if you know or suspect that you have any such infection is to tell your lovers. 'What, *all* of them?' asked one man, aghast. 'But I'd have to send out a circular letter!' Yes, *all* of them. It's socially irresponsible not to, as they will need to be treated too, before they have the opportunity to pass on the infection to other partners. Initially, it's always a bit embarrassing having to ring up and tell your lovers the score, but most adults these days accept that contracting some sort of sexually transmitted disease is an occupational hazard of enjoying a varied sex life. The best way to approach the matter with your lover is to discuss the matter in a light-hearted manner in the early stages of your affair, before there's any likelihood of your having STD. Then if it happens, you'll both be more prepared and less likely to feel unnecessarily ashamed and guilty.

You can find out the address of your local VD clinic (also called Special Clinics or Departments of Genito-Urinary Medicine) by ringing your GP's surgery or your nearest hospital. You'll save yourself a lot of time and aggravation if you telephone the clinic before you go to establish the days and times it is open, as some clinics prefer to see men and women on separate days.

Treatment at the clinics is fully confidential and no report will be sent to your GP. The doctor at the clinic will have to ask you intimate questions about your sex life and your recent partners. Try not to be shy and hold back any information as this only makes it more difficult for the doctor to establish the exact nature of any infection you may have. Rest assured, the doctor is not going to be censorious about any of your sexual activities or raise an eyebrow at the number of your partners. You will then have a medical examination – an internal examination for women. This doesn't take long and usually doesn't hurt. All that remains is for you to give small samples of urine and blood for routine tests. You will probably be informed of the diagnosis on the same day and given some tablets. The usual course of treatment lasts about four weeks, but you will be asked to come back for check-ups to ensure that the infection has fully cleared up.

For further advice and guidance – for women *and* men – on all these matters, a book like *The Women's Health Handbook* is invaluable. There are excellent and reassuring chapters on all aspects of contraception, pregnancy, sterilisation, VD, thrush, cystitis, the menstrual cycle and the menopause. Another reassuring paperback is *STD – Sexually Transmitted Diseases* by Maria Corsaro and Carole Korzeniowsky, published by Sphere Books.

When Your Lover Has Gone

Getting the push is never easy to bear. It may be a sudden, dramatic parting, after a blazing row followed by silence, with your notes and phone calls ominously not returned. Or you may have seen it coming for ages, but ignored the warning signs – your lover is busy at weekends . . . has to work late . . . looks glazed when you start making future plans . . . arrives later and later, then not at all . . .

Whichever way it happens, where relationships are concerned you can be sure that there is no such thing as a clean break. Despite those gossip column pictures of celebrated couples brightly asserting that their split is completely amicable, they are still the very best of friends and wish one another every happiness, the truth is that at any given time there is usually one of them who wanted out more than the other.

Being rejected by someone you care about is always painful and a shattering blow to your self-confidence. Just as being in love does wonders for your appearance, endowing you with a radiant vivacity, so being jilted tends to make you look as jaded, dull and off balance as you feel inside.

Friends are essential here. The best kind of friend will understand what you're going through, come round with a bottle or two, listen while you agonise, scream, weep and moan, then tip you into bed and throw the empties in the bin. But in the end, of course, the friend will go home and you'll be left in an empty room, just you, miserable as hell, missing your lover like mad. Experience and common sense tell you that time really does heal and in six months' time you'll be able to hear your lover's name and shrug. But that doesn't help at this immediate time. It hurts *now*, this minute. What can you do?

Don't fall into the trap of trying to blot out the pain with a long binge on booze or dope. It's bad enough getting over a love affair without doubling the aggro by giving yourself a drink or drugs problem as well. And whatever you think now, in a year's time you'll agree that no man or woman in the world is worth suffering that much for.

What does help is to hurl yourself into something physical. Paint your bedroom and whitewash your lover out at the same time. Dig the garden, play squash, any hard, exhausting activity which will expunge your anger and resentment and tire you out so you don't lie awake night after night moping. It won't bring your lover back, but at least you'll feel you've achieved something: a new-look bedroom or clearer skin and eyes from the squash, which with the rest of your world in disarray will be a gratifying boost to your morale.

Another solution is to try a spot of self-analysis and work out exactly what it is you feel you've lost along with your lover. It might be sex, status, self-esteem, social activities or a combination of all four. But none of them is irreplaceable. And remember, you may have lost a number of things you liked along with your lover, but you've also rid yourself of much that irritated you too. Think positive. Remind yourself of all the activities you are free to pursue without him or her. Dwell on your lover's annoying habits and mannerisms. Enjoy being free to plan your life for yourself instead of having to pander to your lover's tastes and whims.

You won't get over it overnight, of course. There's bound to be a period of mourning, bitterness and self-pity. But bear in mind, in your darkest moments, that just because he or she didn't want you, it doesn't mean no one else will. Everyone, but everyone, gets the elbow at least once in their lives. Eventually you will meet someone else and find your emotional balance and confidence gradually restored.

Softly as I Leave You

When it's your turn to say 'on your bike' it can be almost as agonising as getting the push yourself. It's amazing how many affairs start or drag on because one or other of you can't muster the courage or tactful turn of phrase to bring the liaison to a halt. Sometimes, especially in the early stages, the most obvious approach can be the most effective.

'One of my men is threatening to give me a T shirt with *Can't We Just Be Friends* printed on it, I've said it to him so many times,' Pat A. laughingly told me. 'It may sound a corny line, but it works. If they still come on heavy, I tell them they are great guys, very attractive, fantastic, terrific, but I happen to be in love with someone else. I think most of the men I know must be incredible romantics at heart, because they always accept that, and lay off.'

The art of the lighthearted turn off is well worth cultivating, especially when it comes to handling the amorous spouses of friends, who seem to believe (particularly if you're newly divorced or separated) that you must be missing out sexually. It's a difficult situation, as obviously you don't want to stop seeing your friends, or cause strain within your relationship. The wisest dodge is to avoid, if possible, being alone with these predators. If you are cornered, be pleasant, firm, slightly shocked and disappointed. Bring your friend's name immediately into the conversation. Hopefully the predators will be so scared of you spilling the beans that they will back off quickly – though be prepared for a resentful backlash as for a time they may try to influence your friend against you.

When it's a long standing affair that's burnt out, how you get the message across to your lover depends very much on your nature, whether you're the devious or the direct type.

A devious ploy is to throw a large party, invite all your most attractive friends and try and get your lover off with one of them. Or endeavour to turn your lover off you. Think back to what drew them to you in the first place. Was it your mutual interest in Renaissance art? Then renege, and rave over Picasso's cubist period. If you were loved for your fall of shiny, healthy hair, screw it into a knot and don't wash it until your lover has checked out for the last time. Talk endlessly about subjects you know bore them and stop laughing at their jokes.

If you're thinking hell, what a callously underhand approach – at least I'd have the guts to tell my lover straight out that we were finished, bear in mind during the showdown that honesty is not a licence to kill. Having shared your most intimate moments with your lover, you will be acutely aware of all his or her vulnerable points. Be kind. Be generous. Take all the blame yourself and accept too the inevitable backlash as they wade in with the verbal chain saw and decimate your character. Just grit your teeth and agree with every insult that's hurled at you. Then get out.

And stay out. The most cruel thing you can do, having ditched someone, is to dangle yourself in front of them again, just popping in to 'make sure you're OK' . . . 'hear how the interview went' . . . 'see if the cat got over that flu'. Your ex-lover will get over you a lot faster if you stay out of sight and give him or her the space to form a new relationship. An extremely distraught lover might refuse to leave you alone, causing noisy, embarrassing scenes on your doorstep, or making recriminatory phone calls through the night. Living alone, this sort of terrorism is particularly alarming. The best way to avoid it is to drop out and stay with friends for a while after the split. Your lover will soon tire of phoning an empty flat, or banging on a door that never opens.

In the end, of course, everything shakes down and you either stop seeing one another completely, or you keep in contact out of habit or just plain curiosity. Whatever the reason, the important thing to accept is that your relationship now has a new set of rules. Many men, accustomed over the years to regarding women as possessions, like the car or the Black and Decker, can't believe after the split that the little woman is capable of organising her own life. 'Annie's just hopeless with money. I've told my accountant to keep an eye on her and let me know when she gets in a muddle.' . . . 'It isn't that I mind Sheila having lovers. The reason I tear into her about it is that she will pick men who are so bad for her.' And women are often guilty of refusing to accept that men can manage domestically, or choose their own clothes. They can, they can.

After the split, it's important to have the courage to stand back and learn to let go. Hopefully, when all the bitterness and resentment have faded, you'll be able to meet again as friends, and smile, 'Thanks for the memory – of all the good times.'

* * *

Some Useful Addresses

British Pregnancy Advisory Service, 1st Floor, Guildhall Buildings, Navigation St. Birmingham 2. (Birmingham 643 1461)

Brook Advisory Centres, 233 Tottenham Court Road, London W1P 9HE. (01-580 2991 and 01-323 2991)
(They give advice on contraception and abortion and are specially geared to young people. Their London office will give you the address of a centre near you.)

Family Planning Association, 27-35 Mortimer St. London W1A 4QW. (01-636 7866)

Release, 1 Elgin Avenue, London W.10. (01-289 1123)
Emergency number outside office hours: (01-603 8654)

Further Reading

Women's Health Handbook, Ed. Nancy MacKeith (Virago)
Games People Play, Eric Berne (Penguin)
Sexually Transmitted Diseases, Maria Corsaro and Carole Korzeniowsky (Sphere)

CHAPTER 5

ENTERTAINING

Guess who's coming to dinner?

The most important person you'll ever entertain in your home is *you*. Yet for many single people, eating alone is such a miserable experience that we fall into the trap of saying with a shrug, 'Oh, it's only me, so I'll eat my soup straight from the saucepan . . . it's no fun cooking for yourself – I'll just bolt down a cheese sandwich for my supper . . .'

But why save the best china, silver and your culinary expertise for guests? Don't you deserve the best too? Of course there's no need to go to all the palava of setting the table if you don't feel like it. But an attractively laid tray with gleaming cutlery and a glass of wine will do wonders for your morale. (Pick up a box of wine from your off-licence. It allows you to enjoy a single glass at a time.) After a while, this ritual of pleasing presentation will become a habit, and you'd no more dream of supping from the saucepan than you would off the floor.

Mealtimes are often especially difficult for those who find themselves suddenly and unexpectedly on their own. We are accustomed to thinking of eating as a social occasion, and after years of having another face on the other side of the table, someone to talk to over the meal – even if it was a screaming row – it comes hard when overnight mealtimes become a solitary experience.

When Vera was widowed, eating alone was the aspect of her new life she found most painful to come to terms with. Because he rose very early, her husband preferred to have his main meal at lunchtime, and she was accustomed to him returning home every day at one on the dot and regaling her for an hour with amusing stories of his morning's business activities. At first, after his death, she found herself setting the table in the dining room as usual and unable to swallow a mouthful of lunch because the room was echoing with memories of all those years of shared meals, and shared laughter.

Sensibly, she decided to combat this by changing her routine. She now has a light, soup and sandwich lunch in her sunny kitchen and eats her main meal in the evening, off a tray in front of the television. This not only stops her feeling depressed at the absence of her husband, but also, she finds, gives her much more free time during the day. Although she never minded it when her husband was alive, she admits that it is something of a relief now not to be obliged to break off in the middle of a morning's gardening to come in and make a steak and kidney pie for lunch. She accepts that although her years with her husband were extremely happy and she was content then to organise her life around him, now she is on her own there are positive advantages in being free to arrange her routine to suit herself.

The principle of treating yourself like a special guest applies particularly to food. Of course it's a pleasure to know that, being single, you can enjoy a frozen pizza for your dinner if you feel like it without anyone screaming with outrage that you haven't steamed up all the windows and yourself preparing their favourite boned stuffed lamb. Fast foods are now an accepted part of the culinary scene and no one leading a full and varied life would possibly be without them. Even so, it's not fair to your body to fuel it with junk food all the time. No one's suggesting that you make with the Magimix every night, whipping up a succession of gourmet feasts, but even if you only cook a proper meal once a week – say at weekends – it's a good start, and your health and appearance will benefit. In any case, it's a prudent idea to keep your hand in at cooking, so that when you have friends round, or someone you particularly want to impress, you aren't thrown into a panic at the notion of feeding them.

It's much less nerve wracking if you've tried out a few dishes on yourself.

Choosing a cookery book is a very personal business, but for myself, I prefer coloured pictures showing each finished dish and no lofty assumptions that I know what a roux or béchamel sauce is. For anything basic, like how to make pancakes, I find my hand automatically goes out for my faithful Mrs Beeton. Another enduring favourite is Katharine Whitehorn's *Cooking in a Bedsitter* which has the bonus of being a hilariously funny read. If you shop at Sainsbury's, pick up a copy of *Food for One* by Deanna Brostoff. Apart from excellent recipes, it contains realistic advice on marketing for one and also the wisdom of organising an emergency food store cupboard. As with any other skill, cooking comes a lot easier if you are able to watch a demonstration. Several men I know have been inspired to become avid cooks through watching Delia Smith's cookery course on television. Her approach, they tell me, is pleasantly basic and although things never actually do go wrong, you are always left with the reassuring suspicion that they could, quite easily.

When it comes to food, something everyone living alone should do from time to time is consume a meal while sitting in front of a mirror, It's a salutary experience! Think of the number of times you've been put off someone by the revolting way they stick out their tongues like flycatchers while forking up meat pie. If you dine alone a great deal, it's easy to get lax and not realise your tie is floating in the gravy and you're eating as if you've stuck your head in a trough.

Likewise, it's sensible to watch the way you look when you're alone. Obviously, in your own place you want to feel free to relax in your most comfortable clothes and not wash your hair if it doesn't suit you to. But if you find you're spending days slopping around in an old dressing gown, or without shaving, then for the sake of your morale, this is a rut you should heave yourself out of. Subconsciously, it's depressing if every time you pass a mirror, you're viewing

114

yourself at your worst. Give yourself a treat occasionally by making yourself easy on the eye. Comfortable gear doesn't have to be old and tatty. And most people do feel more toned up after a bath and a splash with cologne. Don't save your cologne or scent to use just when you're with other people. Why not enjoy smelling good for yourself? Women travelling to the States could pick up a bottle of Senchal, a perfume that's been created specially for singles.

The big night for dressing up and going out is, of course, Saturday. And nearly every single person I've talked to has confessed that Saturday nights are the big bogey about living alone. 'Thank God it's Friday!' scream the radio DJs. 'Have a *great* weekend!', conjuring up visions of a hectic social whirl with you as the glittering centre of attention. If you don't happen to have anything arranged for Saturday night it's so easy to feel swamped with self-pity, imagining the rest of the world revelling at a roaring party to which everyone but you has been invited.

But instead of moping about, convincing yourself you're a social failure, why not take a more positive attitude towards your free weekend? At first, the notion of spending a weekend by yourself may seem daunting, even boring. How are you to fill the time?

To a large extent, that depends on how you spent your week. Anyone who's been cooped up in a stuffy office for five days will probably want to devote some of the weekend to getting out in the fresh air and doing something active. Walking, gardening, swimming, roller skating – whatever your choice of activity, the essential thing is to get out and *do* it, instead of just thinking about it. Alternatively, if life's been hectic during the week, you might be inclined to treat yourself to an unashamedly self-indulgent weekend. Buy yourself delicious treats in food and drink. A stack of new paperbacks and cassettes. Sleep late. Wallow in long, hot baths.

Elaine Paige, star of *Evita* and *Cats*, spoke in the *Standard* about the pleasure she derives from weekends when there is no one else around: 'I buy all my favourite things and they are always the same: different cheeses, white warm fresh bread, a box of Twiglets, a little pot of caviar, and prawns – which I fry in butter and garlic.' She takes the phone off the hook, and spends hours reading the papers and pottering in her garden.

If you're really feeling adrift and incapable of settling to anything, it might help to draw up a timetable of things you want to do and achieve over the weekend. On Saturday morning, for instance, you might decide to clean your flat and car, promising yourself a half bottle of Mâcon with your lunch, as a reward. Afternoon: Shop for materials for shelving you're intending to put up on Sunday/Phone your sister/Sort out and label that jumbled heap of cassettes. Evening: Prepare supper, with remaining half of Mâcon/Write up diary for the week/Watch TV, with new golfing magazine to hand to cover the boring bits/Make real coffee to accompany Bailey's Irish Cream.

The idea of making a timetable might seem an over-structured aproach, but for many people, especially those unused to living alone, it does work. At the end of the weekend, they feel that the planning has paid off and instead of spending two days drifting from one unfinished activity to another, they have done something constructive with their time.

However you spend your time, the experience of the first few enjoyable solo weekends will make you wonder how you could ever have viewed them with alarm. For once you've learned to entertain yourself, you'll find that a weekend on your own is something you'll look forward to and cherish.

Party Politics

One sure way to make entertaining a misery is to attempt it on a scale, or in a style, that's beyond you. Just because *they* invited you to a five-course banquet, it doesn't mean you have to reciprocate in kind. If you hate cooking, don't attempt an elaborate dinner party. Instead, invite your friends to share a take-away Chinese and a video tape, or suggest that everyone who comes contributes one course. Remember, people are always pleased simply to be invited. No one expects you to trade daube for daube. Anyone who's slimming, for example, will be delighted to attend a diet supper with tempting low calorie dishes and refreshing white wine. Anyone who's not will enjoy your outsize pot of spaghetti, washed down with gallons of chianti. Conversely, don't let the poverty of your friends put you off throwing a lavish bash if you have the space and the money to spare. Gerald and Grizelda may unfailingly offer you bean stew on a tin plate when they ask you round, but that doesn't mean they'd tear up your engraved invitation to the ball of the year. They'd adore every extravagant second of it. (If you want to be seen going wildly over the top, you hire a party psychologist who advises you on how to space your guests at the table in your £10,000 marquee – you maintain a plate distance of twenty-seven inches – and a party architect who orchestrates the event, co-ordinating roving flautists to draw the guests outdoors for the firework display and ensuring that the car of each departing guest is waiting as he reaches the door.)

The number of guests you can comfortably cram in to your pad is vital . . . as is having the right mix of people. The couple who were such a hoot on your Greek island holiday will look quite different when you see them dressed, and the boss you've invited to impress with your air of cultured sophistication won't be enamoured by their insistence that you repeat your hysterical holiday trick with the tumblers on your head and the table between your teeth.

Don't automatically expect all your friends to like one another. Colleagues from work, golf club cronies, old school pals and ex-lovers just might not gel – and you'll be left with the sneaking suspicion that all the way home they'll be muttering, 'God, who would have thought old Chris would have such awful friends?'

It's important to invite enough people to cover for those who don't show and those who've had a row on the way there and aren't displaying much *joie de vivre* initially. This is a hazard of entertaining in suburban areas where guests tend to arrive early and head straight for the buffet because they've been so busy fighting over who should put Junior to bed that they missed out on supper. If you live in this kind of area you'll find your rooms empty magically at a quarter to twelve, as they roar off into the night frantic because the babysitter charges double time after midnight. You should also allow for those guests and their uninvited friends who turn up after the pubs have closed showing rather too much of the party spirit.

Forget about trying to balance men and women guests. It's the blend of personalities that makes a party go, not an equal balance of male and female voices.

Entertaining, of course, does not have to take place in the evening. If alcohol gives you migraines, but you're a dab hand at making mouthwatering toasted teacakes and short-bread, why not hold a traditional tea party complete with lovely delicate china, old-fashioned plate stands and several delicious varieties of tea. Or if Gerald downstairs is likely to ruck up at a boisterous evening party at your place, throw a lunch-time do. Then everyone can sleep it off on your floor during the late afternoon and sweep you off for a thank-you dinner in the evening. Magazines are fond of urging us to throw Sunday brunch parties, but the only place I've ever witnessed one was in the magazine photographer's studio, at five p.m. I don't know any real people with either the enthusiasm to prepare such a feast, or the energy to get up on a Sunday to attend one.

Whatever form of party you decide on, it seems to me a basic essential that you should like the people you are inviting. This may seem too obvious to need stating, but you must have noticed the recent spate of magazine articles in which the writers assume you hate all your guests and have only asked them round in order to return, as cheaply and nastily as possible, the hospitality they have given you. If you rate your friends so low that you deliberately give them such revoltingly sweet sherry that they won't ask for seconds, why bother inviting them in the first place? Besides, the downwards repercussion spiral when they return your invitation is horrible to contemplate.

It's only considerate to make it clear to your guests exactly what form of hospitality you're offering them. Are they being invited for drinks, a snack, supper, after-dinner drinks or what? If you just say, 'Do come round on Thursday for the evening', you'll leave your guest wracked with indecision about what to wear and whether to eat first at home.

Entertaining needn't be expensive. Twenty-three-year old Iain likes to have his friends round for a meal but finds his forester's pay won't stretch to *haute cuisine*. 'The answer,' he says, 'is to serve your guests the very best of what you can afford, in food and drink. The cheapest food is likely to be what's fresh and in season. I have a passion for escargots, but my budget will never run to them so instead I serve flat mushrooms in garlic butter with crusty French bread. And nursery fare is always surprisingly popular. I frequently end my dinners with a crisp-topped bread and butter pudding, and everyone fights for seconds. As for booze, well I make my own wine. Most of it is pretty grim, but I do have a superior chilled gooseberry, which when artfully decanted tastes just as good as French wines costing ten times as much!'

If you're throwing a bottle party, don't expect your guests to supply all the booze. You don't have to lay in a full armoury of spirits, just an encouraging array of wine and beer to show willing. Avoid paper cups. Off licences supply glasses free (you pay for breakages, naturally) if you order your wine from them. In colder weather, a mulled wine is both welcoming and cheap to make. And don't, please, persecute the non-drinkers by offering them a choice between tap water and tap water. Jugs of fresh orange juice, Perrier water or fruit punches will be most gratefully received.

On the subject of booze, something you can't avoid is the question of how you handle drunks at your party. I don't mean normal conviviality, but those frightening occasions when you realise you've got guests in your pad who are hell bent on destructive drinking – destructive both in the sense of maltreating themselves and abusing you, your other guests and the home you've spent time and money putting together. Some people who live alone are so fearful of this kind of situation that it puts them off entertaining altogether, so I canvassed some hardened party givers about their solutions – short of calling the police and having the revellers thrown out, which doesn't make for a conducive carnival atmosphere. I found there were various schools of thought on what to do:

   * To ensure that you go on enjoying your party, the most positive action you can take is to get rid of the drunks. It helps if you've thought ahead and invited some heavyweight friends who can if necessary act as bouncers and manhandle the carousers into a taxi home. The taxi is crucial (if you can persuade the driver to co-operate) as if you just heave the revellers out into the street you're in danger of them banging on the door or attempting to climb back through the window, and the ensuing disturbance is hardly calculated to endear you to your neighbours.

   * It's useless trying to reason with anyone who's sloshed. And it's no good hoping that as soon as they've demolished that last bottle of Scotch they'll calm down and accept a nice mug of black coffee. With certain brands of hardened drinkers, once the Scotch has run out they'll move on to the gin, vodka, sherry, even Brasso if that's all you've got and they're still conscious enough to imbibe it. If it's either physically impossible for you to throw the person out, or socially indelicate for you to do so (he's the boss's brother) all you can do is take a calculated risk, and pump as much

alcohol as you dare into him in the hope that he'll pass out.

    * If the winebags are very rich, sit back and let them do their worst. Then go round the following afternoon when their hangovers are just beginning to subside, but they're still feeling fragile, and present them with a bill for the damage.

Even for the most spontaneous bedsit bash, some forward planning is vital. In fact, the more confined your space, the more you and your guests will enjoy the do if you've thought through a few organisational details beforehand.

Where, for example, are all the empties destined to go? Will your landlady create about the fire hazard if you dump them on the landing? Where is everyone going to put their coats? Twenty guests arriving in the middle of winter can soon make your one room resemble a jumble sale. Can your neighbour be persuaded to offer her place as a cloakroom for the evening? Is the shared bathroom/loo going to be available that evening? If Grizelda downstairs who has declined your party invitation is in the habit of soaking for four hours in the bath every Saturday night, you're going to have a tribe of extremely desperate guests on your hands. Is there enough loo paper? Are the spare rolls *visible*? Have you enough glasses, plates, cutlery and rolls of kitchen paper to mop up spills and double as napkins? Even if you don't smoke, remember to provide plenty of ashtrays for those who do, otherwise you'll find fag ends stubbed out on your precious Sèvres plates.

Precious things you have to make a policy decision about. I tend to put away anything breakable, but I don't go as far as some people I know who cover their carpet and expensive Heal's sofa with polythene before a party. To me there is always the lurking threat that if I don't behave myself they'll wrap me in cling film as well.

You'll set the mood with lighting and music – it's worth experimenting with both beforehand to ensure that the speakers work and that the intimate, floor level lamp doesn't reflect up a sinister light that will make your boss' wife look like a ghoul. Soft lighting is, of course, flattering and romantic, but it can be irritating blundering about in the gloom unable to see to whom you're talking. Bear in mind that all lightweight lamps at elbow level are bound to get knocked over. It's always pleasing if you are able to create a vista. Even if it's too cold to use the garden, string some lights in the trees, or fill your windowboxes with candles in jars. (Avoid candles at large gatherings. They look lovely, but not when the curtains go up in flames.) I am always saddened at the way we in Britain shut out our glorious sunsets and the moon and stars. If there's a full moon, why not draw back the curtains and delight your guests with the vision of the garden bathed in silvery light.

Music is very much a matter of personal taste. However hard you try, there will always be some guests who groan that they can't possibly dance a step to that antiquated rubbish on the tape, or those like me who complain they can't hear the people they're talking to and could you please turn the sound down to a more acceptable dull roar. In general I find that people respond most to the music they danced to in their youth. For those of my generation, it's the Beatles who start us bopping, whereas my mother's foot begins to tap if we put on Joe Loss, and my nineteen-year-old niece gyrates to groups like 10 CC.

Whether you invite people by phone or via an engraved card, it does help if you give them clear instructions on how to find your place. It's incredible the number of people who seem to have no idea of exactly where they live. 'You know that archway opposite the brewery – oh, you don't know the brewery, well, actually I think it's a furniture warehouse now but everyone round here still calls it the brewery, anyway, just opposite is an arch and you go under that and bear left, no, hang on, Jean says it's best to take the right hand fork by the mountain ash, it's a local landmark, and then you'll approach our house from the opposite end if you get my meaning and we're the third one down on the left, no sorry the right if you're coming from that end, no there isn't a number and the local hooligans have smashed up the Mon Repos name plate but we've got a teak front door, you can't miss it . . .'

When you're giving instructions, stick to landmarks like churches or pubs which are unlikely to have changed and won't have been vandalised beyond recognition. And take pity on townies who wouldn't know a mountain ash or teak front door if it fell on them, and could spend hours driving round arguing the toss about it.

It's a great asset if your front door (if that's the one you use) is clearly visible and the bell works. Russell Harty tells a salutary story when as a sprog teacher, he was invited to dine with the elevated personage of the Second Master of his school:

'I fumbled for the front-door bell, pressed it, tightened the knot in my tie and huddled inwards from the fury of a wintry gale. Nothing happpened. I rang again and rehearsed the possibilities of grave social error. Still nothing happened.

'I pressed my cold ear to the oak. I heard voices. I kept my finger hard upon the bell. Nothing happened. I kept now one finger on the bell and banged upon the oak with a flat wet hand. Eventually the slapping became rhythmic, hypnotic almost. It became obvious that this particular Englishman's castle had been closed down for the night. Then came the sound of chains clanking and heavy-weight curtains being swished aside and the peeved tones of the Second Master "all-righting" it as the great door swung open. This created a natural vacuum which blew me into the centre of the sitting-room where a circle of surprised faces, presided over by the hostess, gave dreadful note of social indiscretion.

' "What an original entry," said the Second Master, as previous invitees glanced knowingly at their dinner partners. "One never uses the front door," he said, meaning 'one doesn't whistle the Magnificat' or 'one doesn't pick the eyes out of one's whitebait.'

' "Perhaps," he continued, "you would help push this sofa back against the door and my wife will help you then to a drink." I drank to forget, and eventually left the party in the highest of spirits, through the back door, having bored the guests with a presentation of the limitless possibilities of anagramatising "Hare with Four Legs." '

It's surprising how quickly your initial anxiety that no one is going to turn up escalates to blind panic as an avalanche of guests surges over your threshold engulfing you with coats, bottles, flowers, funny stories about the drive over and how your front door handle came off in their hand. It's at this stage that most hosts feel like leaving them all to it and sliding off by themselves to the movies. It is, of course, quite impossible for you to manage opening bottles, pouring drinks, changing tapes, mopping up spills and making amusing conversation all by yourself. Tell yourself that most shy folk welcome the opportunity to have something to do, and delegate as many tasks as possible to them.

But however fiendishly you plan and delegate, there is always the wild card, the unexpected event which you could never have anticipated. At the last big party I gave, I felt pretty smug about my organisation. On the day, my team of helpers arrived prompt at two o'clock and I reasoned that all I would have to do would be to drift round, issuing instructions on what they were to do with the garden lights, the amplifier, the buffet, the drinks table. What I had completely overlooked was that it was Wimbledon Finals Day. Not only that, but it was the classic, never to be forgotten first final between Borg and McEnroe. My aides were so paralysed with excitement as they huddled round the TV that I was obliged to rush in all afternoon with trays of stiff Martinis, in between earning blisters on blisters as I strung fairylights, heaved wine crates round the kitchen, carved up sides of ham and beef and cursed everyone, particularly McEnroe and Borg.

Dinner Parties

The sitting at the table dinner party is one of the hardest forms of entertaining for the single person to carry off successfully, especially if you're beset by lack of space. People's knees will be interlocking Lego fashion under the cramped table and you're likely to end up poleaxed with all the fetching and carrying – for having artfully wedged everyone in round the dining table, the people you've delegated as Chief Helpers won't be able to get out without dismantling the bookcase hemming them in.

You are also putting yourself at a slight disadvantage with regard to the menu. When people (OK, I mean men) are invited to sit down at a table and eat, they subconsciously expect a higher standard of cuisine than if they're asked to serve themselves from a buffet. Place men round a formal table, plonk down a Lancashire hotpot and watch their faces fall. Yet a steaming dish of it for them to help themselves to will be greeted with cries of delight.

On all counts, an informal buffet supper is a much easier affair to handle. But if your promotion or your inheritance hinges on entertaining the boss or Aunt Maud to a formal dinner, here are a few tips:

The Day

Obviously, Saturday is the most convenient day to entertain as it affords you more time to get everything ready. But if you have to entertain mid-week, prepare as much as you can the night before, and lay the table in the morning, before you set out for work. Then if you're caught up in a crisis at the office or your bus is held up in a traffic jam, you won't be in a panic at the thought of having to organise everything from scratch when you arrive gasping on your doorstep.

The Menu

Choose a cold starter and sweet which you can prepare in advance, so you only have a hot main course to worry about. Don't experiment, stick to dishes you are familiar with – and try the entire meal and wines out on a few friends the week before. Ask the friend who is impersonating the boss's wife to advise you on the comfort of her chair, the draughts, the jutting table leg and the view through the kitchen door of the Pet of the Month.

Backstage

Clear the kitchen of all non-essentials to allow you ample surfaces for cooking paraphernalia and reviving gin. Work out in advance what plates, dishes, cutlery and glasses you will use, and clean them all up the day before. Bear in mind that you'll be weak with exhaustion by the end of the meal, so work backwards and have the coffee cups ready on a tray, and the cheeses laid out, under cover. If this elegant little gathering is taking place in the kitchen, then heaven help you. Those glossy magazine pictures of intimate kitchen dinner parties with the rustic pine table laden with wine and pretty pots of daisies never seem to show any real people cluttering up the scene – or the sight of the sink brimful of greasy pans and smeared with blood where you cut yourself grappling with the roast goose. (Avoid food which calls for major surgery if you come out in a cold sweat at the sight of a carving knife. And it's no good calling on your Chief Helper to carve. All that happens is that the rest of the meal grows cold while he makes a hash of dissecting half the goose, and then waves the knife at you accusingly: 'God, haven't you got a sharpener for this thing?' The sharpener, of course, is one of the non-essentials you cleared out and stuck in the cupboard under the stairs . . .)

Clothes

Steer clear of any garment with wide sleeves which catch on door handles as you come sweeping in with the soup. Keep your make up, mirror, comb and perfume spray in the kitchen for touch-ups between courses. Some people prefer to cook with the kitchen door and all windows flung wide to prevent a festive flush, but during a howling gale green powder works just as well instead.

The Table

Don't leave setting it until the last minute. Do it well in advance or early in the day. Then if you do find yourself in a flat spin as your guests arrive, at least they will be encouraged by the sight of a laid, hopefully gleaming table, rather than you rushing round hurling the silver like a circus knife thrower. A pretty tablecloth or even a sheet can do wonders for a sordid table. Flowers and candles look charming, but calculate if there will be room for them when the meal is in full flow, remembering the space required for wine bottles, serving dishes and all those elbows.

The First Half Hour

The worst period, when you whirl, Dervishlike, 'twixt sitting room and kitchen, pouring sherry, handing round nuts, arranging the flowers your boss's wife brought, basting the duck, tasting the sauce, throwing logs on the fire, and throughout it all contriving to look ecstatic at the entire experience. One way to lower your blood pressure is to stagger the arrival times of your guests, and invite everyone ten or fifteen minutes apart. They won't, of course, all arrive promptly at their appointed times, but it usually works so that they don't all come flooding over the doorstep together, thus giving you some much-needed breathing space.

Serving

Trolleys, despised by the offspring of my mother's generation, are now coming back into style. And for good reason. Few of us are adept at balancing trays of avocado vinaigrette on our heads, or ranging rows of plates up our arms – and neither does much for the suave image we are attempting to convey to our boss. A trolley also comes into its own at the end of each course, allowing you to shoot all the debris onto the lower level and wheel it swiftly out of sight.

After Dinner

This is where your Chief Helpers earn their medals. Promise them anything if they will just keep the coffee pot going for you for the remainder of the evening. I have to confess that the coffee stage is usually my undoing. By the time the coffee mill has spewed beans all over the kitchen, I've staggered in with the tray, poured out blacks, whites and 'something just on the palish beige side for me, dear,' handed round *petits fours* and liqueurs, I'm apt to collapse with a sigh of relief on the sofa and fall promptly asleep. You, of course, with your job or your inheritance at stake, will be made of sterner stuff.

Less stressful for the single person to manage are dinner parties where each guest brings a dish – starter, main course or sweet – leaving the host or hostess to provide only the wine and a welcoming ambiance. Or why not invite your friends round for after dinner drinks, and serve a deliciously gooey sweet with coffee, followed by a selection of unusual liqueurs.

Buffet Suppers and Lunches

Having guests help themselves to food saves you an enormous amount of hassle. Some points to bear in mind:

*Buffet fare doesn't have to be lavish. You don't need one thousand and one varieties on the groaning board. Concentrate on a few dishes, of fresh ingredients, beautifully presented. But keep it simple. Why have your tomatoes masquerading as waterlilies, or your radishes as rosettes? Allow ample time to prepare everything. A cold glazed ham, for example, can take an age to carve without an electric knife.

*Paper plates are a boon – but not paper cups.

*Keep two big plastic sacks ready to shoot all the debris into.

*Borrow several pepper and salt sets so people don't fight over your single cruet.

*Eliminate traffic jams by working out in advance the most expedient way for your guests to move round the buffet table.

*If your space is limited, don't attempt to bring out all

the food at once. Keep some in reserve in the fridge. (Late-comers will be grateful.)

Tea Parties

It's important at the outset to decide the tone of these. Is it to be a muffins round the fire and mugs of tea from a big brown pot occasion, or are you going to bring out the Royal Doulton and great grandmama's lace cloth? If you decide to put on a show with the latter, it presumably isn't the sort of thing you do every day, so it's wise to go over each detail first to ensure you're not going to make a slip over the finer points. When a friend of mine entertained her Aunt Maud to tea she brought out her best china, a hundred-year-old embroidered cloth and the Georgian silver teapot. Yet Aunt Maud seemed unimpressed. It was only when the lady had departed that her niece realised that throughout the visit she'd been resting the tea strainer in a Ponds cold cream jar.

Entertaining the Family

This form of 'entertaining' merits a section on its own, because however much you may love your kith and kin, welcoming them to your home can be a fraught experience. Especially if you're living in a small space that isn't equipped as lavishly as the large family homes they have come from. Your family probably think you're a bit odd for wanting to live alone in the first place. Unlike your friends, who will accept you for what you are, families tend to feel they have a right to impose their standards and way of life on you. They know best. This applies particularly to single women (of any age) who find that despite the fact that they are financially independent, perhaps holding down executive jobs, involved in a fulfilling social life and taking full responsibility for their lives, despite all this, their mothers still persist in treating them like backward seven-year-olds. It applies, too, to the widowed, who have to fight against being overwhelmed with brisk, sensible advice from brisk, sensible daughters.

Little wonder that as the day for a family visit approaches, single people feel as if they are under siege. It's easy to over-react at the thought of the impending invasion, and mutter rebelliously, 'Sod them. I always have an orgy on Sunday afternoons. Why should I change my routine for them?' The trouble is, if you stick to this defiant attitude, you know full well that after they've gone you're only going to be wracked with remorse about your piggish behaviour . . . and then you'll find yourself picking up the phone and asking them over again, next Sunday.

The answer, inevitably, is to compromise. But not over everything. It's your home, and it will pay you to have a clear idea right from the start what you're prepared to be flexible over when the family come, and where you're going to draw the line.

Let's get the really boring bit over with first. You simply have to make the effort to tidy up. Even if you just shove all your clutter under the bed, remove your dripping shirts from the bathroom and whizz round with the Hoover, it'll help to smooth the path for a harmonious family afternoon. Remember, most mothers have a way of mentally equating the amount of dust with your own state of mind. If you want to convince your family that you're content on your own, and leading just as fulfilling a life as you would be if you were married, try giving the place a touch of shine and gleam before they arrive. It works.

It's also worth going to the bother of borrowing some comfortable chairs for the afternoon, or some fat cushions for the divan. Anyone over thirty feels foolish and uncomfortable sitting on the floor.

Then there's the question of food. This is definitely not the time to experiment with recipes for your new wok. Indigestion makes fathers extremely bad tempered and prone to start conversations hinging around your sallow complexion and the dark circles under your eyes. Stick to simple, familiar, reassuring food and if they want to nod off in those comfy chairs you've provided, well why not?

Naturally, they will be curious about your surroundings and will appreciate a guided tour. You showing them round is one thing. Them poking in drawers, reading your letters or peering into wardrobes to see if any clothing belonging to the opposite sex is hanging there, is definitely not to be tolerated. Under no circumstances should you permit any invasion of your privacy and this includes all references to your bed: its size, its situation, what it's used for. People who live in conventional houses with conventional bedrooms are frequently embarrassed to enter a small flat and find the bed taking up a large portion of the living area. Just steadfastly ignore all snide comments on the subject. After a while they'll get used to it, and probably find it quite handy for that afternoon kip mentioned above.

Overnight Sensations

Of course you'd like your friends to stay over, especially if it means they can relax and not worry about drinking and driving. But if you're living in a confined area it has to be faced that you won't have the overnight facilities of a larger household.

The considerate guest will suss out the situation before-hand and arrive with sleeping bag, duvet, pillow or hot water bottle. But when, after the sixth brandy, you warmly press the couple on the sofa to stay the night, there arises the question of whether or not to offer them your bed. Some people have no objection at all to turfing out of their bed and camping down for the night in the cupboard under the stairs. Others (count me in) deeply resent being parted from their bed for a single night.

However tired and emotional you are the night before, it pays to fill your overnighters in on the morning routine of the house. If you share a bathroom, advise them when Grizelda will be hogging it. Above all, make sure they know

131

the exact location of the loo. Everyone has a horror story of waking up at 3 a.m. in a strange house with the urge to throw up and blundering around in a panic not able to find the bathroom. I heard of one man who, feeling something rectangular and cold, assumed it to be a handbasin and gratefully brought up half his host's wine cellar and duck a l'orange. Next morning, the host's bonhomie evaporated as he let it be known that it wasn't a handbasin, but his typewriter . . .

It helps, too, to make it quite clear what the breakfast situation is. Are you the type who will cheerfully rise with the sun and cook bacon and egg for eight? Or will you stay buried under the bedclothes, incapable of uttering a coherent word until midday?

With guests who are staying for a few days, it's a good idea to have an extra newspaper delivered, so they don't steal yours to read over breakfast. For some odd reason, when you're staying at someone else's pad, you tend to get hungrier than you do at home, so a considerate host will make it clear what the eating arrangements are. Some people feel a reluctance to 'invade' anyone else's kitchen, so it's up to you to encourage them to make themselves a snack whenever they feel like it. This is especially important if you're working, and have to leave them during the day. If you say something like, 'I'll leave you to have a lie in and get yourselves a late breakfast. For lunch there's some chicken in the fridge, or the pub down the road does a tasty ploughmans. Do help yourselves to tea, coffee, cake, whatever you like . . . I'll be back around six and then I thought I'd take you to my favourite Italian place round the corner,' your guests won't be left in a state of limbo, wondering if they can eat the chicken, or are you saving it for tomorrow? And should they be helpful and lay the table ready for when you get home from work?

If you are eating in, by all means encourage them to set the table and help wash up afterwards. Attempt to do everything yourself and you'll end up worn to a frazzle and resenting your guests. You might find that some guests need educating that a single person can't provide the range of facilities offered by a couple when they entertain. As one man put it after two of his married colleagues had been to stay for a stag weekend: 'They brought their own towels, because they thought being a single bloke I wouldn't have anything so civilised as spare linen. Then once they realised that I wasn't camping out on bare boards, but could provide most of the basic home comforts, they proceeded to sit around, expecting me to wait on them. Occasionally, they'd move a leg to allow me to get past to make up the fire. Breakfast times were the worst. I even had to pour the milk on their Weetabix.'

Living alone, you're more susceptible than is a couple to guests who decide it would be pleasant to make themselves literally at home in your pad. Naturally, you want to offer your guests a comfortable, restful environment, but not to such an extent that they won't go away. Check tactfully on their departure time, and if they show signs of digging in, tell them you have a man arriving within the hour for a lengthy job sorting out the sewage overflow. Or your cousin has just rung to say she's on her way, accompanied by her three children under five.

Whatever type of entertaining you're involved in, it's crucial never to apologise for the lack of space, facilities or the presence of a live-in partner. If you look happy and relaxed in your own surroundings, then you'll help your guests to feel equally at home with you.

Eating out

'One of the things I've given up since my divorce is inviting people round for meals,' a busy Fleet Street journalist told me. 'Working the erratic hours that I do, I simply don't have the time or energy to do the dinner party scene properly, so now when I want to entertain, I take my friends out to a restaurant. I enjoy my friends more that way, as I'm far livelier company than I'd be if I had to rush home from work and go through all the panic and hassle of laying on dinner for six singlehanded.'

Taking people out to eat needn't be prohibitively expensive, especially as an increasing number of pubs and country inns are now serving excellent food at competitive prices. There's no fuss or frills – just good simple fare served in congenial surroundings. If you don't happen to have a copy of one of the good food guides handy, a useful rule of thumb when looking for somewhere to eat is to choose a pub that sells real ale. A CAMRA recommendation· and good cooking usually seem to go together.

It helps if you have sufficient time to decide on the restaurant well ahead of the day itself, to enable you to check out the best tables and get to know the manager and waiters. It pays to call in personally to make your reservation as you can then discuss the matter of the table with the manager and make quite sure that your guests are not going to be placed next to the kitchen, the street door or en route to the Gents. Traditionally, men get a rough deal when it comes to seating, as it's customary to place them with their backs to the other diners. When a woman has invited a man to dinner, it's a considerate gesture for her to reverse this procedure, and give herself a view of the wall for a change.

Women often find restaurant entertaining particularly daunting, partly because they aren't accustomed to it and partly because the waiter will probably assume that the eldest male in the party is the host, and defer to him over all decisions on food and wine. When you're acting as hostess, you probably will find it helpful to ask someone else in the party, male or female, to choose the wine as this then leaves you free to ascertain what everyone else has chosen to eat. (Again, if you're a regular at the restaurant, you'll be in a position to make recommendations on the menu.) With the decision made, waiter Mario will snap to attention beside the aforementioned eldest male guest and await instructions.

This is where you, as a woman, should assert your authority by cutting swiftly in and giving the order. You will find that from then on Mario will ignore EMG and kowtow to you as the one who's obviously paying the bill and, hopefully, leaving the tip.

Men should not make the mistake of assuming that all their women guests are on diets and only want small portions. Some of the most fragile-looking women I know have enormous appetites and do not take kindly to their hosts waving away both Mario and the sauté potatoes on their behalf. Remember, too, that if you're drinking a fair amount, your guests will need to visit the john from time to time. The thoughtful host will ensure that his guests have the benefit of a clear way from the table, uncluttered by sweet trolleys and wine coolers. It also helps if, as your women guests are being seated with their backs to the wall, you discourage Mario from imprisoning them by pushing the table in to a point one inch from their sucked-in waists.

Regardless of the amount of heel clicking you receive from Mario in recognition of yourself as an old and valued customer, it is not considered good form for you to enthuse at length to your companions about the legion of scintillating evenings you have enjoyed at the restaurant. Your guests want to feel special, not that they're in competition with the brilliant crowd you were entertaining here last week.

When the bill arrives, always take the trouble to check it. It is not unknown, even in the classiest of establishments, for managers to gauge how much wine you've consumed and load the bill accordingly, assuming that you'll be too merrily muddle-headed to notice. Don't be fooled if the total is crossed out and a lower sum written in. This is a common restaurant ploy to fog the fact that the second, lower total has still been topped up and you're paying over the odds. Most restaurants now have VAT-inclusive menus. If so, check that the waiter hasn't tried to make you pay twice by sticking in a VAT charge at the end of the bill. If you're suspicious about what those mysterious 'sundries' are – ask. Look to see if there is a service charge. If there is, don't leave a tip unless the service has been spectacular. If service isn't included, leave 15% of the bill if you want to use the restaurant again, otherwise 10% will do. If the service was lousy, try not to leave anything. (Not easy. More than once I've been stopped at a restaurant door by a belligerent manager demanding to know if I realised that service was not included.) By far the simplest way to pay is by credit card, if the restaurant accepts your particular brand.

Before you leave the restaurant, it's considerate to think ahead about transport home for your guests. Make a diary note of local mini cab services, last train and bus times, and where the nearest all-night petrol station is situated.

Who to Take Where

Ex-spouses Should be lunched somewhere a) not extravagantly priced, in case the ex suspects you of squandering the alimony or is resentful they didn't milk you for more b) with a tranquil establishment atmosphere, to help defuse the situation if the conversation becomes acrimonious c) fairly busy, but with no secluded alcove tables, so if you do get soup thrown over you, there will be other diners nearby to help mop you up.

Avoid a) all your old haunts b) those areas where you're likely to run into your current lover c) any place teeming with excitable Italian waiters, who love nothing more than fuelling the flames of a domestic drama.

Parents Take them to a venue that sounds glamorous or cosmopolitan, so they can impress the neighbours, but which has an all-in price that will reassure them of your eye for the value of money.

Teenagers Hard up and fed up after an unremitting diet of fast food, they'll appreciate a stylish whirl round some American style cocktail bars, followed by a blow out at the current *in* place.

Uncle Fred Since you know after two sips of wine he's

136

going to insist on performing his vulgar party trick with the pickled walnuts, give in gracefully and take him somewhere with sawdust on the floor and rude waiters, where eccentricity is the norm.

Aunt Maud The last thing you want, of course, is actually to be obliged to converse with Aunt Maud, or have her talk to you, so invite her to tea at a rooftop restaurant in the hope of rendering her speechless with the transfixing view.

Potential Lovers Potential because when you're actually in the throes of a steamy love affair you either don't go out at all or regard a cheese sandwich in the back of a parked van as an orgiastic feast. Potential lovers, however, require either a dreamy, romantic setting or a zany one to draw them together in shared laughter.

Further Reading

Cooking in a Bedsitter – Katharine Whitehorn (Penguin)
How to Cheat at Cooking – Delia Smith (Coronet)
Food for One – Deanna Brostoff (Sainsburys)
Quick Cook – Beryl Downing (Penguin)
Mrs Beeton's Cookery and Household Management (Ward Lock)
Hamlyn All Colour Cook-Book (Hamlyn)
Just a Bite – Egon Ronay (Penguin)
Stop for Tea – (English Tourist Board)

CHAPTER 6

FESTIVE OCCASIONS

The animals went in two by two . . . .

Christmas

Most single people admit that Christmas is the worst day of
the year for them. A day to be endured rather than enjoyed,
a time when everyone, but everyone, seems to have someone to go to.

'What are you doing for Christmas?' they all ask one
another.

'Oh, I shall be spending it with my family of course,' is not
just the stock reply, but the only acceptable response.
Actresses who devote the rest of the year to jetting between
raunchy lovers in L.A and New York are pictured on Christmas Eve swanning through Heathrow, looking fragile in
furs and murmuring demurely that of course they will be
spending Christmas with mummy and daddy in Croydon.
Friends who regularly ring you up at 2 a.m. to recount the
latest slanging match with their parents, magically make it
up on December 24 and disappear into holes labelled family,
leaving you high and dry. Even those friends on whom you
were sure you could rely, having no family and not appear-
ing to care a hoot about it, even they in Christmas week
invariably seem to receive a letter from a long-lost cousin,
urging them to join the family hearth for the festive
season.

It has to be admitted that however successful you are at
living alone for the rest of the year, and however much you
enjoy your own company, Christmas Day is one time when
you need to be with other people. It's all very well asserting
staunchly that you intend to ignore the whole thing and

treat Christmas as just a day like any other. You probably won't succeed, because in the end, something will get to you. It might be the sound of jollity next door . . . people rushing past with their arms piled high with gift-wrapped packages . . . carol singers . . . Christmas trees glimmering with lights. All conspire to make you feel Left Out.

When I spent Christmas on my own, everything went fine until I sat down in the evening to eat my shepherds pie. I like shepherds pie, and had chosen it in a spirit of revolt against the traditional Christmas fare, which in previous years I'd always found too rich for my palate. After a day at my typewriter, I was hungry and looking forward to relaxing over my supper. I turned on the television. Inevitably, I found myself gazing at the happy family scene – beaming faces over succulent turkey, cranberry sauce, crackers . . . It mattered not a jot that I dislike turkey, find cranberry sauce too sweet and crackers childish. I sat and sobbed into my shepherds pie, consumed with self-pity because I wasn't with my family, being my usual wet blanket self and refusing to wear a paper hat.

I wish I'd had the foresight to plan ahead more sensibly for that Christmas. Unfortunately, too many of us regard Christmas in much the same way that British Rail react to two inches of snow. Suddenly it's upon us. We've made no plans. And the system is thrown into complete disarray.

The first essential, then, is to plan well ahead. If you're one of the growing number of people choosing to celebrate Christmas at a hotel, you must be prepared to think up to six months in advance as the best hotels get very booked up and, as always, single rooms are at a premium. The English, Welsh and Scottish tourist boards all have excellent free brochures detailing hotels, guest houses and farms which extend a traditional Christmas welcome. Another useful brochure is that issued by the Heart of England Tourist Board, which covers the counties of Gloucester, Hereford, Worcester, Shropshire, Staffordshire, Warwickshire and the West Midlands.

Or why not extend your horizons and persuade your

friends to sample a European Christmas with you? Lucerne and Vienna have a fairytale magic about them in December and it's a refreshing experience comparing continental festive customs with our own.

If you're stuck for company, don't hesitate to contact one of the singles clubs like Group 25 or City Circle, who organise houseparties and outings to cover every day of the festive season. Senior citizens looking for a comfortable, houseparty atmosphere at a private hotel or guest house should take a look at the Saga Holidays brochure. All age groups are welcome on Club One holidays. They specialise in breaks for single people and provide an action-packed programme over Christmas.

Alternatively, you could offer your services to the local hospital, or one of the voluntary organisations, for the day. Or you might decide to throw open your home to someone who's in the same position as yourself. Your local students' hostel, voluntary services or DHSS will be pleased to put you in touch with people who would be glad to accept your hospitality.

Above all, don't be too proud to tell people you are going to be on your own. It's a busy time of year, and people will probably just have assumed that you were fixed up with family or friends for the holiday. Don't be deterred by the belief that they will only be asking you round out of pity. You'd be surprised the number of people who spend Christmas very quietly and would welcome your company.

Not everyone, however, is enamoured with the idea of the time-honoured Christmas. But it's a festival so steeped in tradition that people tend to be shocked if you suggest you want to do something a bit different this year. It's like proposing that instead of Christmas pud you serve up a refreshing lemon sorbet. There's nothing wrong with lemon sorbet. Most people find it delicious. But at Christmas? Not quite right, somehow, is it? The stranglehold of the 'right' way to spend Christmas seems to evolve first from the need of children aged from two to one-hundred-and-two to indulge themselves with presents from the tree and discovering silver coins in the pudding. And second from the days when most of the population didn't get enough to eat during the year and Christmas was the one time they could rely on to have a satisfying blow out.

But what about those of us who have chosen to leave childish things behind – who relish being adults? Those of us who don't want to spend two days eating ourselves into a stupor on food we don't particularly like. Why is there no acceptable alternative way for us to enjoy a brief December holiday? One of the best Christmases I ever had was when four of us rented a cottage on the Suffolk coast. There was no television, no tinsel, no bowls of dates stickily gathering dust, no Christmas cake that everyone is usually too full of turkey to eat. We decorated the house with daffodils, and gorged on smoked salmon, caviare and a crate of champagne. We played golf, walked by the sea and sat by roaring fires dreaming, reading, talking, laughing. It worked because we had the courage to jettison those aspects of Christmas with which we felt jaded, and created instead a mood, an atmosphere, a style which suited our needs and personalities at the time.

Many people who hanker after an alternative Christmas plan a trip abroad for the duration of the holiday. At first sight this seems an excellent idea if you can afford it, but you need to think carefully about not just your destination but also your choice of hotel. Wherever it's situated in the world, if the hotel has a large and valued European clientele, then it will probably lay on a traditional Christmas celebration. I heard of one man who attempted to get away from it all in a hotel stuck right at the edge of a desert, and on Christmas morn was appalled to witness Santa Claus wading towards him across the sand, beaming grittily through 100 degree heat. (There's no escape at Easter, either. On Easter Monday, this same hotel imports live bunnies to hop between the palms in the foyer.) In theory, a Communist country should be a safe bet, but you'd still be advised before you book to check with the hotel management for advance warning of any likely festive surprises.

Back in Britain, outdoor types might be attracted by the working holiday offered by the National Conservation Corps. You'd be involved in interesting and valuable conservation tasks – but it's not all hard graft, as at the end of the working day the festive spirit is well in evidence. The Youth Hostels Association, too, has a full and varied diary of events over Christmas. For a houseparty holiday, with the emphasis on walking, rambling and simple wholesome food, contact the Holiday Fellowship, who extend a warm welcome to single people. Or why not book into a health farm for a few days? Think how smug you'll feel after Christmas, patting your trim waistline while the rest of us are doomed to diet.

Another alternative is to throw a Boxing Day party, and occupy yourself on December 25 getting everything ready. People are often so disenchanted with their families by the evening of Boxing Day that they'll rush round to your place with cries of relief. Many of your married friends, in particular, will welcome the opportunity of a change of environment, as along with the tinsel and mistletoe, another traditional feature of the festive season is the marital slanging match – as the police know only too well. They are called out to more domestic disputes over Christmas than at any other time of year.

For those who are absolutely stuck with their own company over Christmas, planning is even more vital. The first essential is to stock up well in advance with all your favourite treats in food and drink. Don't leave this to the last minute or you'll collide with the rest of the world merrily heaping trolleys full of festive fare and tying Christmas trees to mistletoed roof racks. (Actually, they won't be merry at all, they'll be snarling and ready to strangle one another with the fairy lights, but you'll be in no mood to appreciate that.) On the day, get up as late as possible so you don't have to watch everyone else setting off to relatives for their Christmas lunch. Spend the day doing something you enjoy, and which absorbs you. On no account should you turn on the television, and if you can, tune in the radio to Russia. Any continental radio station will be into the jingle bells scene which will only conspire to make you feel suicidal. And if you do sink into the pits, remind yourself that Christmas Day is only one day out of 365. It will pass.

New Year

In many respects, New Year doesn't present so many social pressures as Christmas, as it is considered more a time you spend with friends than exclusively with family. Even so, it can be galling when married colleagues at work loudly assume that your mantelpiece is groaning with invitations to New Year parties when in reality all it's heavy with is dust. If you haven't been invited to a New Year bash, remember that, unlike Christmas, pubs, restaurants and many public places are open. A place to avoid, however, is Trafalgar Square. People tend to throng there in groups and if you're on your own you'll only feel crushed, in more ways than one. Best bet is probably your local as it's bound to have a New Year's Eve extension, which in Britain is enough in itself to promote a welcoming atmosphere of warmth and bonhomie.

Happy Birthday to Me

I'm a great believer in celebrating birthdays, as I think everyone should have one day in the year which is special to them and on which they unashamedly indulge themselves. It's the ideal time to invite all your friends round, as there's no better excuse than a birthday for a party.

But it may happen that your friends are unavailable, or you find yourself cut off from everyone – because you've moved to a new area, perhaps, or you're working in a distant part of the country on that day. If you live on your own, it can at first sight be something of a facer, the prospect of celebrating a birthday alone. You may think there's no point and decide to regard it as just an ordinary day.

But there is a point. It is that you aren't ordinary. You're you. You're special. And you merit some special attention. If there doesn't happen to be anyone around to share your birthday with, then you owe it to yourself to give yourself a splendid day. It may sound crassly obvious, but whatever age you are, you're never going to have the opportunity of celebrating that age again. If you're 25 now, think how deadly it would be to look back in five years' time and remember how you spent your 25th birthday huddled miserably under the duvet, eating cornflakes. How much more inspiring to recall that you treated yourself to a gift of a day.

Buy yourself an extravagant present. Go to the races. Invest in a top to toe massage or beauty treatment. Hop on the hovercraft to France. Splurge on a ringside seat at a big fight or a Stones concert. Or why not make it a day of rebirth, when you start something new – write off for that coveted job, take up hang gliding, fix up those driving lessons. It's important, surely, to create memorable landmarks in our lives – and if a birthday isn't a landmark I don't know what is.

If you're eating – no, dining – at home, indulge in your favourite gourmet foods, eased down with a glass or two of Buck's Fizz. Never lose sight of the fact that you're celebrating your arrival in the world x years ago, and you've survived. There's only one you. You're utterly unique. After the third glass of Buck's Fizz you'll probably come to the conclusion you're damned well fantastic. Cheers! Happy birthday. Have a wonderful day. You deserve it.

The Family Way

Talking about birthdays, I mentioned to student teacher Julia that instead of expecting presents on their birthdays, some people prefer to give their mothers a gift, on the basis that they did all the hard work on that day, all those years ago.

'Oh I wouldn't do that,' replied Julia firmly. 'Since I moved into my own flat I hardly see my family at all. I've tried it, but it just doesn't work. I never invite them here, because they won't make the effort to understand the way I like to live. That I don't need a washing machine, for instance, because the launderette is just round the corner. And if I go home for a birthday party or family tea, they're all bonded together in pairs, taking it in turns to ask me when I'm going to get married. Never if. Always when.'

I know many people who'd agree with Julia. What's the point, they argue, of continuing to pitch up at family functions, when the whole affair is geared as a celebration of the married state and everyone is going to make it obvious they think you're a freak because you're single?

And yet, like it or not, you do have a great deal in common with the members of your family. You may look at the assembled tribe and balk at the notion that you're related to any of them but of course you are, through a brilliant mishmash of genes and chromosomes. It's a fact that most people who cut themselves off completely from their families come to regret it in the end. However bizarre, or dull, they may seem to you now, your family is the only one you've got and it seems foolish not to make the most of the benefits of belonging to a family, just because of some misunderstandings about your life style.

People who are glued together in twos are bound to find your singular way of life somewhat odd and, to their eyes, unnatural. The worst thing you can do is aggressively argue the toss about it. If you shout, 'No, Aunt Maud, I am not on the constant look out for Miss Right, I can manage perfectly well without her, thanks very much!' Aunt Maud will look pointedly at the purple vein throbbing on your forehead and tell your mother if you don't find the right woman to marry soon you'll be heading for an early grave. More effective than all the well reasoned arguments in the world is a demonstration from you – in your appearance, your style, your behaviour – that living alone suits you and is something you positively enjoy. You can always tell people who are well adjusted to solo living, because the phrase 'when you're on your own' rarely drops from their lips. It never occurs to them to say it, because they lead such full lives, enjoying being with other people but appreciating their own company also.

Your family will take as it finds. If you turn up for Sunday tea looking and sounding pathetic, you're asking to be treated as the socially poor relation. You'll speedily be tagged 'poor Annie' or 'poor Bill' and once stuck with that label it's a stubborn one to prise off.

Make a point, first of all, of looking good. Families do tend to judge your state of mind by the state of your fingernails. Frayed collars may signify to you that you've been leading such a marvellously hectic life that you haven't had a minute to spare to buy a few new shirts, but to your mother, they will indicate that your life is coming apart at the seams. She will worry. And because she is worried she will nag, or hassle you. For relatively little effort – clean, well-pressed clothes, freshly washed hair and polished shoes – you'll help yourself to create a harmonious atmosphere.

Parents, remember, don't have the same values as their children. They worry about different things. Mothers tend to be concerned about their son's supply of hot dinners, whilst fathers fret about their daughter's morals. Make the effort to reassure them on these points, and it will ease friction at home.

In conversation, make it plain that you enjoy an active social life. You go out frequently, you have lots of friends, you entertain, you have a marvellous time. Be careful not to overdo this, to the point where you sound frenzied and your father starts muttering about all those late nights. And if you are a woman, emphasise that you are meticulous about not being out alone after dark. You have an unrivalled opportunity here to make all those smug married couples

146

turn the same colour as the lettuce adorning their family ham salad tea. The restaurants you've been to . . . the shows . . . the parties . . . the outings . . . the concerts . . . Naturally, if you overplay this you must be prepared for a bit of needle from your discontented married relatives who, secretly jealous of your freedom, can only retaliate by trying to make you feel inferior because you're single. We're going through a bad patch, is their attitude, so why don't you hurry up and get married and have a bad patch too?

It's vital to retain your sense of humour at these times, and parry their jibes with a lighthearted, 'Oh, I'm waiting for Prince William to grow up', or 'I'm still looking for a girl with eyes as lovely as yours, Aunt Maud'. Sometimes, admittedly, it can be hard hanging on to that sense of humour. I greatly admired the restraint of the single girl who came home to find her mother laying out a wedding dress on her bed, 'in case you ever need it, dear'. Instead of setting light to the dress, and her mother, the girl merely put it back in the box, commenting mildly that it wasn't quite her style.

Most single people are intensely irritated at the way families assume that being solo is no more than a temporary phase. Conversations are littered with '*when* you get married'. . . . '*when* you have a wife and children of your own'. An extension of this is the manner in which many mothers insist on regarding single sons and daughters as mere children, giving gratuitous advice and even buying items for their homes, in a manner that would be regarded by all as grossly intrusive if the same sons and daughters happened to be married.

This is a tricky one to deal with, as mothers do like to feel needed. It probably gave her immense pleasure to hunt round the shops and find an ali baba linen basket that would just fit that corner in your bathroom. You, meanwhile, are speechless with rage because you have said a million times you don't need a linen basket cluttering up the bathroom as you stuff your soiled clothes straight into the blue bag you take to the launderette every week. The only answer seems to be to accept with gratitude the small gifts, acknowledging that they were kindly meant and will help your mother to feel needed. But if it gets to the point when your mother begins to feel it's her right to choose everything for you, firmly draw the line. Women might take this opportunity to point out that the winner of a recent Homemaker of the Year competition was a single woman. In the finals she breezed through all the practical tests, eclipsing the efforts of what the *Daily Mail* described as 'five experienced housewives who have been looking after their families for years'.

One of the advantages of being a single person at family gatherings is that when the flak starts to fly between couples, you know you can escape to the peace of your own four walls. They, however, are stuck with one another. It helps if you make a point of not taking sides in domestic disputes, however much the protagonists may try and drag you in to add weight to their individual points of view.

It may be that the row concerns you. One of the most common causes of family feuds is the question of who is going to be responsible for mum or dad if they become infirm. If you are a single woman, you'll almost certainly find the eyes of all the family turning to you. You will be expected to give up your career to look after an ailing parent. And should you think of moving home to a more distant part of the country, you will be made to feel like an arch traitor. But if your married sister has to move because of her husband's work then that, of course, is perfectly acceptable.

Here again, you have to be firm, which isn't always easy in the face of all the emotional blackmail. But you must make it clear that you value yourself, your job, your home and the life you have made for yourself.

'You have no family of your own, no responsibilities, no ties', they will cry. Tell them that this makes it all the more difficult for you, as you have no one to support you. There are two (or more) of them, so with the load spread, surely one of them could spare the time to take a share of caring for an ailing parent.

It's a fraught situation, as obviously you don't want to appear callous or hardhearted, and naturally you don't want your parent to suffer through lack of care. It helps a great deal if you establish your attitude very early on, before the crisis occurs, so that if and when it does your relatives will know the score and won't automatically expect you to throw up everything to act as unpaid nurse.

For men and women it's an aid to better understanding if you invite your relations to your home, so they can see you against your background and understand that you do have a life, demands and pressures of your own. Otherwise relatives are apt to regard you as something which drops from the sky for the occasional family Sunday lunch. What you have to beware of is your married relatives finding your pad so attractive that they start using it as a bolt hole after rows, or as an afternoon love nest. Watch out, too, for frisky aunts and lecherous uncles who take to popping in, always while they happen to be on their way somewhere else. You'll effectively douche their ardour if you make it plain in the course of your lighthearted conversation that you place them in the same age group as your parents.

Don't neglect the children in your family. Even if you don't want children yourself, it's worth making friends with family youngsters, for as they grow up you'll probably come to value their company. Your single status gives you a unique advantage: often you can establish a special relationship with children, giving them the attention and interest which their parents may be too busy or too tired to bestow. You also bring a new perspective into their world, providing them with vital proof that you don't have to be married to lead a fulfilling life. So many children grow up believing that marriage is not just inevitable, but the only *normal* way to live. It's good for them to be able to look at you and realise that there is an acceptable and desirable alternative.

If you do want children, but can't or have no inclination to bear them yourself, there is no discrimination against single people adopting. Each case is considered on its own merits and you would be subject to the same enquiries as would a married couple. For further information on adoption, write to the Association of British Adoption and Fostering Agencies.

For anyone who has lost contact with their family and wants to keep it that way, there is a service called Message Home which you can use if you just want to let your parents know you are all right. You don't have to speak to them direct, or give them an address or phone number. All it does is reassure them that you're not dead or in the hands of a white slave trader. What you do is ring one of the numbers listed below and your message will be recorded on an answering machine. A representative of the Mothers' Union, who run the service, will then ensure that your message is relayed to your home. The Mothers' Union stress that the service is totally confidential.

The numbers are: London – 799 7662
                             Birmingham – 426 3396
                             Liverpool – 709 7598
                             Bristol – 504 717
                             Portsmouth – 691 964
                             Scotland – 0968 76161

Some Useful Addresses

Association of British Adoption and Fostering Agencies 11 Southwark St, London SE1.
City Circle 43 Vicarage Lane, London E15. (01–555 1279)
Club One Holidays 23 Abingdon Road, London W8. (01–938 1011)
English Tourist Board 4 Grosvenor Gardens, London SW1. (01–730 3400)
Group 25 P.O. Box 15, 232 Gershwin Road, Basingstoke, Hants. RG22 4LP. (0256 23636)
Heart of England Tourist Board P.O. Box 15, Worcester, WE1 2JT.

Holiday Fellowship 142–144 Great North Way, Hendon, London NW4 1EG.

National Conservation Corps 10–14 Duke St. Reading, Berks. (0734 596171)

Saga Holidays P.O. Box 6, Folkestone, Kent.

Scottish Tourist Board Caravan Abbey Place, Murray Green, Jedburgh, Scotland.

Wales Tourist Board Brunel House, 2 Fitzalan Road, Cardiff CF2 1UY.

Youth Hostelling Association Trevelyan House, 8 St. Stephens Hill, St. Albans, Herts. (St. Albans 55215)

CHAPTER 7

PART-TIME SINGLES

Making the most of the meantime

Single people aren't the only ones who live alone. Lots of married people do too for much of the time – those whose partners' jobs or studies take them away, or who are temporarily separated because of housing problems or family commitments.

Anyone who has never experienced such a relationship tends to imagine that it must be one long honeymoon, with the agony of parting being richly compensated for by the heady delights of each reunion. But as those living in this situation are only too well aware, being a part-time single presents its own special problems.

While your partner is away, you become accustomed to running your own household and making all the decisions. It often comes hard, when she or he returns, not only to relinquish some of the control, but also to ride the carping from a partner who has been put on the aggressive defensive as he or she struggles to redefine his or her role in the household. It's not all roses sexually, either. After a time apart, many couples feel uneasy with one another, needing time to talk, to touch and adjust to one another's presence again.

Vicky is married to a businessman who divides his time between offices in London and Bonn. 'When we were first married, we always had a blazing row every time he returned from a trip to Europe,' she told me. 'Then I realised that the root of the trouble lay in my own resentment about the way we were living. When Ken went away I'd sit around moping, feeling only half a person, waiting for him to come home and make me feel real again. Then when he did walk through the door he could never live up to all my hopes and expectations, and I'd feel so let down I'd start picking on him over all sorts of stupid little things.'

The way out for Vicky was first through a part-time job which made her feel valued for herself and, as she says, 'made me take an interest in the world around me, and stopped me thinking obsessionally about Ken all the time.' The second step was for Vicky to accept that as Ken's job dictated her lifestyle, she may as well take advantage of it, rather than feeling lost and only half alive whilst her husband was away. 'When Ken goes off on a long trip, I rearrange the house to suit myself. I make the place mine. Ken is a light sleeper, so our bedroom is at the back of the house, away from the traffic. But I like waking up with the sun on my face, so when he's away I take over the spare room which faces east. When Ken's at home, one corner of the sitting room is usually cluttered up with all his marquetry gear. After he leaves, I put all his stuff in a box and take over the area for my sewing. With no one else tramping through the room, I can cut out material on the floor and leave my sewing machine threaded up and ready for action whenever I feel like it – day or night. Then the morning he's due home, I put everything back again and switch to my role as half of a pair.'

Vicky admits that this dual life took some getting used to initially, but her approach has a lot going for it. If you hate that vase his mother gave you, or if you always quarrel over whether the dining table should be near the window for the view, or in the alcove out of the draught, this is your chance to have things the way you want them for a time.

That's Entertainment?

When your partner is away, it's infuriating to have someone ring up and declare, 'Oh, it would be lovely to see you – when Chris comes back you must both come round to dinner.'

153

Similarly, it's absurd for you to stop entertaining just because your other half isn't there. You don't stop eating or drinking in the absence of him or her, so why blow the whistle on inviting friends to share a meal and a jug of wine with you? The bonus is that during your partner's absence you're free to have round all the people he or she can't stand. The point to watch here, so I'm informed by an experienced hand, is to work out in some detail just how much you're going to tell your partner later. You may swear, with a perfectly clear conscience, that you and Grizelda sat ten feet apart on hard-backed chairs drinking lemonade and discussing Proust. But will your partner believe you? `

The same experienced hand advises me that it's vital for you to know where everything is located in the house. If your partner usually takes responsibility for the booze, it's maddening to find you have a roomful of thirsty guests and no idea where the corkscrew is hidden. It's also helpful if you can encourage your other half to make calls home at a regular time and not out of the blue. From the point of view of the absent partner, it puts a strain on the best of domestic relationships if at the end of a gruelling day in Dusseldorf you fall into your lonely bed, dispirited because you didn't win that valuable contract and your job will now be on the line, and phone home to hear what sounds like all of Northern England merrily pouring your waning bank balance down their throats.

Money

Anyone left keeping the ranch running during their partner's absence should ensure right from the start of the relationship that they are the one with their finger poised on all the financial buttons. Don't leave it to your partner to sort out and pay all the bills on his or her return. If he or she is delayed on a return flight, or gets slung into a foreign jail for nude sunbathing, it's infuriating for the one at home to have the phone cut off because you can't locate the building society pass book to draw funds for the bill.

In a relationship where your partner is the breadwinner it's essential to ensure that:

* You know the name and address of the company he/she works for.

* His/her salary is paid through the bank into a joint account that doesn't need both signatures for either of you to draw money.

* Filed away is one of his/her pay slips giving social security number and tax details in case of emergency.

* You know where he/she is in the world at any given time.

All this may sound alarmist. But a friend of mine who was living with an oil man was left destitute when he disappeared into some foreign blue leaving no address, no clue to the name of his employers and no money for her to pay the rent.

The Part-Time Affair

It is not the purpose of this book to expound on the morality of having an affair whilst your partner is away. Obviously, it's something only you can decide – and much depends on your individual guilt threshold. If you're like divorced actress Felicity Kendal, who says she's faithful to one man 'not because I'm good, but because I blush easily', then clearly, the straight and narrow is the path for you. But many people I spoke to with live-in partners came up with an interesting variety of reasons for opting for part-time affairs:

'We've talked about it and agreed on complete freedom for both of us while Mary's away on one of her business trips.'

'We haven't talked about it but I know perfectly well he's going to be screwing himself silly in New York so I thought what the hell, why shouldn't I enjoy myself too?'

'It's for the good of my health. If I don't have regular sex I suffer from agonising stomach cramps.'

Everyone agreed that the ideal solution was to have a regular lover who understands your domestic situation.

'Richard is marvellous,' the wife of an airline pilot told me. 'He's always very understanding when I ring up and explain that my husband's outgoing flight has been delayed 24 hours so we won't be able to meet that day. He knows it cuts both ways, and he's just as likely to get a call saying my husband's been unexpectedly held up in Los Angeles so Richard and I can treat ourselves to an unscheduled dinner together. Having Richard around on what you might call a semi-permanent basis is perfect, because if you're in my position and you go in for casual affairs, your lovers only get frustrated, resentful and sometimes jealous. That's fatal, as of course the last thing you want is your lover making a scene on your doorstep.'

Russell lives with an actress. He does not have a regular mistress, but says that when he occasionally does have a fling whilst his partner is away on tour, he follows these guidelines:

* Never give your lover your home phone number or address. Try and meet at their place.

(Sound advice, this. Many women have mentioned that it's not so much that they object to their partner having an affair, but they do mind if the action takes place in their own bed, mucking up their favourite sheets. If you do take your lover home, use the spare room, the fireside rug, the sofa. If you must use the bed, don't rip the sheets off five minutes before your partner is due home and stick them in the linen basket. Wash them and *put them back*.)

* Don't be tempted to instal your lover at your home while your partner is absent. Apart from the obvious danger of the lover leaving rings or cufflinks on the bathroom shelf, there are scores of other ways you'll get caught out. Neighbours, for instance, are notorious tittle-tattlers. And one woman homed in on her partner's infidelity by checking on

the amount of toilet paper he'd got through in a week when he was allegedly on his own.

* Try not to rush straight from your lover's bed to pick up your partner at the airport. You may think you look the picture of innocence but to your partner you'll reek of deceit. 'Try to put 24 hours between your lover and your partner,' advises Russell. 'It sounds so much more genuine if you can say you spent last evening watching some dreary programme on TV.'

* The most effective way to keep an affair secret is simply to tell no one at all. If you have to take a trusted friend into your confidence – as an alibi perhaps – try to choose someone outside your normal domestic and work circle.

CHAPTER 8

FACING UP TO FEARS AND PHOBIAS

*The gloom and doom aspects of living alone –
and how to handle them*

Every situation in life, whether we're single, married, divorced or widowed, has its positive and its negative side. So far in this book, we've concentrated on the upbeat aspects of living alone. But it's pointless to run away from the fact that the single state does present its own special problems, both emotional and practical. The purpose of this chapter is to drag all our fears and phobias out of the closet and shine a spotlight on them. I'm not promising that by the end of the chapter you'll never again feel lonely, depressed, frightened of falling ill or terrified of being raped. But by acknowledging and sharing our fears and exploring ways of dealing with them, we can lessen their impact while at the same time lending one another the courage to be more self-reliant.

Loneliness, Depression and Solitude

'But don't you get lonely living on your own?' is the question most asked of single people. Usually by a married couple sitting snugly by the fire, domestic hatchets conveniently buried for the moment as they contemplate cuddling up in bed together while you go home to an empty flat, and silence.

The straight answer is yes, of course you get lonely. There are bound to be things you miss from the family or relationship you were part of before. Someone to greet you when you come home tired from work ... to giggle with over a favourite comedy programme ... to share your joys and fears ... someone, above all, to talk to, especially when life starts rearing up and kicking you in the face. Whether it's something small but irritating like the car playing up, or a larger issue such as the threat of redundancy, having someone loyal there to listen can make all the difference between a temporary black mood and a full-scale depression. It's not so difficult dealing with problems alone when they come separately. But when you wake up shivering with the start of flu, the pipes are frozen, you miss the train, have a row with your boss, get soaking wet and return home to a cold empty flat with a companionless evening stretching ahead, that's when you're likely to give in to misery.

At the most desperate extreme, some find loneliness so unbearable they opt for suicide. A girl who has fought for the independence of her own bedsit might now run back to the home comforts provided by mum. Divorcees often fling themselves back into marriage with the first person who puts a pair of reassuring arms round them.

Even the most successful and celebrated people are prey to such agonies of self-doubt. 'I don't feel the need for marriage,' proudly independent superstar Jackie Bisset has said, 'although it has gone through my mind – usually when I've been depressed.'

When in her mid fifties, novelist Elizabeth Jane Howard left her author husband Kingsley Amis, she admitted, 'I was really frightened that I could not earn a living. But even worse was the terrible fear of loneliness and the knowledge that at my age it is quite likely that there will never be anybody else for me again.'

Eventually, Elizabeth Jane Howard found a new lease of life in living alone, discovering that her own company was far preferable to being with someone who 'didn't even like me very much. He only seemed to want me there for security.'

Kingsley Amis, meanwhile, has moved back in with his first wife. 'What he hates,' commented Elizabeth Jane Howard, 'is to be alone.'

But grabbing the first person who comes along to 'take you away from all this' is hardly the basis for a sound relationship. All you're doing is running away from yourself. It's an escalation of going out all the time because you can't stand the place in which you live. It's a cliché, but a true one, that until you've learned to live with yourself – and that includes feeling lonely – you're not fit to live with anyone else. For marriage is certainly no cure for loneliness. If they're honest, most people in a permanent relationship will confess to the hell of lying wrapped in a partner's arms, and still feeling utterly, desolately lonely.

The plain fact is that *everyone* feels lonely at times. Whether we're single, married, divorced or widowed, we all know loneliness, just as we all know fatigue, hunger, cold. They are all occupational hazards of life on earth. But when it hits you, it helps to remember that loneliness, just like fatigue, hunger and all the rest, is not permanent. *It will not last for ever. It will pass.*

What can you do to make it pass? When you're hungry you eat, and if you're tired you try and get some sleep. What's the remedy when you feel numb with loneliness?

The obvious answer is to defy your languour of despair and get up and do something. If you long for company, refer back to the chapter on socialising, and start to get yourself back into circulation. Alternatively, tackle something that's going to make you feel virtuous, like clearing out the spare room, mowing the lawn, enrolling on a course or mugging up some phrases for your Greek holiday. Anything you have to throw yourself into wholeheartedly either physically or mentally is excellent therapy, as at the end of it you'll feel you've achieved something instead of wasting time feeling sorry for yourself. Another bonus is that the sense of triumph you'll feel at having beaten the blues will give you the strength to face another attack head on next time.

Another solution is to think positive. Revel in your solitary state, and indulge yourself. Splurge on a pile of magazines, an LP, some pretty plants or new denims. Relish the thought that there is no one to tell you the magazines are a waste of money, the record is junk and just shows what poor taste you have, the plants will die under your blackfingered neglect, and in order to get those denims to fit you'll need to lose half a stone.

What you should avoid when the pall of loneliness falls on you is going to places where you're likely to be surrounded by apparently idyllically happy couples. (They're probably not idyllically happy at all, but in your present mood nothing will convince you otherwise.) Don't go for a walk in the park, or stroll by the Embankment. Instead, this is an ideal time to whizz round the supermarket and stock up on delicious treats for your weekend suppers. One look at those tense women pressured by fractious children and a husband who's either bossily organising or standing looking bored by the window watching her struggle to load the trolley should be enough to make you thankful you're married to your independence.

If it's still the lack of Someone Else causing you to feel lonely, try and analyse exactly what you'd want from the other person if he or she were there. It's tempting to imagine the perfect partner as responsive, attentive, totally tuned in to you and your needs. In reality, of course, they'd probably be in a black mood themselves, with their heads buried in a book, or absorbed in action replays on TV. Or wouldn't they be nagging you to cut the hedge and clear up that filthy mess in the bathroom?

Film star Burt Reynolds, dubbed Mr Macho and with an earning capacity of three million dollars a film, could be considered one of the world's most eligible men. But he chooses to remain unmarried. 'The life-mate I'm looking for is someone on a hill singing the Sound of Music. She doesn't exist,' he has said. 'I am also not easy to live with. I am selfish. I have formed habits which I cannot easily break, even if I wanted to. When I have been working all day, I want to have someone to come home to with whom I can be silent – and who will still love me.'

But getting up and doing something isn't the only remedy

if you're feeling lonely and/or depressed. One of the great advantages of living alone is that being free of domestic pressures and responsibilities, you have the time to monitor your own physical and mental rhythms – and how they inter-relate. If you think about it, you'll realise that on some days you feel bursting with physical energy and have no trouble at all running for the bus. On other mornings, just considering getting up makes you feel exhausted.

It may be, on those down days, that you'll be able to rationalise your condition once you accept that there does seem to be a pattern to your moods, emotional needs and responses. If you've woken up feeling low and lonely, you might recognise this as a period when you're feeling much more vulnerable than usual. Should someone accidentally slam a door in your face, you take it as a personal insult. If the train is full and you can't get a seat, you almost burst into tears. Knowing that it's just that time in your personal cycle, and you'd probably be feeling like that if you were in a permanent relationship, or back home with mum, can be a great help to a single person feeling all alone in the world.

Women, of course, are more accustomed than men to recognising the signals of their cycle. Most women accept that premenstrual tension will probably make them bitchy for a few days before their period. (PMT is, at last, a medically recognised condition. If you suffer severely from this, ask your GP to refer you to one of the countrywide PMT clinics, or to a PMT consultant at the Chelsea Hospital for Women; Royal Infirmary, Glasgow; Sinbec Centre, North Wales; Radcliffe, Oxford.) Quite often during menstruation women feel very emotional, cry easily and long to be mothered and smothered in protective warmth. If you know your depression is caused by PMT you may find that simply rolling with it and indulging in a good cry will make you feel heaps better. It's not unusual, also, for many women to feel very randy or broody in the middle of their cycle.

But women don't have the monopoly on cycles. Men experience them too. The men I know who've taken the trouble to chart their feelings and responses for six months or so have confessed themselves quite intrigued as a pattern gradually emerged. They say it's a great help in understanding why they feel emotionally raw occasionally. 'I try to avoid making any major decisions on those dog days,' one man told me, 'because I know from experience my judgment will be impaired. Whereas if I just hold off for a day or two, the phase will have passed and I'll view the world more objectively.'

A top Fleet Street journalist who admits to going through hell learning to live alone after she broke up with her husband, made the point that, 'Living by yourself and coping with loneliness requires a lot of courage. But courage needs to be nurtured with kindness. In order to get through those depression days, we make strenuous demands on ourselves, on our inner resources. So it's crucial, at such times, to make a conscious effort to be kind to yourself.'

Being kind to yourself could be to take a taxi home instead of waiting in the rain for the bus. Stop off for a top to toe massage. Instead of flogging round the supermarket for provisions for your dinner party, dump all the arrangements on a firm of caterers. How you choose to nurture yourself depends on your character and your lifestyle. The important thing, when you're feeling low, is to acknowledge that the effort of fighting it is draining, and you deserve a bit of pampering as a reward.

Novelist Penelope Mortimer, divorced for many years from playwright John Mortimer, carried the theme further in a perceptive piece for the *Sunday Times*:

'I have reached the rather obvious conclusion that loneliness equals missing mum; mum lost and mum longed for. Mum may be, or may have been, a monster. It's the fantasy of being part of someone else's body that's missed, and the fantasy of continual company that's missing ... I'd maintain that the only effective remedy is to be a better mother to yourself than your mother was ... The first step is to go back and start at the beginning, long before sex came on the scene. Indulge childishness. Comfort the deprived baby, feed it, talk to it, pet it; as it grows – which it will do remarkably quickly given the right attention – let it, as far as possible, do exactly what it wants. Listen to its opinions, respect its tastes – they may be different from yours, but they are more reliable. It may be bored by your oldest friends, and enjoy the company of people you've never noticed – because it has never been lonely and is relatively fearless, its motives are sounder than yours ever were. It may even have talents you never had, and thoroughly disapprove of the way you make your living. At first it sounds unpredictable, and there are times when you will automatically tell it to say it's sorry and mind its manners, remember "please" and "thank you".

' "Why?" this alter-ego child will ask. No good telling it that apology, pleading and gratitude are necessary for survival, they aren't. For the first time in your life, probably, you can tell yourself the truth and get away with it.'

If you can achieve it, this development of an alter ego, or inner life, call it what you will, helps you make the crucial transition between loneliness and solitude. The former, as all know who've suffered from it, is negative and debilitating. Solitude, however, is a positive and restorative state. It gives you space to reflect, to gather yourself together. Times of solitude are times to treasure, conscious that you are free to live in your own skin as you, instead of accommodating others and having others nag you because you're not responding to them or communicating with them as they want.

Quentin Crisp has said that he never feels lonely because 'once you've abandoned the idea that to be alone is to have failed, then you're in the clear. . . . I've learned how to live by myself. I *have* to be alone. To come home tired in the evening and find somebody sitting opposite you saying, "And what are you thinking now, beloved?" would drive me mad! The way things are, nobody can ever say to me, "You're not going to sit there all evening doing nothing, are you?" Because I am.'

Learning to turn negative loneliness into a positive state of being alone takes time and practice. As Quentin Crisp points out, the first step is to jettison the idea that to be alone is to have failed. Once you accept this, you'll never again be thrown by situations which previously left you feeling lonely and bereft. Public situations, such as no one talking to you for a while at a party. Or private times, like having nothing to do on a Saturday night.

Once you adopt a positive perspective on being alone, and come to view it as a pleasurable experience in its own right, you stop hankering after what isn't immediately available, and enjoy instead the advantages of being by yourself. We've discussed the value of indulging and cossetting yourself when you're alone. Don't be afraid of talking to yourself, too. You'll probably find you are fascinating company – and so what if people give you curious stares if you do as I do and have long chats to yourself in the car as you wait at the traffic lights. Talk out loud. Ask yourself how you're feeling, and why. Even better, write it down. A daily diary, even if it's only a few lines, can prove an enormous long term asset. Apart from making riveting reading in years to come (was it Mae West who remarked, 'Always keep a diary – and one day it will keep you'?) next time the being-alone-blues strikes you, you can flick back over the pages to compare how you felt last time with this, how long it lasted, and how you got yourself out of it.

Most people I know who've approached being alone in this way say they feel so much stronger, more secure in themselves as self-reliant single people, rather than half a couple or part of a crowd. Like anything else in life, the technique of achieving serenity through solitude is not going to happen overnight. At first, you may make absolutely no headway at all and end up hurling this book furiously across the room. (Try not to hit that lamp you treasure so much – it'll only make you even more depressed.) But it's worth persevering. It's worked for a lot of single people, so why not for you?

The Blues in the Night

However rationally we may approach problems during the day, it's at night that our fears take on a more alarming, often sinister perspective. You know the scene. You're tossing, panic stricken in the dark, convinced you're going to lose your job, your home, your family and your friends. You're going to end up unloved and unlovable, down and out and sleeping under hedges. You *know* the wart on your ankle is cancerous and the pain in your chest is heralding a heart attack and if you don't die of that you'll choke to death because your throat is all tight and you can't *breathe*. Your head is boiling, you ache all over and you'd sell your soul for a warm, comforting body in the bed beside you, someone to put their arms around you and make everything all right.

But there isn't anyone there. So you must comfort yourself. Here are some proven strategies culled from friends who confess to being all too familiar with the 3 a.m. blues.

* Learn to relax. Easier said than done, admittedly, when your body feels more tightly strung than Jimmy Connors' Wimbledon-winning raquet, but tell yourself that at least you'll give it a go. Lie on your back and, starting with either your head or your feet, concentrate on each part of your body in turn. Say to yourself, 'forehead relax ... eyes relax ... jaw relax ... neck relax' repeating it four times for each separate part of your body, and as you work down or up you'll experience the relief of gradually feeling yourself letting go. The importance of the repetition is that it helps to stop your mind wandering, while at the same time it induces a rhythm which lulls (some would say bores) you to sleep. It's a technique worth trying, because it really does work.

* Herb and hop pillows are soothing. Or there is a calming 'sleep cassette' called *Good Night Talk/Good Morning Talk* by Dr Claire Weekes, available by post from Mrs Skene-Keating, 16 Rivermead Court, Ranelagh Gardens, London SW6.

* Don't just lie there in a stew. Turn on the light, open the window, switch the radio on, fetch yourself a warm milky drink and a hot water bottle. Straighten the sheets, plump up the pillows and flick through a magazine. Have at your bedside an emergency cache of inspiring biographical reading about people who've survived apparently unsurmountable odds. Encourage yourself to develop a sense of proportion, by pinning up that glorious 'blue planet' picture of the earth taken by the first men to land on the moon. Ponder on the relevance of you and your problems, in relation to the rest of the universe. Think back five years, and remember all the things that worried you so desperately then. Most of them will seem laughable now. And you survived, didn't you? You may have swallowed a few mouthfuls of water on the way, but you didn't go under then and you won't sink now.

* When Judy Garland felt swamped by the 3 a.m. blues she used to ring Dirk Bogarde for solace and support. Personally, I think this is pushing the bounds of friendship too far – which just goes to show that Dirk Bogarde is a much nicer person than I am. Not everyone will agree, but I feel that if you get to the point where you must, absolutely must, talk to someone, then unless you have very understanding friends the best answer is to talk to a trained listener who isn't going to yawn down the phone and begrudge you their beauty sleep. The Samaritans are the first people who spring to mind here, and you'll find their number in your local phone book. If you live in London, City Circle, a leading singles club, has a section for members who don't work normal hours, and a Night Owls club where insomniacs can meet and chat into the small hours.

Usually, after a night in the emotional pits, you feel

better in the morning. Occasionally, you don't. You wake up feeling leaden and, however sunny the day, it's as if you're viewing the world through thick fog. You feel you can't cope any more. Nothing interests you. Life has lost its savour, and you your appetite for living.

When you're in the throes of this kind of depression, it's worth hanging on to the fact that you're not alone. Everyone feels like this sometimes. Women and men. Married and unmarried. Simon was a top publishing executive I worked with who'd have sessions, every few months, of arriving hours late at the office. 'Cleared up a lot of paperwork at home. Quieter there,' he'd inform me briskly as he breezed in just as I was leaving for an early lunch. Years later, his wife confided that Simon had spent those mornings with the blankets thrown over his head, sobbing that he just couldn't go on. He was terrified of his boss. He resented his children. No one loved him. And the pain across his forehead wasn't an ordinary headache, dammit, it was a brain tumour.

The sad thing is that in our competitive, success-orientated society, it's taken as a sign of weakness and failure if we admit to feelings of insecurity. Talking with trusted friends, changing your routine, taking a short break and, yes, visiting people less privileged mentally, financially, physically than yourself all help to lift you out of a temporary depression. So will anger. If you can develop a fighting spirit, and tell yourself you're not going to allow life or events to push you down like this, you're half way to heaving yourself out of the pit.

Sometimes, though, it becomes impossible to help yourself. If for weeks you find yourself in a state where you can't sleep, eat or stop crying, have no interest in your appearance and your home, are gripped by apathy and keep finding excuses for not going to work, then it's vital to recognise the warning signs of a serious depression and seek help. Not tranquillisers. They'll just dampen your responses and do nothing to get to the root cause of your depression. You need to talk to someone qualified to help you. Ask your doctor to refer you to a counselling service, psychotherapist or psychoanalyst. Or approach one yourself through MIND (National Association for Mental Health) or the Women's Therapy Centre. In London, an experimental Psychiatric Day Hospital has been set up at the Charing Cross Hospital, where you can walk in off the street for immediate counselling in a relaxed, informal atmosphere. The unit doesn't deal with adolescent problems, however. For those, there is a separate hospital organisation: The Project Upstairs at 229 King Street, London W6.

If seeking psychiatric help seems an alarming decision to make, remind yourself that this may be the Age of the Strain but no, you are not going round the bend. What you are doing is taking a positive step to regain your emotional and physical equilibrium.

When I first met Alex he seemed to have everything going for him. An energetic man in his mid twenties, he had recently been promoted to a stimulating job in TV production which entailed travel to glamorous locations and contact with a crowd of attractive, like-minded people. He'd also just moved into the kind of penthouse flat which leaves the rest of us breathless with envy.

'When I first met you I was a mess,' he told me years later. 'After my marriage broke up I just couldn't cope with living alone. I rocketed all over town, going to every party, blazing a trail of riotous destruction. Then I'd come home and lie awake till dawn, counting the swallows on my expensive, interior-decorated bedroom wall. I couldn't sleep. I lost my appetite. I cried a lot. I felt lonely, disorientated and out of kilter with the rest of the world. I knew I was painting the town red to escape from the black despair that was always threatening to engulf me. I knew I needed people, friends, but I was behaving so badly towards them I was driving them away from me. I *knew* I was doing it. But I couldn't help myself. And there seemed to be no one I could talk to. I'd lost touch with my family, and my friends were all connected with my job. I work in a competitive field, and I suspected that if I let my live-wire image slip, I'd not only lose face, but my place on the promotion ladder as well.'

Alex had the sense to get himself to an analyst. It took a year of once-a-week sessions. Then he gave up his rented luxury flat and bought a house in a residential area where, as he says, he's surrounded by 'couples and kids, Monday morning washing lines, the bustle of shoppers in the High Street, and darts in the local on Saturdays. Evidence of normal, everyday life which is just what I need to bring me down to earth after my frenetic, often fantasy-filled days in TV films'. With the analyst's help, Alex realised that as a single man he was suffering from a surfeit of options. Because he was totally free to go anywhere and do anything, he felt confused at all the choices open to him. By taking on the restraint of a mortgage and organising a regulated home life, he found he felt more at one with the world and with himself.

Alex admits that during the darkest days of his depression, he thought often about suicide. There are four thousand suicides in England and Wales each year, and psychiatrists take the view that the majority of these people were severely depressed. Amongst women, the divorced and separated have the highest suicide rate, although the number of men trying to kill themselves is lessening. In addition to those who succeed in killing themselves, there are over 2000 a week who make the attempt and fail – often as a cry for help. But this sort of self-abuse only increases your sense of worthlessness and physically can leave you permanently injured. Overdoses of paracetamol and aspirin, for example, can cause irreparable damage to the liver and kidneys – and having your stomach pumped out is painful and degrading. As Dorothy Parker put it,

> *Razors pain you,*
> *Rivers are damp;*

Acids stain you;
And drugs cause cramp.
Guns aren't lawful;
Nooses give;
Gas smells awful.
You might as well live.

If you don't find that verse at all amusing, and go on not finding it funny for weeks or months, ask yourself if you could be experiencing a severe depression. If so, seek help. Go to your GP, the Samaritans, MIND, or the Women's Therapy Centre. Unhappiness may be a condition of life which we all have to learn to cope with, but because you're living alone, it doesn't mean you need to suffer alone as well.

The Healthy Way to Cope with Illness

Actress Jackie Bissett has confessed that her great fear 'is not being alone – but being ill'.

However rich and famous we may be, however glamorous our lives, the spectre that haunts everybody is the prospect of being sick, weak, helpless, even dying – and having no one there to care, cosset, sympathise, ring the doctor, make food and fetch the prescription.

'Huh,' commented a married friend, reading this over my shoulder. 'You think single people are the only ones who have a hard time when they're ill? When I have a headache it always transpires that my husband has just swallowed the last aspirin, because he has a headache too and his, naturally, is always worse than mine. And if I'm stricken with flu I'm not allowed just to lie there. I still have to run the household from my sick bed!'

Her remark brought home to me once again the advantage we single people possess. In being free of domestic pressures, we have the time to monitor our own natural rhythms and cycles. If you look back over the years at your illnesses, you may find that they fall into a rough pattern and that you seem to be affected by the same ailment at the same time of year. I've lost count of the number of times I've suffered from throat infections during the last weeks of July and December. It varies from person to person, but there do seem to be certain periods in the year when each individual feels out of sorts, and prone to ailments like colds, flu, headaches and backache. By monitoring yourself and when these low times occur, you may not stop yourself going down with flu, but at least you'll be prepared. (I'm beginning to realise I should have suggested that all hypochondriacs skip this chapter. They'll be rubbing their hands with glee, thinking oh goodie, next Thursday I'll have a wonderful day popping pills and wallowing in my blocked sinus.)

Stress, as we all know, is the cause of many ailments. How many times, having caught a heavy cold, have you subsided into bed with a sigh of relief, secretly rather glad to have the excuse to lie there and do nothing for a few days? Again, it's worth taking the trouble to understand and come to terms with our own metabolism, because when we inflict too much strain upon ourselves, the body is often quite relentless about saying, 'I want a rest now, and if you won't relax of your own accord, I shall break down and force you to become inactive.' With some people, a cold or headache is enough to make them take to their beds and let go for a while. But other, more restless souls, still won't relax even if afflicted with these ailments and in such cases the body often takes more extreme measures to make sure it gets the rest it needs.

One highly charged friend of mine, who always seems to have ten times more energy than the rest of us, was mystified at the way, two or three times a year, he was poleaxed by a slipped disc, necessitating frustrating weeks lying flat on his back. Then he realised that each bout of trouble with his back followed a time of crisis in his personal or work life. He taught himself to ease up, and his incidence of back trouble has decreased.

Having accepted that stress can trigger sickness, the next

question of course is what causes stress? Naturally, it varies according to the individual. If you're what psychologists call a Type A person, you'll probably be ambitious, pushy, impatient and volatile. You'll be susceptible to stress diseases, including peptic ulcers, heart attacks and high blood pressure. If, however, you are more introvert, shy, tending to swallow your anger rather than express it, you're a Type B. Some forms of cancer are commoner in Type Bs, and you'll be prone to emotional afflictions, such as depression.

Statistics do point firmly to change – even if it's for the good – being the main generator of stress. A recently divorced person who has just moved home should be aware that the incidence of physical disorders in the year following divorce is twelve times higher than the norm, and that a change of residence has been shown to correlate with disease. That is not to say that every single time you experience some sort of change in your life you are going to feel ill. But if you do find yourself suddenly below par, it helps if you understand why.

'After my much longed for divorce I expected to feel on top of the world,' one woman told me, 'but instead I was utterly wrung out. For months, I crawled home from work just wanting to sleep and sleep and sleep. I was going to bed at 5.30 in the afternoon and waking up the following morning, exhausted.'

Looking back, she realises that she was suffering from mild depression – a reaction after all the hassle of the split from her husband and moving to her new flat. 'I wish I'd understood then that it was a perfectly normal reaction,' she says. 'I think I made myself feel worse by fighting my fatigue. It might have been better just to have rolled with it.'

When you're afflicted with minor ailments like colds and flu which merely require soothing drinks and bedrest, living alone can be a positive blessing. There's no one to tell you how ghastly you look, to try and force feed you when you don't want to eat, to wake you up when you're enjoying an afternoon snooze, to remonstrate that three whisky toddies on the trot is carrying things a bit far.

But when the illness is something more serious, then of course it's worrying being on your own. Especially for the elderly, who quite naturally imagine that every unexpected chest pain is IT.

The vital action here is to take reassuring preparatory steps *before* you become ill. Buy a good First Aid kit. Pin up your doctor's day and night phone numbers, and the address and telephone number of your local hospital. Keep handy a leaflet on how to cope with sudden emergencies like burns, electric shocks, and bleeding. Write down and keep in your wallet your blood group and the name of any pills you may be taking. Stock up not just your medicine chest but your larder, too, with emergency supplies of soothing, easy to prepare meals. Remember, the milkman will deliver not just milk, but eggs, bread, potatoes, poultry – a whole range of basic foods. Establish a good rapport with the milkman, the postman, paperboy, anyone who calls every day and could call assistance for you if necessary. *Never be afraid to ask for help.*

If you can afford it, private medical insurance such as that offered by British United Provident Association (BUPA) or Private Patients Plan (PPP) provides great peace of mind. Although you would always receive immediate treatment under the National Health Service in an emergency, or if your life was in danger, private medical insurance covers you for those conditions which are not urgent, but for which there is often a long NHS waiting list. Some insurance companies also cover you in case you need nursing care at home while you're convalescing.

One way to stave off illness is to keep your body in good working order, and that means eating sensibly and exercising regularly. You owe it to yourself; if you don't keep yourself physically tuned up you'll become depressed, tired and eventually you'll break down. Apart from being unpleasant, illness can cost you time and money – money which you need to support yourself. Take the trouble to organise a regular shopping routine – an hour spent whizzing round the supermarket to stock yourself up for the week is time well spent. Eat plenty of fresh fruit and vegetables and drink as much water as you can; if you loathe the taste of tap water, try mineral waters or herb teas. Keep a supply of peppers, cucumber, carrot, white cabbage, mushrooms, celery and tomatoes in the salad drawer of the fridge, and use them for salads and instant snacks. Buy a blender, and make a supply of nourishing soup to last you all week. If you go out a great deal, don't buy anything that won't keep, like fish or avocado, unless you know you're going to eat them the same day.

Watch that you neither diet so much that you start to look haggard, nor overeat to compensate for things you feel are lacking in your life. And with no one else around to warn us that our breath smells after that garlicky supper last night, its vital for everyone living alone to be especially fastidious about personal hygiene.

A trolley on wheels will ease the strain of lugging your shopping home, and the walk to the shops will do you good. Most people now accept the importance of taking some kind of exercise every day, even if it's hopping off the bus a few stops earlier and walking part of the way to work. Jogging has enjoyed a vogue for some time and has the advantage that it's free, you don't need a partner, and you can do it where and when it suits you. But whether you choose to kick a ball, swim, run or tap dance, you'll only benefit if you do it regularly. Regular exercise not only lessens fatigue, it also builds up your stamina – an asset when a crisis occurs in your life, as it means you'll have more strength and resilience to cope. If you're fit and healthy, you'll look good as well, which does wonders for the morale.

But like all intricate machines, your body is bound to develop a fault occasionally. Just as we ensure that our cars or washing machines are regularly serviced, so we should pay the same attention to our physical selves, by arranging to have annual medical check ups. Apart from the value to your peace of mind, if there is anything wrong with you it's always better to know about it sooner rather than later.

Home Security

Everyone is familiar with the chilling experience of lying rigid in bed, listening to the creak, thump, click which convinces you the burglar is now half way through your bathroom window. Even if you've lived in the house for years, and common sense and experience tell you that those noises are only the wood in the place contracting after the heat of the day or the radiators knocking, it still doesn't stem the rising panic at the knowledge that you are all alone and what happens if . . .

It's even worse for people who are new to the single state, accustomed to the reassuring presence of another body in the bed, someone who will laugh off their fears or grab the torch and investigate. This is where a phone by your bed is an invaluable reassurance aid. Just knowing you can pick it up and ring a friend, or the police, is often enough to calm your pounding heart. It's worth taking the time to follow the instructions in the front of your telephone book and learn how to dial 999 in the dark – not as obvious as you might imagine, if you take a look at your telephone dial. Never be afraid of worrying the police unnecessarily. They are only too well aware that every minute of every day someone somewhere in Britain is being burgled. A horrifying statistic, but one which should goad us into ensuring that our homes are properly protected. When you're lying there listening to those ominous creaks, it's at least a comfort to know that if someone is trying to break in, they're going to have their work cut out getting through the barrage of locks on your windows and doors.

The number and variety of security devices on the

market is at first sight baffling. The British Insurance Association will, in return for a stamped addressed envelope, send you some excellent explanatory leaflets on home security. Or call the Crime Prevention Officer at your local police station. His advice is free. Not only will he save you time in sifting through all the various safety devices on your own, but he'll save you money too by stopping you being pressured by a salesman into buying expensive apparatus you don't need.

The best time to take a look at your home security arrangements is as soon as you move into a new place. It's always a good idea to change all the locks, as you never know who before you had a free and easy attitude to handing out keys.

Doors

These should be fitted with deadlocks. That is, locks with bolts that can't be forced back, but have to be turned by a key. There are two types of deadlock: mortice, which is fitted into a hole cut in the door; and surface mounted, which juts out, fixed to the inside face of the door. What is not adequate is the most commonly-seen form of door protection, which is the surface mounted nightlatch, with a little knob which you click down from the inside. These should always be used in conjunction with deadlocks, because all an intruder has to do is break a pane of glass to the side of the nightlatch, flick up the knob to unlock the door, and your house is then his home. Fit safety chains to your outside doors and get into the habit of using them. A peephole is another good device to enable you to see who's ringing your bell. They don't look obtrusive, and some of them are now incorporated into brass doorknockers. Look in John Lewis in London, or your local hardware shop.

Windows

Most of us remember to shut our windows at night or when we go out, but for total security they need locks on as well, for more thieves break in through windows than they do through doors. Each window should have a mortice bolt or surface mounted casement stay with a locking device. They don't look obtrusive, and they're easy to fit yourself onto wooden windows. For metal framed windows you'll probably need a locksmith's help and you may have to drill holes in the frame. If you have louvred windows, seek professional advice, as it's sometimes possible for prowlers to lift out sections of the glass from the outside.

Keys

It's always worrying when you're obliged to leave a key (for a repairman, or Aunt Maud) with someone you don't know very well, especially as so many high street shops now offer an on-the-spot duplicate key cutting service. One way round this problem is to have your locks fitted with registered, or numbered keys. The safeguard is that a new key can only be cut via the manufacturer, who has a list of owners and key numbers, and who will only act on order of your signature. But of course if you lose a key, you have to suffer an inconvenient delay while you write to the manufacturer and ask for another one to be cut. (It's a good idea always to keep a note of the numbers on all your keys.)

Since most burglaries are committed not by professional thieves, but by opportunists, tempted by open windows or doors, one of the most effective deterrents is to make your house look occupied at all times. Leaving the hall or bathroom light on is not enough. A better idea is to connect a table lamp or radio to a plug-in timer, to produce light or voices at intervals determined by you. If you're away for longer than 24 hours, a seven-day plug-in timer will operate on a similar on-off sequence set by you, which will deter anyone who is hanging around checking. Another device, Securiswitch by Smiths Industries Time Controls, has a photocell sensor that puts the light on when it gets dark. It'll stay on for six hours and then switch itself off automatically.

For extra security, you may think it worth investing in a burglar alarm. They aren't cheap. The simplest alarms cost upwards from £250 to have professionally fitted, but you have to balance this against the aggro of having your home turned over, the loss of your valuables and the price you put on your own peace of mind. Do-it-yourself kits are less expensive – upwards from £60 – but they won't be accepted as a satisfactory deterrent by your insurance company. For advice on burglar alarms, and a list of recommended installers, write to the National Supervisory Council for Intruder Alarms.

It has to be admitted that all this changing of locks and setting time clocks is a boring chore and you might be tempted to think oh, why bother, I'll take my chances. But once it's done, it's done and you then have the reassurance of knowing you've effected everything possible to protect yourself and your property. It's better than being wise after the event and wishing you'd taken the trouble to phone the Crime Prevention Officer, as you go through the hassle of filling in insurance claim forms and clearing up the debris the intruders have left.

Finally, don't forget the everyday, simple measures you should take to be effectively protected. Some of them seem glaringly obvious, but when you're in a rush it's easy to forget that last minute precaution – which could cost you dear, as I found out when I carefully locked all my doors and returned to find someone had entered my house through the kitchen window I'd left wide open.

* Remember, you're being watched even when you don't realise it. Try not to leave or return to the house at the same time every day. The occasional half hour variation may be enough to confuse that hawk-eyed potential intruder.

* It helps if you can make the exterior of the house look the same whether you're there or not. It's a giveaway to the hidden watcher if you always leave the same upstairs window open when you're at home, but close it when you go

out. Similarly, there's no point in remembering to cancel the milk and newspapers if you then leave the garage door open revealing to the world that you're away from home.

* Remove keys from inside locks, so they are not accessible via an adjacent window, or letterbox. Don't hang keys by string from the letter box, or put them under mats, flowerpots or on top of windowledges. These are the first places a thief checks. Foil sneak thieves by locking up every time you go out, even if it's just for five minutes.

* Never open the door after dark unless you know who your caller is. Always ask to see the credentials of people like gas, electricity and insurance men. Don't let your callers know you live alone. Refer to 'we' rather than 'I'.

* If you have a cat, don't leave the window open – instal a cat flap.

* Don't leave garden tools or ladders lying around. It's pointless supplying the thieves with the equipment to climb up and break in.

* Take photographs of your valuables, to help in insurance claims and assist the police to recognise your treasures should they be stolen. Make a note of the serial numbers on your TV, camera, stereo, car chassis, etc. It will aid the police to recover your goods if you write your name and address on valuable items with a security marker, such as the Volumatic pen from W.H. Smith. The ink is invisible to the naked eye, but shows up clearly when monitored by special police equipment.

* Make sure your house and its contents are adequately insured. For advice, write either to the British Insurance Association or the British Insurance Broker's Association, or look in your Yellow Pages.

* Try geese. A Scotch whisky firm haven't had a single break-in since they set one hundred geese to patrol their warehouses.

* If you're still being kept awake by all those creaks, bangs and knocks, put the light on and read all about it in

an excellent book by Dermot Walsh, called *Break-Ins*.

If You're Attacked

'I don't give a damn about my stereo or fur jacket,' said Joan, newly divorced and nervous of living on her own. 'My main concern is me. When I hear those things that go bump in the night I shake with fright, thinking is this it, will I be knifed, raped or clubbed to death?'

Quite. Most of us, especially women, the elderly and the infirm, have been prey to such fears. We know we've taken every possible precaution – locks on our windows and doors, the telephone by the bed and a shriek alarm in our handbags. Even so, it's only natural to wonder, if the worst came to the worst, how we'd react under attack. Would it be freeze, flight or fight?

If you do wake up and find an intruder in your room, the most sensible course of action is to get the hell out and then scream for help. If that's not possible (and it often isn't, especially if you've assiduously locked all those doors) what should you do?

This was the situation Jenny faced when she was a student. Foolishly, she'd left her bedroom window open one summer's night. She woke up and found a man rifling through her dressing table.

'I was so startled, I screamed,' recalls Jenny. 'That, of course, alerted him and he moved towards me. I wished with all my heart I'd kept my mouth shut and feigned sleep. But I gathered my wits, and started talking to him, quite gently. To my relief, he responded. He sat down by my bed, and we talked for over two hours – mainly about his childhood and his family. Then, quite suddenly, he got up and went away. Almost crying with relief, I dialled 999.'

When the police arrived, they asked Jenny for a description of the man. After all, he'd been sitting next to her for two hours, and the police quite naturally reasoned that

Jenny would be able to provide them with a detailed run down on his physical appearance.

'But I couldn't,' wails Jenny. 'My glasses were on the bedside table, and while the man was in the room I didn't have the nerve to ask him to pass them to me . . .'

Jenny was fortunate. It isn't always possible to do as she did and talk your way out of trouble, especially if the intruder is beyond the stage of being prepared to listen to anybody. It's difficult giving advice on how to handle a situation like this as, inevitably, you'll act on instinct. *The police advise that you should avoid engaging in a physical confrontation with an intruder.* Providing he (or she) is not trying to harm you, and you can't run away, then do nothing and say nothing to provoke him or her. The intruder may have no intention of injuring you but if you startle him he might attack you out of brazen self-defence. If, however, you find yourself in a desperate situation where you have no choice but to fight back remember that legally you are permitted to use as much force as is necessary to defend yourself. Try to stay cool and bear the following in mind:

* Break a window to attract attention or provide you with an escape route.

* Remember you have an enormous advantage, in that you are on your home ground, whereas your attacker is unfamiliar with the layout of your home.

* If you have the time, and the presence of mind, utilise anything in an aerosol can as a deterrent. Squirting hair spray or fly killer in his eyes might put him off long enough for you to get away.

* Don't be squeamish about inflicting pain. You've got to if you're going to win. Don't waste your energy pushing and shoving. Attempt at all costs to keep your hands free. If he makes a grab for them, twist his fingers back – until they snap if necessary. Go for his vulnerable points. Jab your thumb in his eyes. Smash the side of your palm up hard under his nose. Twist his ear. He'll be ready

for the knee in the crotch, but probably not quite so prepared for a kick on the kneecaps. Use every natural
weapon at your command: your nails, teeth, knees. Again,
because you're on home ground, you have the advantage
of being aware of all the other potential weapons in your
pad. Not just obvious items like scissors, breadknife and
brass poker. Anything can be used to inflict pain if it's got a
sharp edge, a point, or is heavy – a metal ashtray, keys, a
pencil, a paperweight.

   * Be alert for signs that your attacker is weakening,
and becoming more vulnerable. But don't give up. Keep
jabbing, poking, kicking. If he doesn't turn tail and run,
wait until he is momentarily winded, and effect your
escape. It helps to have prepared your mind for such an
eventuality, so you know which way you'll run, which well
lit house, pub or shop you'll rush to for help. Start
screaming as soon as you're clear of your attacker. It's a
regrettable fact that you'll evoke more response from the
public if you shout 'Fire!' rather than 'Help' or 'Rape'.

   Many people of both sexes are now taking advantage of
the excellent evening classes in self-defence. You may not
want to be a karate black belt, but it's useful to have your
reflexes sharpened up, so that under attack you react
instead of freezing. You learn what evasive action to take
when threatened, and being in a mock fight helps to make
you less afraid if the real thing should happen to you. This
is especially important for women, who are generally
encouraged from girlhood to believe that any form of
aggression is unfeminine, and who often lack the confidence to defend themselves in an assertive manner.

Funny Phone Calls

It's not amusing at all, of course, to pick up the phone and
suffer heavy breathing, or someone mouthing obscenities
down the line. I was surprised to learn that it isn't just

private individuals who are plagued with this. A woman who runs a marriage bureau tells me that her office staff receive these calls – and there's a season for them. In the Spring, with the sap rising, it's not just love, it seems, that a young man's fancy turns to. The occasional one-off call is worrying, but not too alarming. What really gets under your skin is the regular caller. My marriage bureau friend solved this by making a scratching noise on the mouthpiece with her nail, and arranging for a male friend to say authoritatively into the receiver, 'That's all right now, madam. We've managed to trace the call.' After that she had no more bother.

If you don't have a heavy-voiced friend around, the most effective remedy is simply to put down the receiver on a table, then go off and have a bath or watch TV for half an hour. People who make obscene phone calls get their kicks out of shocking you, and if you're not responding down the line, they'll soon get bored and ring off. (How do people *afford* these calls with phone charges so high?) You could also try blowing a police whistle down the mouthpiece. I'm told the noise has a shattering effect on the ear drums.

Some people recommend listening to the caller's suggestions, and then yawning boredly, or outgunning the caller with even filthier suggestions of your own. Personally, I'm not prepared to waste my time doing this – and you run the danger of the caller enjoying your competitive streak and ringing up again for more verbal titillation.

It's always wise for women to conceal their sex in their telephone directory entry. J. Smith is preferable to Miss J. Smith. If you continue to be besieged with unwelcome calls, you may find it best to go ex-directory. Then when the phone rings, you'll know it's someone you want to talk to.

Outside Attack

It's bad enough being menaced in your own home. But it's when we're out, especially at night, that many of us feel most at risk. (Although with regard to rape, more than half the cases reported to the Rape Crisis Centres during 1981 happened indoors.) Again, thinking ahead and exercising common sense are the key safety factors.

* Come home by taxi if you can afford it. Radio cabs are cheaper than mini cabs.

* Avoid isolated bus stops and short cuts down dark alleys. Where possible, keep to well-lit streets, but if you have to walk down a dark road, carry a torch, and walk facing the traffic.

* Wear flat shoes so you can run away fast.

* Get to know the phone boxes and police stations on your route home. Don't be afraid to knock at a nearby house and ask for help.

* Don't hitchhike, or give lifts. If you're absolutely stranded, ring the police. Obviously, you can't use them as a taxi service, but they will get you home in a dire emergency.

* Try to keep amongst a crowd.

* Women should never enter an empty train compartment, or one with a sole male passenger. If the carriage empties, move to another one. If you are pestered, complain to the guard or driver.

* Don't drink too much. If you get fuddled, you're more likely to miss the last bus and take stupid chances which could be disastrous.

* Avoid eye contact with kerb crawlers. Don't speak to them at all. Above all don't shout 'fuck off' as this will only goad them on.

* Carry a weapon. Scream alarms are legal, pepper is not. Lapel pins and brooches can inflict effective damage on an attacker.

* Keep your keys in your hand as you approach your house.

* Carry money and valuables in a shoulder bag, strapped across your back, under your coat.

* Scream, scream, scream.

In Your Car

* Travel on main or well used roads and park in well lit areas.

* On entering, check the interior, especially the back seat. Lock the car when you get in.

* Callous though it may sound, it is wiser not to stop if you see an accident. Drive on and report the incident by phone.

* If you break down on an unfamiliar, deserted road at night lock yourself in and wait until morning rather than blundering off by yourself in the dark.

* If you are followed home, don't get out but attract attention by flashing your lights and sounding your horn.

* When you get home, leave your car lights on until you have switched on your house lights.

If you are attacked, however shaken and upset you are, however much you just want to blot the whole ghastly incident from your mind, do take the time and trouble to report it to the police. Only ten per cent of all attacks are reported, but it's important to do this, even if the episode was comparatively trivial, because your account might be a vital link in a dossier of such cases which the police have been building up. Try to report the attack the same day or night that it happens. Don't leave it till the next day. Those few hours could be crucial to the police in tracking down your assailant.

Don't just concentrate on clothing in your statement, as your attackers can easily alter their entire appearance by changing their apparel. Think of height, colouring, build, voice, whether their breath or bodies smelled, and what of. When they ran off, how did they move? One of the hardest things for anyone to disguise is the way they walk and run. What direction did they go in? Did they have a car? Can you recall anything of the registration number, the colour, the shape? The smallest detail could be important.

Rape

Any rape victim will naturally be in a state of extreme shock and distress. Some women feel so unclean after such an attack that they find it impossible to talk about, fearing a reaction of hostility and recrimination even from those closest to them. But if it happens to you, it's vital that you don't suffer in silence at such a time. You must talk to someone about it. If you can't bring yourself to go immediately to the police, or talk to a close friend or relative, then contact your nearest Rape Crisis Centre. There are centres in England, Scotland and Ireland, and their service is free and confidential. You'll find them sympathetic and reassuring in that they will be able to give you both emotional and practical support. They will explain about police, court and medical procedures and, if you wish, accompany you to the police station.

When you report the rape to the police:

* Do so as soon as possible.

* Don't have a bath or tidy yourself before you go, as you may be destroying evidence.

* Don't take any alcohol or drugs.

* Take a friend or your mother with you for support and be prepared for an internal medical examination by a police surgeon. (A day or so later you may need to have photographs taken of any bruising, which takes time to show.)

* Take a change of warm clothing with you – the police may keep some or all of your original clothing for tests and evidence.

No rape victim should ignore the dangers of venereal disease and pregnancy. Go for a VD test after about a week (someone from the Rape Crisis Centre will accompany you if you wish) and for a pregnancy test 10 – 14 days afterwards. You have no automatic right to an abortion on the National Health Service as a result of rape, although you could be eligible for a termination under Section 1 of the Abortion Act, which takes into account risk to the patient's life and mental health. The Rape Crisis Centres or your local Citizens Advice Bureau will help you with legal advice, should you require it.

Emergencies

Fires, floods and frozen pipes can happen to anyone, whether they're living alone or not. But such emergencies always seem more alarming when you're by yourself. If there's someone else around (even if they're in more of a turmoil than you are) at least you have the comfort of another human presence. On your own, even if you're normally the ice cool type, a sudden chip pan fire could throw you into such momentary confusion that you're either rooted numbly to the spot or goaded into doing quite the wrong thing by tipping water over the flames. Just a few seconds of blind panic. But those precious seconds could cost you your life.

You're less likely to panic if you're mentally prepared for the emergency. Knowing what to do, and when to do it will help to keep you calm and prevent damage both to yourself and your home. On a quiet evening, take the trouble to read through the following section, and familiarise yourself with the course of action to take in each situation.

Fire

Before it happens, walk round the house and plan your escape route. Check out staircases, where doors and windows lead to and how easy they are to open. If you live in rented accommodation, enquire what fire regulations apply to the building and whether the landlord is vigilant about enforcing these. Is the fire escape staircase accessible or has Gerald from downstairs pushed his unwanted wardrobe up against it? Make sure you know where the fire alarms and extinguishers are sited in the house and *how to use them*.

Remember, if a fire does start, you'll naturally be in a bit of a panic and this is no time to have to start peering distractedly at the instructions.

One of the most common causes of fires in the home is the chip pan, so never leave one unattended. Make sure you extinguish cigarettes properly and try not to smoke in bed, especially if you've had a few drinks. Bedlinen catches light at an alarming rate and you might not notice the tell-tale smell if you've dropped off to sleep. When you buy upholstered furniture, watch out for the swing tickets which should by law be attached, warning you that the item is made from inflammable material. Most of our foam-filled sofas, for example, will ignite in eight minutes from a carelessly thrown cigarette and send off toxic fumes into the bargain. If you have an open fire, never leave it, even for a minute, without putting a guard in front – and don't be tempted to use the guard to air or dry clothes. Never stand too close to a fire, especially if you're clad in a gauzy garment. And place your mirror somewhere other than above the mantelpiece.

For added peace of mind, you could invest in a Firecheck package, made by Hoover. It contains a smoke detector, a fire extinguisher and a fire blanket to smother flames.

TACKLING FIRE

The Fire Service recommends that you should never attempt to fight a fire yourself unless it is in its earliest stage and there is not the slightest risk to yourself or others.

* If you suspect that there is a fire behind a closed door, don't open it.

* Remember that smoke can be as dangerous as flames.

* If a chip pan catches fire, turn off the heat, smother the flames with a lid or damp cloth, and leave for half an hour.

* If your clothes catch fire, roll on the floor to extin-

guish the flames. Should another person's clothes catch fire, lay him or her on the floor and roll them in blankets, rugs or a thick coat.

WHAT TO DO IF A MAJOR FIRE BREAKS OUT

* Close the door of the room where the fire is – this will help to contain the fire and restrict the spread of poisonous fumes.

* Alert the household, and get everyone out by the safest route. Flatdwellers should *not* use the lift.

* Alert neighbours and call the fire brigade. (Don't leave it to someone else.)

* To call the fire brigade, dial 999. You don't need to put money in a public call box. Remember to give the full address of the fire, e.g. 12 Smith Street, New Town.

* Try to reduce draughts that may fan the fire. Close all doors and windows (even in rooms away from the fire) if this can be done safely.

IF YOU ARE CUT OFF BY FIRE

* Close the door of the room, close any fanlight or other opening and block up the cracks with bedding, etc.

* Go to the window and try to attract attention.

* If the room fills with smoke, lean out of the window. If smoke outside prevents this, try lying close to the floor where the air is clearer, until you hear the fire brigade.

* If it gets so bad you must escape before the fire brigade arrives, make a rope by knotting together sheets of similar materials. Tie one end to a bed or other heavy piece of furniture.

* If you cannot make a rope, drop cushions or bedding to break your fall. Get through the window feet first, lower yourself to the full extent of your arms, and drop.

* If the window will not open, break the glass with a heavy object. Try to clear jagged glass from the lower edge and, if possible, place a blanket over the sill before escaping.

Water

Before the flood occurs, make sure you know where the stop cock is situated. This is a tap which controls the mains water supply into the house. In modern houses, this is usually sensibly sited underneath the sink, but in older properties you may have quite a merry search, probably finally running it to earth underneath the floorboards. In an emergency, first turn off the water at the stop cock, following the rule which applies to all taps: clockwise turns it off and anti-clockwise turns it on. Then phone the plumber. Ideally, you will have located a reliable plumber before the emergency, otherwise you run the risk of falling prey to a cowboy outfit who will exploit the situation by charging you an inflated price. If there is no one locally who can recommend a plumber to you, write to the Institute of Plumbing for a list of those in your area. Should it be impossible during an emergency to find a plumber, ring your local Water Authority (under Water in the phone book) who will come day or night to turn off the main outside stop cock.

When you go away for a few days in the winter, leave the heating on and sinks plugged up to guard against frozen pipes. If they do freeze, thaw them out gently with a hair-dryer. Make sure all your pipes are lagged, and attend immediately to dripping taps. In some areas, the local water authority will rewasher dripping taps and ballvalves for you on request, free of charge.

Water is a ruthlessly efficient conductor of electrical current, so never take anything like an electric fire into the bathroom and don't touch any electrical appliance with wet hands. For your own safety, get into the habit of letting the water run away before you get out of the bath. Then if you should happen to slip and bang your head you won't fall face down into the water.

Electricity

Be prepared. Find out where the mains switch is (again, in older properties it could be hidden anywhere, from the larder to the garage) and lay in a supply of matches and candles. Put these somewhere accessible that you can reach easily in the dark. You also need a powerful torch – buy one that stands up on its own, rather than the sort with a tendency to roll off the table at the crucial moment.

Use good quality plugs that conform to British Standard 1363, and make sure they are wired correctly, with the blue wire to the Neutral terminal (marked N), the green/yellow wire to Earth terminal (marked E) and the brown wire to Live terminal (marked L). When you buy a plug you'll probably find that it's been fitted with a 13 amp fuse. This means that it will pass a mighty 2750 watts before it blows. Yet most of us cheerfully, and rashly, fit these hefty 13 amp plugs to small appliances like sewing machines and blenders which in fact need only a 3 amp fuse. Appliances rated at 700 watts or more need a 13 amp fuse. Anything less than 700 watts and a 3 amp fuse will suffice. If you're in doubt about how to choose the correct fuse for the job, pick up a leaflet called *Plugs and Fuses* from your nearest Electricity Board showroom.

Have frayed, split or worn flexes replaced at once. Never staple a flex to the wall or skirting, or run it under carpet or linoleum. Extension cables should be fully uncoiled, and not left lying in a tangled heap – twisted wires can cause fires. Unplug your television at the socket before you go to bed. Electric underblankets should be taped smoothly to the bed to avoid wrinkling. Switch them off before getting into bed, and never use an underblanket as an overblanket, and vice versa. Have electric blankets serviced every year by the manufacturer.

For complete protection at home it is best to have a qualified electrician fit an Earth Leakage Circuit Breaker (ELCB) into your house wiring circuit. This detects any small leakage in the current and will immediately break the mains circuit before it causes a fire or gives you an electric shock. The Electricity Board recommends that you have your house wiring circuit tested every five years – they will do this for you free, although of course you have to pay for any rewiring which may be necessary.

If you don't know anyone who can recommend a qualified electrician, contact The National Inspection Council for Electrical Installation Contracting who will give you a list of approved practitioners in your area. Anyone unsure about the jobs it's safe for them to tackle themselves should take advantage of the one-day courses run by the Electrical Association for Women on electricity in the home. The Association is based in London but will organise a course for ten or more men or women anywhere in the country.

Gas

If you smell gas:

* Extinguish cigarettes. Don't use matches or naked flames.

* Don't operate electrical switches (including doorbells) – either on or off. If the electrical appliance is faulty, it could spark and cause an explosion.

* Open doors and windows, to get rid of the gas.

* Check to see if a tap has been left on accidentally, or if a pilot light has gone out.

* If not, there is probably a gas leak. Turn off the supply at the mains gas tap (usually situated near the meter) and call the gas service: Listed under Gas in the phone book.

If you are over 65, or disabled, and you live alone, you are entitled to a free gas safety check on your appliances. This free check includes any necessary adjustments as well as materials up to the cost of £2.50 (inc. VAT.)

Oil

You'd be surprised the number of people who've discovered the foundations of their houses flooded with domestic heating oil. It's only when it happens to you that you find you belong to a whole fraternity of fellow sufferers, each competing with horror stories about who had the most oil lapping about under their houses. In my case, I had converted from oil central heating to gas, when I noticed a lingering smell, rather like Brasso, pervading the house. I prised up a floorboard, and saw this unmistakeable layer of oil lying on the foundations. Convinced I was sitting on a time bomb, I completely lost my head, pausing only to douse the roaring log fire before rushing screaming from the house.

The fire brigade arrived, clanging impressively into the drive, clearly under the misapprehension from my hysterical 999 call that they were being challenged to combat an oil slick with flames dancing round the edge. The head fireman, when invited to view the paltry smear of oil under the floor, was extremely patient. He put some of the oil in a saucer and held a lighted match over it. The match went out. Domestic heating oil, I learned, is not highly flammable. If anything similar should happen to you, ring your oil suppliers; they will put you in touch with a firm who clean up the mess and pour gallons of lavender scented goo on the foundations to get rid of the smell.

The moral here of course is that quite often emergencies, though frightening, inconvenient and time consuming, may not in the end turn out to be disasters. And you'll probably be covered for any damage under your insurance policy.

First Aid

We're all frightened of having an accident and there being no one around to help. Here again, knowing what action to take in the emergency will do much to keep you calm. But an equally vital aspect of first aid is knowing what *not* to do. Most importantly:

* Don't take any alcohol.

* Don't attempt to treat or diagnose every injury yourself. A knowledge of first aid is only intended to help you deal with minor emergencies, or to enable you to hold

the fort until medical assistance arrives. If you have any doubts or anxieties about the seriousness of your injury (whether you're suffering from a minor sprain or a major fracture, for instance) do not hesitate to call for your doctor or in severe cases dial 999 for an ambulance. If possible, open your front door or advise the doctor or ambulance service over the phone how they can get in.

THE FIRST AID BOX

You can obtain a fully equipped first aid box very reasonably from a chemist such as Boots. Make sure that the container is waterproof, and keep it either in the kitchen, which is where many home accidents occur, or in the bathroom. It's useful, too, always to keep a torch handy near your box. And don't forget to keep the first aid box topped up with fresh supplies after each item has been used.

BLEEDING

Small cuts — clean under cold running water. Dab on a weak antiseptic solution such as diluted TCP, then apply an adhesive dressing (ie. a plaster).

Large cuts — press firmly on the area with a dressing or clean folded cloth until the pressure has stopped the bleeding. If the cut is too large for a pad to control the bleeding, press the edges of the wound together very firmly with your fingers and thumb, and maintain this pressure for at least ten minutes. Then apply another pad. If necessary, and providing you do not suspect a fracture, lie down and raise the part which is bleeding. If the blood still seeps through the pad, call for medical assistance. *Do not* attempt to apply a tourniquet as you will probably be doing more harm than good.

After any cut, it is recommended that you check with your doctor to see if you need an anti-tetanus injection.

BURNS

Small burns — cool the affected area with cold, not icy,

water, for about ten minutes. A burned finger can be held under running water, or if it's a limb that's burned, immerse it in a bucket, sink or bath. Otherwise, cover the affected area in a thick cloth saturated with cold water. Hold the pad flat over the burn and keep renewing it as it loses its coolness.

Once you've relieved the pain, cover the area lightly with a clean dry cloth, towel, or handkerchief.

* Don't prick blisters or put cotton wool directly onto them. Leave them alone, or protect them with a paraffin gauze dressing.

* Don't apply creams, lotions or antiseptics to a burn.

Large burns and chemical burns — do not treat these yourself. Seek medical help immediately.

INSECT BITES AND STINGS
Cool the swollen area with a cold pad. Smooth on a soothing cream such as Boots Sting Relief. If a bee sting has been left in the skin, pull it out, close to the skin, with fine tweezers.

If you're stung in the mouth or throat, suck an ice cube and seek immediate medical help as there is a danger that severe swelling will obstruct an airway. Wherever you're stung, if the swelling is severe, or you feel ill after a bite, seek medical advice.

CHOKING (on something swallowed)
Try to relax. Make yourself cough as vigorously as possible.

If you still fail to dislodge the swallowed object, try to give yourself a series of abdominal thrusts. Place the thumb side of one closed fist firmly in the soft area *above* the navel and *below* the breastbone. Grasp this fist with your other hand, and give a sharp thrust upwards with both hands into your abdomen.

FAINTING
Either lie down with your legs raised, or sit with your head

bent forward between your knees. Loosen your clothes, breathe slowly, and when you recover, sip a drink of water.

POISONING
Immediately call for an ambulance.

* Do not drink salty water or try to make yourself vomit.

* If possible, take with you to the hospital the suspected poisonous substance you've swallowed.

SHOCK
Shock usually occurs after a severe accident, injury or loss of blood. It's as well to learn to recognise the signs so if you are in a state of shock you'll have the reassurance of understanding what's happening to you and what to do about it.

In shock, you'll probably be very pale and feel cold. You may be thirsty, giddy or sick and feel mentally adrift. Loosen your clothes and, providing you are sure you have not suffered a fracture, lie down with a warm cover over you until you have recovered or medical help arrives.

* Do not take any liquids, especially alcohol. Just moisten your lips or suck on a wet handkerchief.

* Don't try and warm yourself with hot water bottles. An all-over covering is better.

The Elderly

If you're getting on in years, you're particularly at risk from accidents in the home, especially if you suffer from poor sight, so it's only wise to take sensible precautions. Banish polish and small mats from your floors and get into the habit of wiping up grease stains immediately. Make sure none of your stair rods have worn, or the carpets have frayed patches. Above all, do wear well-fitting footwear at home. Slopping around in backless slippers is asking for trouble, particularly if you have any difficulty walking and keeping your balance.

Elderly people are particularly susceptible to hypothermia (very low body temperature). It occurs most often in people who live alone, with little or no heating and an inadequate diet. If you are suffering from hypothermia you will become very lethargic, with icy cold, pale skin. Should you find yourself in this condition, do not just fill a hot water bottle and assume that will warm you back to a normal state.

Call for medical help, and in the meantime sip a warm non-alcoholic drink and keep yourself cosily covered up in a warm room.

Further Guidance

The British Red Cross Society, The St John Ambulance Association and The St Andrew's Ambulance Association all run excellent first aid courses where you can learn all the procedures for dealing with accidents in the home. These organisations also publish useful manuals and booklets on first aid.

Steering the Right Course

(I've concentrated on cars in this section, but of course most of the information applies to two-wheeled transport as well.)

We all know that frustrating feeling when the car won't start, you're late for work and you lunge at it like Basil Fawlty, shouting, kicking, threatening terrible reprisals if it makes that ghastly whining noise just one more time. In fact it's not usually men who rage like this at their cars, but women. Deplorably, there are all too many of us who boast proudly that we haven't the faintest clue what goes on beneath the bonnet. 'I have a marvellous man at the garage down the road who'll whizz out at a moment's notice to help me . . . Oh, if I break down on the road I'll just flag down some passing male . . .'

But the man in the garage could be away on holiday. And flagging down passing strangers is risky and always to be avoided by the solo driver. No, in the long run it saves all of us, men and women, a lot of time and hassle if we make an effort to get to grips with the basics of how our cars work.

Start by reading the handbook and following the advice on weekly routine maintenance. Check the radiator to make sure it's topped up with water, and ditto the battery. (Use distilled water for the battery and don't forget to screw the tops back on.) Check the oil level and tyre pressure. Examine tyres for wear and damage and when either you or the garage attendant puts air into the car wheels and the spare, make sure the dust caps are replaced. Otherwise a bit of grit could get in and cause a puncture. Learn how to change a wheel.

Regular services are a worthwhile investment for your car. I know they're expensive and it might seem cheaper to get old Fred down the road to do the service; after all, he knows all about lawnmowers . . . But if the garage fouls it up, at least you've got some comeback on them, whereas if Fred fits a Flymo part to your Ford there's nothing much you can do except shout at him and pay to have the car serviced properly at a reputable garage.

It's reassuring to keep an emergency kit in your boot, especially if you have to drive long distances or over lonely roads at night. Apart from obvious items like your toolkit, tow rope, fire extinguisher, torch and triangle warning sign, seasoned travellers tell me they also keep with them a first aid kit, an old raincoat in case they have to mend a puncture in pouring rain, and a bag of apples and a novel to while away the time while they're waiting for the AA or RAC man to come.

Both the Automobile Association and the Royal Automobile Club run a get-you-home service. But before you call on your motoring club for assistance, there are simple remedies you could try first if you're having trouble with your car.

If the engine turns over but won't start — Check that you're not out of petrol and that there are no loose or disconnected leads. The ignition system could be damp – wipe the distributor and points with a dry cloth, or spray with a moisture repellent.

If the engine turns over slowly (whines) and the headlights dim — Sounds like a flat battery. Have it fixed to a recharger, or use jump leads to start the car. If it's a manual, you could ask someone to give you a push start.

If the oil light flashes when you're cornering — Top up with oil.

If the ignition light flickers while you're driving — Check to see if the fan belt is slipping and needs tightening. Otherwise, it could be the generator failing to charge the battery. Check that the leads to the battery are not disconnected. If they are secure, call for assistance.

If the temperature gauge swings up to very hot and then drops to cold — The engine is overheating. Stop, and leave the engine to cool. Top up with water. If the trouble continues, you may have a leak and need professional help.

Accidents

Accidents are frightening enough at any time, but especially if you're alone in your car, and the driver you've collided with has a gangful of relatives ready to leap out and assert that it was all your fault. It helps you to stay calm if you're sure in your own mind of the right things to do, and the order in which to do them:

1) Park your car in a safe place and if necessary switch on lights or hazard lights.

2) Immediately you get out of your car, write down the other driver's registration number and sketch a map of the scene, with arrows to show your version of what happened. Include a note of the weather conditions. If you are carrying a camera, take photographs of the scene. This will impress the other driver that you know what you are about, and he or she will then be less likely to try and

intimidate you into admitting culpability. Apart from obtaining the name, address, telephone number and insurance company of the other driver, say as little as possible, as an unconsidered remark could prejudice your case. If, however, the other driver is conscience stricken, encourage him or her to talk and make a written statement admitting guilt. Should he or she offer you money on the spot to cover the damage, don't accept as you might find out later that the damage was worse than you thought.

3) Get the names and addresses of any willing witnesses.

4) If someone is injured, the accident must be reported to the police within 24 hours, and you must show them your insurance within 5 days.

5) Inform your insurance company immediately.

The British Insurance Association has a clearly written leaflet called *When it Comes to the Crunch* which tells you about handling insurance claims after an accident.

Dealing with Authority

After a prang in the car, or when the garbage hasn't been collected for three weeks, many people who have previously been accustomed to their partner being the one to write strongly worded letters to the insurance company, or ring up the council, suddenly feel bereft and helpless at the realisation that they now have to act on their own behalf. For anyone in this situation, a useful book is *People Power* by Tony Gibson which gives a short run down on government and council obligations – like how often the latter are supposed to collect the rubbish.

Especially daunting are those letters you receive from the Council, the Bank, the Insurance Company, stamped with reference numbers and worded in incomprehensible officialese. The first fact to remember, before you're stampeded into a panic and throw the whole lot on the fire, is that for your purposes there is no such thing as the Council, the Bank, the Insurance Company. However intimidating their offices may seem as you gaze up at them from the High Street, the organisation concerned merely consists of people – ordinary human beings who eat, sleep, fall in love and worry about money just like you and I.

'That's all very well,' said Rose, a newly widowed friend, 'but I've just had three letters from the Bank Manager himself and the last one was underlined in red.'

All bureaucracies encourage you to imagine that Mr Kingpin himself is sitting at his impressive desk, frowning over a dossier with your guilty name stamped all over it. Not so. What happens is that the work is delegated to lesser, and then even lesser, minions, but all the letters are sent out in the name of Mr Kingpin. If you rang Mr Kingpin and actually by some miracle managed to get through to stammer out your fears, worries and excuses, he probably wouldn't have a clue who you were or what you were talking about.

If you feel flustered at the thought of having to write a business letter, just copy the style and layout of the letter you're replying to. Make sure you address it to the right person (give him or her their correct title) and include any reference numbers from the letter they've sent you. The reference numbers may not mean a thing to you, but will help a secretary to identify your letter, and, hopefully, speed matters to a satisfactory conclusion.

Be brief. It may be easier to keep what you want to say clear in your mind if you simply list your points rather than trying to construct elegantly phrased paragraphs. Always keep copies of your letter, and don't expect an immediate reply. In a large organisation, your letter may have to travel from the post room, to Mr Kingpin's secretary, to lesser minion, to lesser lesser minion, whose dictated reply will then have to progress back along the same route. This is bound to take at least a week. But if your letter gets mislaid in the post room, has coffee spilled over the vital paragraph by Mr K's secretary, and sits in the lesser minion's in-tray while he's away with flu, then you'll probably find yourself waiting over a month for a reply.

Far better, if you can, to sort the matter out quickly over the phone. (This applies especially to tax offices. The people there are charming over the phone and will also answer promptly if you write to them on one of their own official forms. What they don't respond to are letters.)

When you ring up, always make a point of asking for the name of the person you are dealing with. It makes it much easier if you have to ring back, or if you are obliged to go on to his or her superior and complain. If he or she won't give you a name, just ask, politely but ominously, 'Are you *refusing* to give me your name?' This puts the person on a spot and usually brings results.

Always start off by being polite and reasonable. We're all fallible and we all make mistakes. If you begin by being aggressive, you'll put the other person's back up, and jeopardise all hope of any goodwill that might have been there in the first place.

If you get no joy out of the first person you speak to, ask to be referred to his or her superior. Should they get stroppy over this, revert to the phrase, 'Are you *refusing . . .*'

Again, when you reach the Head of Department, begin by being polite. Don't castigate the minion you've just been speaking to as the H of D will only feel obliged to rush to the defence of his or her staff. Try and promote an atmosphere of mature rapport between you and the H of D – clearly, the minion couldn't be expected to be *au fait* with all aspects of such a complicated matter, but you're confident that the H of D will bring his or her greater experience to bear and resolve your problem with the utmost speed.

If it transpires that H of D has other ideas, now is the time for you to stop being polite and reasonable and start the escalation procedure. Inject a note of abrasiveness into your voice. Interrupt him or her. Allow yourself to get angry. If you're the timid type, *force* yourself to get angry. Why the devil should they treat you like this? Who do they think they are?

Should you find that all you're getting out of the exchange with H of D are a sore throat and soaring phone bill and temperature, then you must resort to the pen. This is where it helps if you've kept a note of all your phone calls and the gist of each conversation. Fire off a letter to H of D with a copy to Mr Kingpin. Hopefully, this will goad Mr K to act on his errant departments like a dose of salts. But if you still draw a blank, you then have to decide if the time and trouble you're taking over the matter is actually worth it. It is? Then there are several more effective escalation techniques open to you, all of which are described in Christopher Ward's excellent, and often viciously funny book, *How to Complain*. If that doesn't help, I suppose you could always ring up Mr Ward at his editor's desk at the *Daily Express*, and complain, reasonably and sweetly, that his book . . .

Some Useful Addresses

British Insurance Association Aldermary House, Queen St, London EC4N ITV. (01-238 4477)

British Insurance Brokers Association Fountain House, 130 Fenchurch St., London EC3M 5DJ. (01-623 9043)

British Red Cross Society 9 Grosvenor Crescent, London SW1. (01-235 5454)

City Circle 43 Vicarage Lane, London E15. (01-555 1279)

Electrical Association for Women 25 Foubert's Place, London W1V 2AL. (01-437 5212)

Institute of Plumbing Scottish Mutual House, North St. Hornchurch, Essex RM11 1RU. (Hornchurch 51236)

MIND (National Association for Mental Health) 22 Harley St. London W1. (01-637 0741)

National Inspection Council for Electrical Installation Contracting 237 Kennington Lane, London SE11.
National Supervisory Council for Intruder Alarms St Ives House, St Ives Rd. Maidenhead, Berks. S16 1RD

Rape Crisis Centres:

ENGLAND
London, 24 hours, 7 days a week (01-340 6145)
Birmingham, 24 hours, 7 days a week (021-233 2122)
Brighton, Tues. 6pm–9pm; Fri. 3pm–9pm; Sat. 10am–1pm (0273 699 756)
Canterbury, Mon, Thur, Fri. 6pm–9pm; Tues, Wed. 2pm–9pm (0227 50400)
Coventry, Mon, 7pm–10pm (0203 57709)
Leeds, 10am–midnight, 7 days a week (0532 44058)
Liverpool, Fri. 6pm–8pm (051-709 1938)
Manchester, Tues, Fri. 2pm–5pm; Thurs. 7pm–9pm; Sun. 6pm–8pm (061-228 3602)
Nottingham, Mon to Fri. 11am–5pm (0602 410440)
Oxford, Wed. 2pm–10pm (0865 726295)
Portsmouth, Fri, Sat, Sun. 8pm–8am (0705 739366)
Sheffield, Wed. 10am–2pm; Sat. 2pm–4pm (074 68480)
Tyneside, Mon to Fri. 10am–8pm; Sat, Sun. 6.30pm–10pm (0632 329858)

SCOTLAND
Edinburgh, Wed, Thur, Fri. 6pm–10pm (031-556 9437)
Strathclyde (Glasgow), Mon, Wed, Fri. 7pm–10pm (041-221 8448)

IRELAND
Dublin, Mon to Fri. 8pm–8am; Sat, Sun. 24 hours (0001 601470)

(At the time of writing, there is no Rape Crisis Centre in Wales.)

St. Andrew's Ambulance Association 48 Milton St, Glasgow G4 0HR. (041-322 4031)

St John Ambulance Association 1 Grosvenor Crescent, London SW1X 7EF. (01-235 5231)
Women's Therapy Centre 6 Manor Gardens, London N7. (01-263 6200)

Further Reading

Break Ins – Dermot Walsh (Constable)
Reader's Digest Book of Do-it-Yourself Skills (Reader's Digest)
Fit for Life – Donald Norfolk (Hamlyn)
First Aid in Mental Health – Joy Melville (Allen & Unwin)
Social Origins of Depression – George W. Brown and Tirril Harris (Tavistock)
How to Complain – Christopher Ward (Secker & Warburg)

CHAPTER 9

MONEY

Accounting for yourself

Budgeting

'I couldn't believe it. After I left home and set up in a bedsit on my own, I went out and bought some detergent, shoe polish, soap, shampoo, toothpaste and deodorant, and got no change out of a fiver. I'd no idea just keeping clean cost such a filthy amount of money.'

'When I was married and we were having a dinner party, I'd buy smoked salmon, steak and an expensive sweet from the deli without giving it a second thought. Now I'm divorced, I've had to learn to do magic things with mince and I'm appalled at what I used to spend, how I never checked the price of anything.'

'After I was widowed, these horrid brown envelopes kept landing on the mat. Rates, electricity, gas, telephone and coal bills all seemed to come at the same time. My late husband used to deal with all this sort of thing. It came as an awful shock realising how much you have to pay out. I just sat down and cried.'

Whether you're seventeen or seventy, learning to budget and manage your money for yourself is always difficult at first. It's especially hard for young people who've just set up on their own and now find themselves bereft of all those freebies they took for granted at home. 'It really is money down the drain,' remarked a student, glaring at the bottle of washing-up liquid which had cost him 57p. 'I was planning to spend that 50p on a phone call to my girlfriend.' The cost of calls from public telephone boxes was another hidden expense which the student had forgotten to budget for. Then there are the bills and money-eating emergencies

207

which sneak up on you unawares, wrecking what you'd thought was a watertight budget. You knew you had to pay rates, for instance, and sensibly arranged a monthly standing order through your bank. Then whack, through the post comes a demand for the *water* rates, which you'd completely forgotten about, and which will soak up the money you'd set aside for a new coat.

Rates, of course, are a particularly sore point with single people, many of whom are now campaigning for a change in the way these are assessed. At the moment, a house or flat is rated according to its value, rather than the number of occupants under its roof. This means that a single person has to stump up the same amount in rates as a married couple with a joint income living in exactly the same accommodation next door.

Obviously, it's impossible to work out an accurate budget until you know exactly what all your outgoings are – and it can take six months to a year for all these to become clear. To start with, the best approach is to carve up your income, apportioning it roughly for essentials and luxuries. The percentage of what you spend on what will vary with your lifestyle. If, for example, travel is a high priority but clothes aren't, you'll naturally divvy up your money accordingly. As a rough guide, mortgage, rent, rates and insurance should take 30% of your income; food drink, household, 20%; fuel bills, telephone, 10%; fares, entertainment, holidays, lunches, 25%, which leaves 10% for clothes and extras.

To put this another way, in 1981 the London YWCA suggested the following basic weekly budget for life in a bed sitter in Inner London:

Rent	£20.00
Electricity/Heat	3.00*
Fares	8.00
Food	10.00
Lunches (plus LVs)	5.00

per week——£46.00

*more in winter

Extras

Chemist	2.00
Clothes	5.00
Entertainment	2.00
Laundry/Repairs	3.00
Holidays	5.00
Miscellaneous	5.00

per week——£22.00

Total Per Week £68.00

(Don't forget to allow for inflation.)

You must remember to allow enough in your budget for food. Don't rely on being taken out most of the time for meals, or hope that one slap up dinner will see you through the week. If you exist most of the time on toast, with an occasional paid-for blow out in between, your health will suffer, which could be costly in terms of time taken off work.

As your bills come in, make a note of each of them. After six months, you should have an accurate record of what you need to put aside for mortgage or rent, rates, fuel bills, telephone, fares, insurance, TV and car licences, car road tax, car servicing, petrol and oil, subscriptions to social and sports clubs, union subs etc. A filing system sounds boring, but it will save you time in the long run, as it's even more boring having to spend an entire afternoon tearing your place apart hunting for that missing insurance certificate. One of those compartmentalised box files is ideal.

Pay as many of these regular bills as possible by monthly standing order through your bank. If you find that bills flood in at certain times of the year, and you'd prefer to spread the load, take advantage of the budget account offered by most of the big banks. Together, you and the bank work out what your bills will be over the year. This is divided into twelve, and you pay one twelfth of the total sum into a budget account every month. Then you pay the bills it covers with a special cheque book for that account. Even if you haven't got enough in the account to cover your bills in a heavy month, the bank won't bounce your cheques, because you are paying into the account regularly.

'My advice to anyone just starting out living on their own is not to get behind with major outgoings,' a single man told me. 'I was stupid. I skipped four rent payments to make a deposit on some stereo gear. I couldn't make the rent money up, so I got slung out of my room. Because I didn't have a reference from the landlord, I found it hard to find another place. Meanwhile, I had the H.P. on the stereo to keep paying. I'd never make the same mistake again. Rule one with me now is to lay out the money to keep the roof over my head. Luxuries like new stereos can wait.'

Credit cards, like Barclaycard and Access, are an enormous asset, providing you possess the discipline to use them sensibly. If you shop at the right time (usually around the third week of the month) it will be about six weeks before you're required to pay up. So you're gaining six weeks' free credit and the money you owe the credit card company can be sitting in your building society earning you six weeks' interest. The way to win with credit cards is always to pay the full amount when the bill comes in. That way, it doesn't cost you a penny. If you elect to pay only part of the bill, you're landing yourself with very high interest charges.

Saving

Don't keep yourself on such a tight financial rein that you have no money left over for emergencies – or for fun. Try and keep something aside every month, so if the cooker finally breathes its last or you feel like splurging on those gold highlights, you have the funds to cover it. Long term saving is important, too. If you're living in one room and can't afford the price of a new kettle, it may seem laughably absurd to suggest that in years to come you'll probably be in the market for a house of your own. But times change, and so will your fortunes and aspirations. When bank and building society funds are tight for mortgage-seekers, managers tend to look favourably on people who have been regular savers, so the pounds you manage to stick away each month will prove valuable both in terms of cash capital and as a long term investment for your future. Make a point of getting to know your bank manager. Don't wait until you need a loan. Establish a rapport when you don't want anything from him, and you'll be building up sound emotional capital, which you'll reap the benefit of later on.

What you should never do is stick your spare cash in a sock and hide it under the mattress. (It's amazing the number of people who do.) Apart from the danger of the mattress, and your savings, going up in smoke, your money is worth a bit less every day it's sitting in that sock. You must make your money work for you, by earning interest. It's important when deciding where to allocate your savings to make sure you're taking full advantage of your tax position. Tax payers will gain most from putting their money into building societies, National Savings Certificates or the Save-As-You-Earn scheme. Non tax payers investing a lump sum should do better with bank deposit accounts, local authority loans or government securities.

I found that a surprising number of the single people I talked to have put their extra cash into stocks and shares. As engineer Peter put it. 'It's a gamble, admittedly, but as I've no one dependent on me financially, I enjoy being able to speculate with my money. If I make a packet, that's great. If I should lose the lot, well it's only me who'll suffer, not a wife and children as well.' For the most part, Peter follows the advice of his broker over his portfolio. But he confesses he gets a kick, too, out of investing in certain companies for the concessions they offer their shareholders. Wheelers Restaurant, for example, give their shareholders a delicious buffet lunch, while if you have shares in the Savoy Hotel you can get rooms there at half price during August. Peter had shares in Heron, and when he bought a car from them he found a case of Burgundy sitting in the boot. For a list of companies which give perks to their shareholders, send a large, stamped addressed envelope to Perks, Grieveson Grant, P.O. Box

191, London EC2P 2DS.

Where to Turn for Help

The best person to advise you on savings and all aspects of
your financial affairs is, of course, an accountant. But we
can't all afford our own tame money man. Yet sound advice
is essential, especially as so much changes every year with
the budget. Many people find their newspapers particularly
helpful here, especially the *Daily Mail*'s Wednesday 'Money
Mail' and the *Daily Telegraph*'s Saturday 'Money Go
Round' section. The Consumer's Association's monthly
Money Which? is invaluable, especially for its easy-to-
understand guide to each year's tax changes. For a general
guide on managing your money, there is the excellent *Penguin Money Book* which sets out briefly and simply the
basic principles of banking, saving, life insurance, tax and
pensions. As one of the authors failed O-level maths five
times, he feels he's in a unique position to understand the
blackout that afflicts the rest of us when we're faced with
columns of figures.

Many newly widowed women, unaccustomed to dealing
with money matters, are plunged into despair at the prospect
of handling their own finances.

'I felt deeply resentful of my late husband for leaving me
with all those bills, and letters from the tax man. It all
seemed such a muddle, and I hadn't a clue how to deal with
any of it,' Vera told me. 'It was a very strange time. Half of
me mourned for my husband, and the other half was
screaming at him for being so inconsiderate as to leave me
helpless in the face of such a financial mess.'

In this situation, the first thing to hang on to is the knowledge that there is no need to be stampeded into action. Despite what all that red ink, underlining and capital letters
would have you believe, you will not be turfed out into the
street if you don't pay the bill or answer the letter by return
of post. Next, bear in mind that the bank manager, or tax
man or woman are really approachable human beings, just

212

like you and me. When my mother was widowed she had a migraine at the thought of going to see the bank manager. She'd never in her life had to do more than pay the milkman. When she finally nerved herself to walk into the Nat West she was amazed to find herself being treated most royally. Doors were opened for her, coffee was offered, her chair was moved out of a draught. She came home and demanded a large sherry, not out of despair, but in sheer relief that the entire exercise had proved so unalarming.

Remember, no one expects you to become a financial wizard overnight. Everyone understands that you've never had to handle your money matters before and that you're a novice at the game. No one is going to shout, accuse, or make you feel a fool because you don't understand how to write out a cheque. The only time bureaucrats get stroppy is if you try to make out you're smarter than you are, or they are. Make it clear that you're not trying to hide anything, but that you simply don't understand what's going on and what you have to do, and you'll find them reassuringly sympathetic and helpful.

For more guidance, the National Association of Widows runs a countrywide advisory service which provides both financial and emotional support. There is also a book called *Beat Your Bank Manager*. Written by a bank manager's wife, it suggests how to win your bank manager's confidence, and how to take advantage of all the services that a bank offers.

Making Economies

The shock of unexpectedly being obliged to manage your money yourself is often exacerbated by the necessity of having to live on a reduced income. For the divorced, accustomed to two pay packets coming in, or the widowed, cushioned by a high standard of living, coping when there's less cash can be a dispiriting and depressing business. Eventually, of course, we adjust and learn to make economies. Though if we're honest, we'll admit that many of our economies are false ones, because what we save on one thing we'll only splurge on another. Because I live in dread of feeling cold, I'll cheerfully spend my winter weekends collecting logs in the forest, to build myself a roaring fire. But what I save on all this industriously collected fuel, I'll blue on taxis instead of taking the bus. Still, we all have to start somewhere (even if we do fritter the savings on luxuries) so here are some belt-tightening tips:

* You're losing around £15 a year in interest on £2,500 take home pay if you're paid monthly. Arrange to be paid weekly instead.

* Have your hair done at home instead of at an expensive salon. Find a hairdresser who moonlights, or someone who's married and wants pin money.

* Don't use your phone before 1p.m., or preferably till after 6p.m. to obtain the cheapest rate. Save those long chats for Sundays. If your phone is out of order for more than two days ask the area office for a rebate on your rental.

* Stop believing the adverts. Do you really need a peanut dispenser? Or curtains that match the duvet that matches the carpet? Be especially wary of electrical gadgets. The fewer you own, the less often they'll break down and the fewer repair and maintenance bills you'll have to pay.

* Give up driving your car in Le Mans style. If you drive a Mini 1000 at 30 mph you'll get 70 miles to the gallon. Driving at 70 mph in the same car, you'll only get 32½ mpg. Let everyone else do the overtaking while you cruise along and pocket the savings.

* Take advantage of last minute cheap holiday booking bargains. Keep an eye on your travel agent's window, the holiday pages in newspapers, or go to The Late Traveller, who specialise in late bookings.

* Look for clothes in charity shops in prosperous market towns.

* You could save over £25 a year by altering your

central heating time switch to come on an hour later and go off an hour earlier.

* Insulate your home. You don't have to instal expensive glass double glazing. Acrylic sheeting, or even cling film works just as well for a fraction of the price.

* In winter, minimise body heat loss by wearing a woolly hat round the house when you're alone.

* Fix up a dartboard in your sitting room. Walking to and fro from the board keeps your feet warm – and keeping score does wonders for your mental arithmetic.

* Avoid bank charges. Most of the big banks don't charge you if you keep £50 or £100 in your current account. (It is not, of course, *free* banking because your £100 in current account is not benefiting from the interest it would earn if you kept it in deposit account.)

* Many big stores now offer free credit on larger items for six or even twelve months.

* Barter your skills or commodities with your friends and neighbours.

* Buy basic items of clothing, like a winter coat, either in sales or when you see the one you want – even if you think you really can't afford it at the time. If you wait until you need the coat, you'll only spend weeks flogging round the shops and even then you'll probably not find one you like.

* Theatre-goers should keep an eye out for cheap price previews. Talking about a play that's just opened impresses people into believing you were invited to the first night. In London, there's a booth at Leicester Square offering reduced price tickets for shows that evening.

* Make your own wine, for a glass to enjoy on your own in the evenings, to slosh into stews, or to concoct a warming mulled punch with. But unless you're really expert at it, don't offer your home brew to friends.

* Take advantage of every concession and perk available to you. Ask at your local Citizens Advice Bureau or Department of Health and Social Security Office for a copy of *Which Benefits*? This lists all benefits you might be enti-

tled to, from free prescriptions to rent allowances and rate rebates. If you're a pensioner, make full use of bus passes, reduced matinee tickets, train concessions etc.

It's a False Economy to ...

* Economise on food to such an extent that your health suffers.

* Purchase 'saving-up' stamps which you buy for 50p to £5 and stick in a book to help with your TV licence, electricity, gas bills etc. You'd do better to keep your money on bank deposit or in a building society and earn interest on it.

* Buy clothes at sales which either you don't need or require skilful altering to make them wearable.

* Be so mean with your heating that you make yourself miserable – especially if you're going to spend the money you save on gin or grub to cheer yourself up.

Borrowing

Most of us at one time or another need to raise cash in a hurry. It may be because we've got ourselves into a financial hole and need the money to keep the landlady at bay. Or it could be that we've seen a bargain car at a price it would be madness to refuse, except that we don't have the funds available yet as we'd budgeted to buy the car in two months' time.

When such an emergency arises, what you don't do is answer one of those newspaper ads which promise you tempting amounts of money on loan at no security. Common sense will tell you that money lenders are not philanthropists. They are not going to hand over large chunks of cash because they like the colour of your eyes and hell, you're such a nice person you deserve a break. Money lenders charge astronomical rates of interest, and if you miss a payment or two the penalties can be stiff enough to turn your blue eyes a blood-shot brown.

The cheapest way to borrow money is from a friend or

relative, interest free. This is also the easiest way to lose friends and turn relatives sour, especially if for the most sound reasons in the world, you discover that you can't pay the money back. Most people find it terribly embarrassing when those close to them try and touch them for a loan. The only way you can avoid this affecting your relationship is to borrow for a short term only, and ensure that you pay back the loan promptly. It also eases the situation if you insist that the transaction is put in writing, with both parties retaining copies of the documents, and you pay them interest at the current market rate. After all, why should you have the use of their money interest free? It means they are losing out on the deal. If you put it in writing, pay up promptly and with interest, you stand a good chance of Aunt Maud being willing to stump up another lump should the need arise. An added bonus is that provided you have formal documentation to prove the deal, the Inland Revenue may give you some tax relief on the interest you've paid.

If Aunt Maud is unco-operative or broke, your next stop is the bank. The advantage here is that lending money is an everyday affair for them, so you won't be curling up with embarrassment as you would with Aunt Maud. Providing you have an account at the bank, you can borrow from them in two ways, either with an overdraft or a personal loan.

An overdraft comes cheaper than a personal loan and is usually used for short term borrowing. The bank allows you to draw out funds as you need them up to an agreed limit and you'll be charged between 3 and 5 per cent over the base rate operating at the time. Personal loans are for larger sums of money – from about £500 to £3,000 – and tend to last from between one to five years. You borrow a set amount for a set time at a set interest rate, and pay it back in equal instalments each month.

Alternatively, if you have a sympathetic employer it might be worth approaching him or her. Employers are no more philanthropic than money lenders, but they do have a vested interest in keeping you working productively, and they know you won't be doing that if you're worried about money. Apart from straight personal loans, many firms also offer advances for heavy outlay on season tickets.

If you should lose your job, or your financial circumstances change, and you find you are unable to meet your commitments, always tell the lenders immediately. Don't just stop the payments and hope they'll forget about you. They won't. But if you approach them and explain your difficulties, you will probably find them sympathetic and agreeable to a temporary rescheduling of your debt.

People in their seventies who own their own home might consider raising long term cash with what is known as a home interest plan. With this, you take a loan from an insurance company using your property as security and you use the money to buy an annuity. If your property is valued at, say, £38,000 you could take a £25,000 loan which would give you an income of about £103 a month. After your death, the house remains part of your estate, but the insurance company loan will have to be repaid, so your house may have to be sold in order to achieve this. For free advice on the pros and cons of home loan plans, contact Hinton and Wild (Insurance) Ltd.

Medical Insurance

Anyone who is self-employed should think seriously about taking out a medical insurance policy which will provide you with an income if you fall ill, either temporarily or permanently. There are two sorts of medical insurance policies:

Sickness and accident insurance which will replace your income in the short term. *Permanent health insurance* will pay you either until you recover or until you reach retirement age. But with most policies, there is a time gap of anything between one month to two years between the onset of your illness or accident, and the first payment from the insurance company. In addition, there are the *hospital cash plans*, such as those offered by British United Provident Association (BUPA) and the Private Patients Plan (PPP) which pay for the cost of any treatment you need and also provide home nursing care while you are convalescing. A plan of this kind is worth considering, for however close you are to your family, however kind your neighbours, it could happen that you'll fall sick at a time when no one can get to you to help. Treacherously icy roads could prevent your family travelling far, for instance, whilst your kind neighbours may be on holiday.

Making a Will

However young you are and even if all you've got in the bank is an overdraft, you should still make a will. If you think about it, you do have some assets – a favourite silver ring, your precious collection of 78s – and it's all very well saying oh, why bother, when I'm gone it doesn't matter what happens to my stuff, because you don't really want things of sentimental value to end up on the scrap heap. Far better to sit down one evening and work out which friends or relatives you would like to have your possessions.

Anyone with considerable assets to dispose of – a house, car, jewellery, silver etc – and many people they want to leave things to, would be well advised to consult a solicitor over making a will. The important thing, especially if your affairs are complicated by trusts, settlements or whatever, is to get the legal jargon right in the will, as one ambiguous or misused phrase could result in your money going to the wrong person. It's estimated that solicitors spend more time (and make more money) sorting out home-made wills than they do drawing up ordinary ones.

But you don't have to go to a solicitor. If your affairs are very straightforward you could use one of the will forms obtainable at stationers. Better still, buy the Consumers' Association book *Wills and Probate* which takes you step by step through the whole will making process.

Some Useful Addresses

Hinton and Wild (Insurance) Ltd, 374–378 Ewell Road, Tolworth, Surbiton, Surrey KT6 7BB
The Late Traveller, 5a Gloucester Road, London SW7 4PP. (01-581 2458)
National Association of Widows, Chell Road, Stafford ST16 2QA. (0785 45465)

Further Reading

Beat Your Bank Manager – Wendy Elkington (Oyez Publishing and Ward Lock)
The Penguin Money Book – Tom Tickell and Eamonn Fingleton (Penguin)
Wills and Probate – (Consumers' Association)
Money Which? – (Consumers' Association)
The Cosmopolitan Money Guide – Lynn Faulds-Wood (Ebury Press)

CHAPTER 10

TRAVEL

Going it alone

'Oh, I'd love to go to Africa, the Scottish highlands, Paris for a weekend . . . but I wouldn't want to do it on my own . . .'

If the words have a familiar ring then you must by now be resigned to the fact that you are probably never going to see the splendour of Victoria Falls, Ben Nevis or the Seine by moonlight. Because if you hang around, waiting for some-one to come along and do things with, you're going to end up doing nothing and going nowhere.

'But it's not the same on your own. Half the fun of travel-ling is sharing the experience.'

Maybe. But the other half of the fun is the relief of not having A.N. Other tagging along. Even if you're fortunate enough to be travelling with the most fabulously right some-one, there are times when he or she is going to drive you screaming mad. Travel with a companion, and you're really stuck with them for the duration of the holiday. You eat at the same table, share the same room and the same bath-room. In the heat you'll become irritable, and all those little personal habits of theirs which at home you scarcely notice, will gradually magnify and send you crazy. There'll be fric-tion when you long to lie on the beach and your companion wants to walk up the mountain. At least when you're involved in a relationship at home – whether it's on a friend-ship or deeper level – your everyday routine of work, shop-ping and leisure activities ensures that each of you has your individual space, and recuperative time away from one another. But on holiday, you're thrown together in the most unnatural manner. Little wonder then, that so many promising romances and friendships disintegrate in the intimacy of a shared hotel room.

Another problem is that holidays are about dreams. For most of us, those two or three weeks in the year are all we're going to get, so they've got to be right. Which means if you share a holiday with someone, you're not just stuck with them, but with their dreams and expectations as well. Travel alone, however, and you are at liberty to be as selfish and as self-indulgent as you wish.

'My ex-wife had a very demanding job and needed a restful, flaking on the beach type holiday,' a divorced man recalls. 'It was only after we split, and I was leafing through the brochures that I realised how much the beach scene bored me. Even so, I nearly plumped for one of the resorts I'd visited with my wife years before. Then I saw how wet I was being, choosing the same type of holiday, going back to the same old place, simply because it was safe, and I felt apprehensive about breaking new ground somewhere else. Anyway, instead of scorching on a Spanish beach, I took myself off on an orienteering course. I loved it, and I'll definitely do something similar next year.'

Travel alone and the choice of venue is yours. Forget all those past arguments about 'what's the point in saying you want to go to Malta again – you know all those pathetic kittens there make you cry all the time.' If you want to go to Malta and sob over the strays, good for you. There's nothing and no one to stop you.

The main thing is to take the plunge. It's futile denying yourself the pleasure of a holiday simply because you have no one to travel with. You're not going to be on your own, anyway. Your fellow travellers are not going to be twined together in pairs, pitying you as the odd one out. Remember, a holiday atmosphere generates good will, so if it's company you're seeking it won't take much effort on your part before your overtures of friendship are fully reciprocated.

Ease yourself gently into the holiday scene. Pick up a stack of brochures from your travel agent, and amuse yourself on a cold winter's evening sorting out where you'd like to go. This is a sensationally luxurious moment. Within your budget, the world is yours. You have no partner's whims or wishes to consider. You're free. In a year's time your circumstances could have changed, and you may never again know the liberty bestowed on you now. Make the most of it!

Where to Go

How you choose your holiday depends on the particular dream you want to fulfil. You might yearn to have the breath kissed out of you by a handsome count in a Venetian gondola. Alternatively, perhaps you long to turn your back on the world and stalk the mountains of Crete alone, in springtime.

Studying the brochures, it's easy to feel overwhelmed by the variety of resorts and hotels on offer, and not know how to set about selecting one. The best way is to start by striking out everything that is unsuitable for your particular needs. Most single people, for example, find they prefer to bypass places and activities which involve a family scene. Clearly, hotels which offer babysitting facilities, and special pools and menus for children will be best avoided by you. It's essential to learn to read between the lines in holiday brochures. If you want somewhere quiet, cold shoulder resorts described as lively, popular, or conveniently situated on a main road, near the airport or above the local taverna or supermarket. On a beach holiday, check out not just the distance to the sea, but whether you have to negotiate steep steps or hills to get to it. (Though it has to be remembered that the most beautiful beaches are always worth a trek to reach.) Don't pay out money for hotel facilities you don't really need. On a beach holiday, is it essential to stay somewhere with a hairdresser, sauna, five-star restaurant and lifts to every room? You might be much better off saving your money and checking in to the cheaper, more basic hotel down the road.

Women travelling alone find it advisable not to stray too far from signs of civilisation. When you're stuck in a traffic jam in Piccadilly, the notion of that remote little villa tucked up high in the olive groves is immensely appealing. But when the disco's over and you have to walk two miles along an unlit and unfamiliar road to climb the hill to your villa, then you realise that a hotel nearer the centre would have been a better and safer bet.

If you're looking for congenial company within your own age group there is a host of travel operators offering singles and special age group holidays. Twentys, Bachelors Abroad, Small World and Club One cater more for the younger end of the market, whilst Saga Holidays and Intasun Golden Days Holiday Club will be of more interest to senior citizens. And with some of these tour operators your holiday isn't over when you arrive back in England, as they'll invite you to winter reunions at riverboat parties and on springtime trips to Paris.

One word of warning. No woman should go on one of these singles holidays hoping to find romance. The women nearly always outnumber the men ten to one, and as one girl put it to me, 'It was mortifying. Sitting in the disco, waiting my turn to be favoured with a dance by a spotty creature I wouldn't have looked at twice in England.' If you're a single bloke, however, it seems you can't go wrong on a singles holiday.

But beaches aren't for everyone. Many single people prefer instead the stimulus of a beautiful or exciting city. Places like Paris, Amsterdam, Venice, Copenhagen or New York are delightful to visit in the spring or autumn. There's masses to do, and you'll come back bubbling with interesting conversation, whereas all the beach brigade will have to relate is a saga about the dubious state of their bowels. The grade of hotel you elect to stay in will depend on your choice of city. If you're somewhere where you need to impress, like

New York, take the cheapest room at one of the best hotels, such as the Algonquin. Everyone you meet will be knocked out at your style in staying there (no need to mention that you don't have a suite, but the cupboard under the stairs) and as you'll be situated in the centre of town, you'll recoup some of the cost of your room on what you save on taxi fares. Alternatively, in a friendly little capital like Amsterdam, you'd be crazy not to stay in one of those charming, tall buildings that verge the canals. When I went, with *Time Off*, I stayed at a two-star hotel with a chandeliered bedroom big enough to hold a dance in, and a wonderful view up the tree-lined canal to the floodlit bridges of the city.

One disadvantage of cities for the solo traveller, is that the sight of all those busy people can accentuate your sense of aloneness. Unless you're mentally geared up for this, it's possible to feel distressingly adrift. To combat this, an increasing number of single people are finding that an activity holiday is the answer. The type and strenuous nature of the activity depends, of course, on your natural inclinations and energy. If you're the outdoor type in search of adventure, Pennworld do camping trips to Turkey, Jordan and Egypt. It sounds appalling to me, but comes highly recommended by those enthusiasts who like their sunshine pleasures rough and tough. In complete contrast, keen gardeners could head for the Island Hotel, Tresco in the Scilly Isles. Tresco is celebrated for its marvellous variety of plants, trees and shrubs and the hotel runs a full programme on topics ranging from sub-tropical plant cultivation to flower arranging.

Whatever your interest, from winemaking to photography, building your own house, rearing goats or windsurfing, it's easy to combine it with a holiday. The big advantage for singles is that you meet a group of like-minded people, there's plenty to do if you're feeling energetic, and the social scene is usually pretty lively. For further information, write for a booklet, *Activity and Special Interest Holidays in*

England, from the English Tourist Board. The Welsh and Scottish Tourist Boards also have booklets covering their areas. The National Institute of Adult Education has a booklet listing residential short courses, covering study weekends, field trips and also courses for the disabled and the elderly. It's also worth looking at an excellent paperback, *The Alternative Holiday Catalogue*, by Harriet Peacock which lists over 150 different holidays to suit all tastes, from antiques to zen.

A big plus about being single is that having no one else's needs or timetable to consider, you can book late for your holiday and often pick yourself up a marvellous bargain. If you've got a week off, and the weather's lousy in England, what's to stop you dropping everything and heading for the sun? Naturally, you have to take a chance on what's on offer, but there are always good holidays to be had if you know where to look. Obvious starting places are your travel agent and the holiday pages of the newspaper. But there is also a club called The Late Traveller which specialises in late booking business. Members get priority, but they handle bookings from non members as well.

It's advisable to cultivate a travel agent who's sympathetic to your individual needs, and willing if necessary to do some work for you. Many of them tend to be lazy, relying on you to study the brochure, read between the lines and fill in the booking form. While they obviously can't be expected to know offhand whether the interior of your villa is decorated in pink or white, it is their job, if required, to make an effort, contact the tour company and find out for you if your hotel is next to a sewage plant, or if 'coastal railway' means an express train roars right across the beach.

Wherever you go and however you book, do make sure you study all the small print relating to surcharges, the cost of cancelling and what the travel and health insurance policies cover. It's a wise move to write down for the travel agent exactly what you want – a single room, air conditioning, your own bathroom – and keep a copy. Insist that

226

the agent confirms to you in writing that the facilities you require will be available. Then take the agent's letter (and the brochure) with you on holiday to slam down on the hotel manager's desk if there's any dispute.

If you can't afford to holiday in a hotel, why not try a home exchange? The hometown you're sick of the sight of may be fulfilling a dream for someone from another country. And from your point of view, taking over someone's house means you get off the hotel tourist beat and learn more about the locality and the way people really live. A list of agencies which specialise in house swaps can be obtained from the British Tourist Authority.

Getting There

I don't know anyone, even the most seasoned of travellers, who doesn't get ten yards away from the house en route for the airport, without panicking that they've left the iron on and lost the front door keys. When you're travelling alone, you're conscious that there's no one else to delegate any of the shutting, locking and cancelling jobs to, and no one else to blame if you did leave the iron on and your flat burns out.

The ony way round it is to make a list of everything, from cancelling the milk to taking the moggy to the cattery. Allow yourself plenty of time and tick off each job as you do it. Try to avoid tearing off in such a hurry that you leave your home in a mess – it's so depressing to come back to. And however rushed you are, do remember to leave someone your holiday address and the name of the travel agent you booked with. A trustworthy neighbour is a godsend, not just to have a key and keep an eye on the place for you while you're away, but also to ring up if you're convinced you did leave the bathroom tap running. If you're at daggers drawn with your neighbours, check in your local paper for organisations who will take care of your home, pets and plants while you're away. Homewatchers is one such country-wide agency, but there are many more.

It's fatal to get so carried away with the euphoria of going away that you forget you've got to come back. Check out the timing and route of your journey home – trains, buses and taxis from the airport. Remember, planes are often delayed until the small hours and the glow gained from a good holiday will be ruined if you're left tired, hungry and stranded at the airport.

Like anything else in life, careful preparation is the key to ensuring yourself a smooth passage. Do everything well in advance. Check that your passport is up to date, whether you need a visa and jabs, that you have adequate health insurance and that you've ordered travellers cheques and foreign cash. Don't forget to pack your cheque book and plastic money too. British bank cheques, backed by a guarantee card, are honoured in Europe – you can make two £50 transactions a day at any bank displaying the EEC Eurocheque symbol. And Access and Barclaycard/Visa are widely accepted in Western Europe and North America.

Comfortable clobber is essential – save your sprayed-on jeans for the disco. Everyone swells up on planes, so wear easy fitting shoes and clothes in a cotton polyester mix, which will keep you cool without getting creased. When you're travelling from one climate to another, dress in layers which you can peel off or add to as the temperature changes.

It depends where you're going and who you need to impress, but I feel it's not worth taking anything valuable with you – expensive watches, jewellery, cameras etc. It wrecks a holiday if you're forever fretting that you think you left your Rolex in the public loo. And I'll never forget the scene at Mombasa airport at eight o'clock one steamingly hot morning: a trail of British matrons sweltering their way across the tarmac, sweat staining their expensively made up faces because they were all clad in the minks they'd had on in sub zero London, which they daren't let off their backs for an instant for fear they'd get nicked.

Neither do you want any dramas en route about missing

passports, money or boarding cards. Invest in a zipped, strong travelling bag with a comfortable, wide shoulder strap that leaves your hands free. For additional security, wear the bag with the strap across your chest. Into the bag put passport, tickets, travellers cheques and cash to ease the way with porters at your destination. (Alternatively you may prefer to carry your loot in a money belt.) Don't forget a phrase book and film for your camera. A jacket with pockets is useful, too, for sunglasses and a pen. It seems to be one of those butter-side-down rules of life that you always get handed forms to fill in on aircrafts when your bag is tucked neatly away under the seat and you can't move an inch for trays of food and the man next to you slumped in a snoring stupor.

Apart from the zipped bag, you also need a sturdy plastic carrier, in which you place your emergency food and drink rations. Most forms of travelling involve hours of hanging around at airports or stations, and it's difficult for the solo traveller to lug a suitcase and a tray of food through a buffet queue. The queues, as we all know, are endless. Then when you finally battle through the checkout with your vinyl sandwich, there is nowhere to sit. A light plastic bottle of orange juice, or something stronger, and a box of your favourite sustaining goodies will preserve your sanity and your temper. Use the empty bag from your emergency rations to carry the sweater, socks etc. you'll be stripping off as the temperature, hopefully, rises on your journey.

Travelling solo, one skill you'll soon acquire if you didn't have it before is the knack of clever packing. The obvious, golden rule is never to pack anything you can't carry yourself, unless you're so fantastically rich you have porters fighting for the privilege of carrying your bags. Stuff your shoes with small items like pants and socks and place them with any books and other heavy items at the bottom of your case. Roll rather than fold your clothes, and put anything that might leak or break in plastic containers or polythene bags. Take extra polythene bags as they're handy for laundry and sandy swimwear. Since luggage goes astray so alarmingly often, seasoned travellers take basic overnight gear – toothbrush, shaver etc. – with them in their hand-luggage.

The type of case you buy depends on the kind of travelling you're doing. If you're going by car or coach, soft luggage is fine and has the advantage of being flexible enough to take without complaining all those last minute items you nearly forgot. But if you're travelling by air and you want your luggage to last, you need a case with a hard shell to with-stand both the rough handling and the contrasts in tempera-ture it will have to endure. (Your case could be sitting out in 90° Spanish heat for two hours and then be wafted away into arctic temperatures in the hold of the plane.) The big disadvantage of rigid luggage is that it's appreciably heavier than soft. Some people solve this by abandoning the notion that luggage should last for years, and buying a cheapish set of mail order cases which they cheerfully chuck out when they split.

If your case doesn't have its own built-in wheels, it's a sensible idea to invest in a set of luggage wheels. The metal framed type are more practical than the sort on straps, as the latter tend to slip off your case. Practice wheeling your case at home, both on the level, round corners and up and down stairs. It's a myth that you can't use wheels to negotiate stairs. It's tricky, but it can be done.

Label all your luggage clearly with your destination. Don't leave on old labels, and don't put your home address outside as it's a giveaway for airport thieves who then know your house is empty.

Make use of the Duty Free on your way through to pick up a bottle of Scotch as an ice breaker with your fellow guests at the resort. Scotch is an ideal drink for this purpose. It doesn't need a mixer, and there's something wicked asso-ciated with it, which means that people who at home would shudder at the thought of drinking the stuff, when in devil-may-care holiday mood will pitch in happily and bless your foresight in remembering it.

Business Travel

One of the perks of being single is that we are often more available to travel on business than our married colleagues. If you're visiting an area that attracts many holidaymakers and your company allows you to choose your own hotel, try and select one that's off the tourist beat. It's hard maintaining a businesslike frame of mind when the dining room is crammed with merrymakers hurling paper streamers at one another.

Once installed in your hotel, don't fall into the trap of spending every night in your room, either working or watching TV. You'll be fresher for the next day's work if you take a proper break. Stroll round the town, or chat to the people in the bar – perhaps someone would like to take in a movie with you, or join you in tracking down that Japanese restaurant you saw advertised in the local paper.

Make a point of getting on friendly terms with the hotel receptionist as he or she will in effect become an extension of your office, arranging cars, taking messages, booking tickets. Get the receptionist on your side from the start and you'll go a long way to making your business trip run smoothly and efficiently. And before you leave, remember to make a note of the names of the receptionist and hotel manager, so that next time you're there you can establish an immediate rapport with them.

With a View to a Room

For all holidaymakers, this is the moment of truth, walking for the first time into the hotel that is to be your home for two weeks, for which you've shelled out a lot of hard earned money. You've pored over the brochures, agonised, rejected, selected and now you're there. Will it live up to the dream? You study the faces of the other residents. Do they look happy with their lot or is there a brooding atmosphere

231

of discontent? If your arrival was delayed and you've missed dinner, do the staff cheerfully serve you something simple but sustaining, or are you treated to the big shrug and the sound of doors slamming as the kitchen staff beetle off into the night?

For the single traveller, this is often the most gruelling period of a holiday, because if you've asked for a single room you've got to ensure that it comes up to scratch. If you discover, as too frequently happens, that they've allotted you the cubby hole next to the asthmatic air conditioning unit, then however late at night it is, however tired you are, it is vital that you complain immediately. Do not unpack. March straight back to the reception desk and tell the manager that the room is unacceptable. Ignore the manager's Oscar-winning display of amazement at your dissatisfaction. He's not daft. He knows what the room is like and he's used to handling aggro about it. As always when complaining, start off by being polite to give the manager a chance, in return, to be reasonable. If you get no joy, sharpen your voice by degrees and be prepared for an all out screaming match. Try to stay in full view of everyone at the reception desk. Resist suggestions that you retire to the manager's office and slug it out in private. Look blank at all expressions of regret that the hotel is full, and there is not another room to be had. There must be another room, even if it's the manager's own. What would he do if the Queen of England turned up and wanted a bed for the night?

As in all arguments of this sort, it's the one who has the most stamina to carry on scrapping who wins and the manager has the advantage here as he hasn't had the hassle of a long journey behind him. Do your best to avoid being fobbed off with the suggestion that you use the cubby hole for one night and he will try to find you something better in the morning. But if fatigue does cause you to succumb, aim to get the best night's sleep possible, so you can return to the desk first thing in the morning fighting fit for round two. Above all, don't give up. If you're on a package, force your courier to assist you. Should your courier be the type who regards holiday makers and their problems in the same light as clouds preventing them getting the tan they took the job for, threaten a telephone call to the head office in England. If necessary, make such a call. It's an excellent way to convince everyone that you mean business and are not to be trifled with.

Anyone sharing a room will naturally have security of money and valuables very much in mind. It's always a vital consideration when travelling, but especially so when you're pitched in with a perfect stranger. The obvious solution is to keep your passport and spare travellers' cheques in the hotel safe, and leave your valuable bits of jewellery at home. But if you're camping, or staying in the sort of villa where the doors don't even close properly, let alone lock, you might consider a coathanger-safe device called a Stowaway. Sling a jacket over it and anyone would think it was a bulky black plastic coathanger, but unlock it and there's space for your passport, wallet, jewellery etc. Available from a firm called Cavalcade, it has a spring steel hook which locks over a wardrobe rail and is impossible to remove without breaking the rail, or using the key.

For those single people who hate eating alone at home, the prospect of dining solo in public can be enough to put them off taking a holiday in the first place. The first thing to realise, of course, is that unless you want to be, you won't be marooned all on your tod, the cynosure of every pitying eye. You'll be seated at a table with others. And as you make friends during the course of your holiday, naturally you'll often eat with them, too.

But that said, yes, there are times when we have to enter a dining room on our own and endure the head waiter's sniffed, 'Just for one, is it?' as he leads you to a table facing a white tiled wall. Canny campaigners don't just say they would prefer another table, they point to the one they want, near the window or on the terrace. As they point, they leave the head waiter standing and move purposefully towards the

233

desired table. If you're quick enough, and resolute enough, firmly settling your belongings on your new territory, the waiter will hardly have the nerve to do a rugby tackle to prevent you getting there, and that will be round one to you.

The next fixation we have to overcome is the conviction that everyone else (in pairs, naturally) is staring at us and feeling sorry for us all on our own, unwanted-unloved-leprous-failures-been stood up-missed the boat-sob, aaaagh! It's calming and confidence building at this stage to ignore the menu, and order yourself a drink instead – an aperitif, or some wine to accompany your meal. This gets rid of the flapping waiter, and gives you something to toy with while you rationalise the situation. Because most of the other diners, of course, are not concentrating on you at all. They are either gazing in dismay at the plate of greasy swill in front of them, or they are involved in a marital wrangle about who left the light on and let all those mosquitoes into the bedroom.

If they have noticed you, they're probably envious at your freedom to eat your meal in peace without being obliged to listen to a partner on the other side of the table sounding as if they have their head in a trough. Or, especially if you're a woman, they'll be intrigued at the sight of you dining alone. To be intriguing, it's essential to have something of an air about you – but that's easy enough to cultivate. Sitting there like a petrified mouse, avoiding people's eyes and making it plain the waiter terrifies you, is not intriguing and will only make your fellow guests feel sorry for you. (On the other hand, some solo travellers make a lot of friends this way. They look approachable and in need of befriending, cashing in on the knowledge that people in holiday mood tend to be kinder than they are at home, eager for their good will and good times to wash off on all around them.) But perhaps your pride won't allow you to encourage others to regard you in this light. You happen to be enjoying your own company and don't want anyone else around for the moment – or if you do, you'd rather choose them rather than be chosen. In such a situation, it helps if you fantasise a bit. A simple accessory like a notebook on the table in which you scribble the occasional phrase (preferably with a wry smile playing around your lips) will be enough to generate in the other guests' minds the notion that you are either a best-selling novelist seeking material (watch them start to preen as they imagine themselves starring in your latest epic) or could you be a Michelin Guide inspector? (Watch the head waiter start to turn cartwheels round your table.)

Tipping the waiter after each meal is an excellent way of ensuring good service. In England, we're accustomed to waiting until the last day of our holiday before dishing out tips. But I've noticed that if you tip in small amounts as you go along, you avoid that soggy patch at the end of week one: 'Are you leaving us tomorrow, madame? No? You are here for another week? Oh how delightful. I was feeling desolate that we would no longer enjoy the enchantment of your beautiful smile . . .' and your coffee takes an hour to arrive because they know they don't need to start chatting you up again until around Thursday lunchtime.

The Right Mix

The dread most people have about holidaying alone is that they'll be stuck on their own for the entire time. That everyone else will be in pairs and they will be the odd man or woman out.

Not so. Providing you look friendly and approachable, you'll soon find other people to link up with. Even if by some ghastly mischance the remote Hebridean hotel you've picked turns out to be a honeymooner's retreat, remember even the most devoted couples get sick of the sight of one another sometimes – especially when they're burdened with one another each day for twenty-four hours solid – and they'll probably be glad of your company to relieve the monotony of their own for a while.

The wise move, especially if you're travelling alone to a big city where you know no one, is to plan ahead. Tell everyone at home about your trip, and solicit names and addresses of their friends and acquaintances in your holiday area whom you could ring up and perhaps meet for a drink. This approach can also provide a boost to your home social life, as it gives you an excellent excuse to call that fascinating man or woman you met at a party last week, to ask his or her advice on where you should stay in Venice.

On a package holiday, make a point of getting friendly with the resident courier at your resort. (If you are the opposite sex to the courier, you may find the matter taken out of your hands, with he or she making a point of getting very friendly with you.) English magazines are usually very gratefully received by any Brit working in a foreign country. The courier should ensure that you are included in all the group activities and outings. But more than that, because they are based in the resort, couriers should know all the best places to eat and visit which are off the tourist beat. They also mix with a lot of local people, so even if you loathe the courier there's a chance he or she will be in a position to introduce you to some acquaintances who are more your scene.

But it's your fellow guests, of course, who are destined to be your extended family for the duration of your holiday. At first, all those strangers look chillingly alien. They're not, of course. They're just reticent, like you. If you start with the people in the rooms on either side of you, and make a smiling enquiry about the best way to the beach, or how you get hot water out of the shower, you'll probably find them amiably responsive.

Even on holiday, human beings are creatures of habit. After a few days, you'll find that a pattern emerges in the drift of social activity and you'll soon be able to locate the focal gathering points for each time of day ... the beach, the harbour taverna, the pool, the patisserie, the bar, the disco ... Have the nerve to take your time over who you want to become friendly with. It's all too easy, feeling adrift at being alone, to land yourself with the beach bore, who throws stones at the Germans floating on their lilos, shouting 'Sink the Bismarck, ho, ho ho!' Lie on the beach with a hat over your face and eavesdrop for a day or so while you sort out the buffoons from the rest.

Once you spot a group of people you think you'd like to know better, it's important that you take your courage firmly in both hands, walk straight up to them and pitch in. I once spent two miserable weeks on a cruise with no one to talk to because I was too hesitant to approach a lively group who seemed to be having a whale of a time. It turned out later, when we all got thrown together during a hassle in the customs clearing shed, that they'd thought I was being offensively standoffish, misinterpreting my mixture of shy pride as a conviction of my own superiority.

Opening gambits are easy on holiday, as you'll find your fellow travellers relaxed, expansive, open to fresh experiences and the company of new people. Having studied the local notice board, you could ask if anyone's been on the trip to the monastery or to the caves ... should you take a sweater ... what sort of shoes? When you're in a place that you're to call home for two or three weeks, there's a mass of local knowledge to be acquired, and shared – from whether the hotel really does stop serving breakfast at 9.30, or if you can roll in at 10 and still get fed, to gen on the peculiarities of the local bus time tables, where you get the best exchange rate for your travellers cheques etc. A question on any of these topics is a sure fire ice breaker. It works in reverse, too. If you spend the first couple of days mugging up on the resort, when you're standing next to someone who's musing over whether to take the boat trip, you'll be able to strike up a conversation by telling them that if they book in the village it's much cheaper than doing it through the hotel. What is vital is that you put in a spot of preliminary groundwork to establish that the group you're approaching actually speaks the same language as you, and your bright line of chat won't

237

be falling on uncomprehending foreign ears. Avoid, too, trying to establish detente with a rash guess as to the nationality of the person you're speaking to. You always get it wrong. The Swiss take great exception to being mistaken for Germans. Australians look in danger of socking you one of you ask if they're from New Zealand or South Africa. And that dusky maiden straight out of the cigar adverts will spit at you that she wasn't born in Costa Rica, but Coventry.

A woman friend of mine who is an experienced and extremely well organised traveller always makes a host of friends by being enviably well equipped with all those small essentials the rest of us meant to pack, but forgot: safety pins, calamine, insect repellent, needle and thread, clothes pegs, bottle opener. She's scrupulous about paying her way, and buying her round, and as she says, there's always your invaluable bottle of Scotch to oil the conversational wheels.

If you find that none of your fellow guests strikes any sparks in you, give them a miss and concentrate on local interest instead. Arm yourself with a phrase book, get off the tourist track and mingle with the residents. Travel on local buses instead of the hotel coach, go to church, visit the backstreet shops, eat at places where the locals eat. As you wander past their houses, admire their gardens, and their children. (Though for your own safety, men should avoid admiring female children over the age of twelve.) Show you are taking a genuine interest in the local people and the way they live, stutter out a few phrases in their language and you will be unfortunate if you do not encounter the most overwhelming kindness and hospitality from the people you meet. I was once taken on a magical trip up into the mountains of Cyprus by a Turkish schoolgirl from whom I had asked directions to the bank, and who then invited me to meet her family. Her family turned out to be every member of the mountain village, who rushed out in force to welcome me. As eagles soared in the blue overhead, I was plied, in the space of two hours, with pistachio nuts, Turkish delight, Coke, grapes, bacon and egg and a plateful of goat's cheese

238

sprinkled with sugar. As I said, the hospitality is sometimes overwhelming, but the experience was ten times more rewarding than tepid moussaka in the hotel dining room with a hundred other Brits.

One way for a single woman not to make friends on holiday is to sashay round the resort in a transparent top and bootlace bikini bottom. You'll only drive the other women to close ranks, barring you from any companionable relationship with them and their men. And despite what the girlie magazines would have you believe, single men are not automatically turned on by women who carry all before them in public. Most men are romantics at heart, and are embarrassed by tart art exhibitionists. Though of course, if what you want is a quick screw with a different local romeo every night of your hol, then this is the ideal way to dress. But don't complain that you had no stimulating conservation, and ended up with a dose of something nasty that you could have got more inexpensively at home.

Staying Well

Being ill at home when there's no one on hand to look after you is problematic enough. On holiday, in an alien country, a strange bed, and with a language barrier, it can be a nightmare.

Prevention is the name of the game here. Whatever else you forget to pack, don't omit whatever pills and potions agree with you to cure headaches (and hangovers) indigestion, constipation, diarrhoea, sunburn, bites and stings. It may sound an awful chore hiking a rattling medicine chest with you and having no room for those flash gold dancing shoes, but it will all make sense if the only bopping you're capable of doing is a frenzied Aztec Twostep to the loo. Women should remember that a severe attack of diarrhoea can cause the Pill to pass straight through the body so take standby contraceptives with you.

Everyone always blames the water for stomach upsets on holiday and of course you should always check that it's safe to drink from the tap, especially if you're in the Mediterranean or North Africa. If you're warned against the water, buy bottled mineral water and don't forget to use it to clean your teeth. Refuse ice cubes, ice creams, and always peel fruit. But it's not always the water that's the culprit. A combination of unfamiliar foreign food, too much cheap booze, plus a surfeit of sun – coming on top of a long, tiring journey – can conspire to upset even the strongest constitution. It's hard to do, I know, but you'll feel in much better form if you take it easy for the first few days. Don't rush about, or drink gallons of the local vino rotto, or lie in the sun for too long – especially after you've been drinking. Give your body time to adjust to the different pace of life and the unfamiliar treats you're shovelling down it, and it'll reward you by not giving way under the strain of the good life.

If real disaster strikes, and you need hospital treatment, this is the point at which to reap the reward of medical insurance. After booking your holiday, ask for forms E111 and SA28 at your local Department of Health and Social Security. These explain your rights with regard to reciprocal health arrangements with EEC and certain other countries. We've all heard horror stories about people who've had to sell their houses in England to pay for medical bills run up while they were travelling in the States. If you're journeying to North America be pessimistic, and make sure you have at least £25,000 worth of cover. £6,000 should be enough for destinations in Europe. This should include cover if you have to cut short your holiday, as well as local doctor, hospital and drug costs.

The Longest Mile . . .

However marvellous a time you've had, it's always good to come home . . . a stack of mail to open, eggs boiled just the way you like them, a soak in your own tub, the newspapers, a cup of tea, a pint . . .

Getting home is great. Once you're there. But a fraught homeward trip will soon wreck all the expensively obtained relaxation of your holiday. For this reason, the most seasoned travellers insist on cossetting themselves on the return journey. They pay porters to cope with the luggage (and usually get them through Customs quicker) and if it's been impossible to arrange for someone to meet them with a car, they take a taxi. If they don't live within taxi riding distance, and it's late at night, they don't bother struggling half way home and then sleeping on a station bench – they check into a nearby hotel and spend the night in comfort. With only themselves, and their own timetable to consider, they sensibly take advantage of the single person's freedom to be flexible.

By far the most pleasant way to come home is to a welcoming atmosphere. If you can, ask a friend to stock up your fridge and turn on the heating for you. Make your holiday last a little longer by sharing with him or her the local delicacies and duty free goodies you've brought back. And when your friend enquires, 'Well, and how did you get on by yourself?' hopefully you'll be able to reply, 'Oh, I had a wonderful time. I'd never be afraid of going away on my own again!'

Some Useful Addresses

Bachelors Abroad, (Blue Sky Holidays) Montilla House, Crowborough Hill, Crowborough, Sussex TN6 2SD. (08926 64466)
British Tourist Authority, Queens House, 64 St James' St., London SW1.
Cavalcade, 100 Chadwick Road, Astmoor Industrial Estate, Runcorn, Cheshire, WA7 1PW. (Runcorn 67272)
Club One Holidays, 23 Abingdon Road, London W8. (01-938 1011)
English Tourist Board, 4 Grosvenor Gardens, London SW1.

Homewatchers, 34 Cheyham Way, Cheam, Surrey. (01-643 1297)

Intasun's Golden Days Holiday Club, Leisure House, 29–31 Elmfield Rd, Bromley, Kent.

The Late Traveller, 5a Gloucester Road, London SW7 4PP. (01-581 2458)

National Institute of Adult Education, 19b De Montfort St., Leicester LE1 7GE.

Pennworld, Broad St, Hereford. (0432 55311)

Saga Holidays, P.O. Box 5, Folkestone, Kent

Scottish Tourist Board, Caravan Abbey Place, Murray Green, Jedburgh, Scotland

Small World, Russell Chambers, Covent Garden, London WC2E 8AW

Time Off, 2a Chester Close, Chester St., London SW1X 7BQ. (01-235 8070)

Twentys, 41 Widemarsh St, Hereford HR4 9EA. (0432 55311)

Welsh Tourist Board, Brunel House, 2 Fitzalan Rd, Cardiff CF2 1UY

Further Reading

Alternative Holiday Catalogue, Harriet Peacock (Pan)
Your Holidays (a booklet for pensioners) Age Concern
The Best of British Pubs (Letts)
Outdoor and Activity Holidays in Britain, Edmund Swinglehurst (Thames Magnum)
Just Off For the Weekend, John Slater (Pan)

A MEMO TO THE MARRIED

Every single person knows how aggravating the married can be about their solo status. Niggling slights and put downs which you're aware may be generated by the married person's envy of your freedom and independence, but that nevertheless react on you like a fingernail scratched along a blackboard. Yet quite often, the culprits genuinely don't mean to offend. They've simply made certain assumptions over the years about single people and they don't realise how much their stereotyped attitudes irritate you. To help you get the message across, overleaf is a page for you to leave open when next in the company of anyone who is confused about how you succeed in living alone – and liking it.

MEMO From: The Owner of This Book
      To: All my Married Friends and Relations

Please . . .

* Don't ask me when I'm going to find myself someone to marry.

* Don't assume I am incapable of feeding, washing or clothing myself.

* If I am separated, divorced or widowed, do continue to invite me round to mixed gatherings. But don't keep telling everyone, within my hearing, how *sorry* you feel for me.

* Don't ask what I find to do with myself at weekends.

* Don't call me a spinster. Especially a dried-up spinster.

* Don't assume I'm gay. And if I am, remember it's my business, not yours.

* Don't invite potential Mr/Miss Rights to partner me at dinner parties.

* Don't assume I have a repressed maternal instinct.

* Don't agonise with my friends over What Is Going To Become Of Me.

* When at my home, don't pry into my private things. And when caught, don't protest you're only doing it because you're worried about me.

* When I am visiting you, don't go in for emotional blackmail to persuade me to stay longer.

* Don't cross-examine me about my love life. If I mention a new man or woman in my life, don't immediately pose the hopeful question: 'Is it serious?'

* If I am getting on in years, don't assume I am a naive halfwit, have no sex drive and only want a small sweet sherry to drink.

Your Loving Mother

Deanna Maclaren

Caroline Lambert can stand most things. She
doesn't mind living in the guilt-edged security
of the stockbroker belt. She can put up with her
husband Len. And she can just about tolerate
having a blooming 16-year-old daughter with
fanciable boyfriends – even if the generation
gap makes her feel like an over-sexed
cradlesnatcher. The one thing Caroline can't
stand is a visit from her mother.

Caroline's mother suspects that her daughter's
marriage is on the rocks (that Len, so coarse,
never really was *one of us*). She suspects that
her granddaughter's been badly brought up (all
those O levels and no Common Sense). But
most of all she suspects that someone
somewhere is having a good time – and it's all
Caroline's fault!

The stage is set for a family row of epic
proportions in this riotous satire of colour-
supplement values spiced with a wickedly
perceptive look at the horrors of family life.

GENERAL FICTION   0 7221 5722 3   £1.50

A selection of bestsellers from SPHERE

FICTION

PACIFIC VORTEX!	Clive Cussler	£1.95 ☐
REALITIES	Marian Schwartz	£2.25 ☐
CHAMELEON	William Diehl	£2.25 ☐
THE CAMBODIA FILE	J. Anderson &	
	B. Pronzini	£2.25 ☐
THE STONE FLOWER	Alan Scholefield	£1.95 ☐

FILM & TV TIE-INS

E.T. THE EXTRA-TERRESTRIAL	William Kotzwinkle	£1.50 ☐
THE IRISH R.M.	E. E. Somerville	
	& Martin Ross	£1.95 ☐
INCUBUS	Ray Russell	£1.50 ☐
THE GENTLE TOUCH	Terence Feely	£1.50 ☐

NON-FICTION

NELLA LAST'S WAR	Nella Last	£1.95 ☐
THE NUCLEAR BARONS	P. Pringle	
	& J. Spigelman	£3.50 ☐
THE HEALTH & FITNESS		
HANDBOOK	Ed. Miriam Polunin	£5.95 ☐
ONE CHILD	Torey L. Hayden	£1.75 ☐

*All Sphere books are available at your local bookshop or newsagent, or can be
ordered direct from the publisher. Just tick the titles you want and fill in the
form below.*

Name _____

Address _____

_____

Write to Sphere Books, Cash Sales Department, P.O. Box 11, Falmouth,
Cornwall TR10 9EN

Please enclose a cheque or postal order to the value of the cover price plus:

UK: 45p for the first book, 20p for the second book and 14p for each
additional book ordered to a maximum charge of £1.63.

OVERSEAS: 75p for the first book plus 21p per copy for each additional
book.

BFPO & EIRE: 45p for the first book, 20p for the second book plus 14p
per copy for the next 7 books, thereafter 8p per book.

*Sphere Books reserve the right to show new retail prices on covers which may
differ from those previously advertised in the text or elsewhere, and to increase
postal rates in accordance with the PO.*